Under heavy enemy fire, U.S. Marines advance inland on Betio Island of the Tarawa Atoll in November 1943. Converted into a bristling fortress by the Japanese, the tiny island—less than half a mile square—was the scene of one of World War II's most violent battles.

ISLAND FIGHTING

TIME® LIFE BOOKS

This volume is one of a series that chronicles
in full the events of the Second World War.

WORLD WAR II · TIME-LIFE BOOKS · ALEXANDRIA, VIRGINIA

BY RAFAEL STEINBERG
AND THE EDITORS OF TIME-LIFE BOOKS

ISLAND FIGHTING

TIME®
LIFE
BOOKS

Time-Life Books is a division of Time Life Inc.

TIME LIFE INC.
PRESIDENT and CEO: George Artandi

TIME-LIFE BOOKS
PRESIDENT: Stephen R. Frary
PUBLISHER/MANAGING EDITOR: Neil Kagan
VICE PRESIDENT, MARKETING: Joseph A. Kuna

WORLD WAR II

DIRECTOR, NEW PRODUCT DEVELOPMENT:
Elizabeth D. Ward
DIRECTOR OF MARKETING: Pamela R. Farrell

Dust Jacket Design: Barbara M. Sheppard

Editorial Staff for *Island Fighting*
Editor: William K. Goolrick
Picture Editor/Designer: Raymond Ripper
Picture Editor: Robin Richman
Text Editor: Henry Woodhead
Staff Writers: Dalton Delan, Richard W. Flanagan,
Tyler Mathisen, Teresa M. C. R. Pruden
Chief Researcher: Frances G. Youssef
Researchers: Karen Bates, Marion F. Briggs, Loretta Y. Britten,
Jane Edwin, Oobie Gleysteen, Catherine Gregory,
Karen L. Michell
Copy Coordinators: Victoria Lee, Barbara Fairchild Quarmby
Editorial Assistant: Connie Strawbridge

Correspondents: Christine Hinze (London), Christina
Lieberman (New York)

Director of Finance: Christopher Hearing
Directors of Book Production: Marjann Caldwell,
Patricia Pascale
Director of Publishing Technology: Betsi McGrath
Director of Photography and Research: John Conrad Weiser
Director of Editorial Administration: Barbara Levitt
Production Manager: Carolyn Bounds
Quality Assurance Manager: James King
Chief Librarian: Louise D. Forstall

The Author: RAFAEL STEINBERG was a war correspondent in Korea for International News Service and *Time*. He spent many years in Japan as a correspondent for *Newsweek* and other publications, and later was managing editor of *Newsweek International*. His books include *Postscript from Hiroshima* (a book about the survivors of the nuclear bombings) and two volumes in the Time-Life Books' Foods of the World series, *The Cooking of Japan* and *Pacific and Southeast Asian Cooking*, as well as a volume in the Human Behavior series, *Man and the Organization*.

The Consultants: COL. JOHN R. ELTING, USA (Ret.), is a military historian and author of *The Battle of Bunker's Hill*, *The Battles of Saratoga* and *Military History and Atlas of the Napoleonic Wars*. He edited *Military Uniforms in America: The Era of the American Revolution, 1755-1795* and *Military Uniforms in America: Years of Growth, 1796-1851*, and was an associate editor of *The West Point Atlas of American Wars*.

HENRY H. ADAMS is a retired Navy captain who served aboard the destroyer U.S.S. *Owen* in the major campaigns of the central Pacific. A native of Ann Arbor, Michigan, he graduated from the University of Michigan and received his M.A. and Ph.D. degrees from Columbia University. After his service in World War II he was a professor at the U.S. Naval Academy in Annapolis, Maryland, and was later head of the English Department at Illinois State University. His books include *1942: The Year That Doomed the Axis*, *Years of Deadly Peril*, *Years of Expectation*, *Years to Victory* and *Harry Hopkins: A Biography*.

ROBERT SHERROD, author of several books about World War II, covered the War from its beginning for *Time* and *Life*. He landed on Iwo Jima with the 4th Marine Division and on Okinawa with the 6th, flew combat missions from carriers in dive bombers and torpedo bombers and endured some "frankly frightening" experiences while dodging Kamikazes. He provided the text for *Life's Picture History of World War II* in 1950.

R 10 9 8 7 6 5 4 3 2 1

Library of Congress Cataloging-in-Publication Data
Steinberg, Rafael, 1927-
    Island fighting

  (World War II)
  Bibliography.
  Includes index.
    1. World War, 1939-1945—Pacific Ocean
I. Time-Life Books. II. Title. III Series.
D767.5754   940.54'26   78-52847
ISBN 0-7835-5707-8

CONTENTS

CALM BEFORE THE STORM

Japanese troops teach songs to New Guinea villagers—a method of indoctrination used during the first year of the occupation.

EXOTIC DUTY IN TROPICAL PARADISES

Waving Japanese flags, aircrews at a Rabaul base provide a ceremonial send-off for pilots on a mission from which many may never return.

In the early days of the War, the Japanese were an invincible force in the Pacific, moving easily from victory to victory—and from island to island. Almost everywhere they came ashore, they found lush realms, with snow-white beaches, frond huts, coconut palms and natives who wore sarongs, grass skirts or loincloths called *lap-laps*.

The conquerors soon settled into a routine that combined the rigors of war with leisurely pursuits appropriate to the setting. By day, pilots flew grueling sorties over New Guinea and the Solomon Islands, while ground crews—not yet equipped with radar—scanned the skies with their field glasses and listened for the approach of Allied aircraft. But duty usually ended at 5 p.m. for most, and after that there were many diversions. The men went fishing in the lagoons or streams, using camouflage nets as seines. They played cards and swam. They climbed palm trees to gather coconuts, and exchanged cigarettes and canned goods with the islanders for fresh fruit—bananas, papayas and mangoes. Until the shipping lanes were cut off in late 1943, vessels from Japan regularly brought news, letters, movies, dancers, singers and packages filled with snacks and other amenities.

So varied were the attractions of Rabaul, Japan's principal air and naval base in the southwest Pacific, that new arrivals often had trouble believing they had come to a war zone at all. But as time passed such euphoria evaporated. The days were scorchingly hot at Rabaul, as at other outposts, and the only water fit to drink was brought in by ship or caught in containers when it rained. Mosquitoes were ubiquitous, and disease was rampant. The men came down with dengue fever, scarlet fever, dysentery and malaria. And as the Allied war machine rolled closer, the Japanese on the islands suddenly faced an uncertain future. The islands they had looked upon as paradises a few months before now seemed likely to become their last resting places.

A group of Japanese soldiers and the women who accompanied them to the islands relax on board a transport headed for the southwest Pacific.

Smeared with body paint and dressed in grass skirts and paper hats, Japanese soldiers prepare to play islanders in a variety show.

13

Refreshing milk from coconuts slakes the thirst of Japanese pilots stationed at Rabaul, where disease-free water was scarce.

A dancer from home performs for Japanese troops at Rabaul during an "encouragement" show—an event like a USO revue.

1

For more than a week the 82 ships of Task Force 61 steamed through the blue waters of the South Pacific. Radio transmitters were silent. Planes from the three aircraft carriers scouted for Japanese submarines that might spot the armada. Aboard the flagships, admirals and generals expressed satisfaction over the lucky weather: low-scudding clouds and tropical downpours shielded the fleet from the threat of prying eyes.

Aboard the transports, 19,000 members of the 1st Marine Division, Reinforced, played high-stakes poker in the ships' heads, got together for songfests featuring such back-home favorites as "Blues in the Night" and "Chattanooga Choo-Choo," and listened to somber know-your-enemy lectures from officers who, by and large, had seen no more combat than their men had—that is to say, none at all.

When they were not otherwise occupied, the Marines sharpened their bayonets, blackened the sights of their rifles, and removed and reinserted the cartridges of their machine-gun belts to make sure there would be no jamming. And they griped—about the food, the heat, their mission. "Whadda we want with a place nobody ever heard of before?" a Marine asked no one in particular. "Who ever heard of Guadalcanal?"

On the night preceding D-day, the loudspeakers on the ships boomed out: "All troops below deck." On board the transport *George F. Elliott,* Marine Private Robert Leckie, a machine gunner and scout with a writer's eye for detail, recorded the scene in his mind. The men filed below, Leckie wrote later, "with little of the accustomed horseplay, without the usual ineffectual insults hurled at the bullhorn that had ordered them down. . . . Packs were checked for the last time, filled with mess gear, clean socks and underwear, shaving gear, rations—here a Bible, there a pack of letters-from-home, an unfinished paperback book, a crumpled photo of a pin-up girl. . . . Now the men were banging the chained bunks down from the bulkheads, crawling into them fully dressed—for no one removed his clothes that night."

In the darkness, the carrier force left the armada west of Guadalcanal and moved toward the island's southern waters. The other ships rounded the western end of the island and split off. Most took station off Guadalcanal itself. The others veered north, then east, toward another target: a

OPERATION SHOESTRING

cluster of smaller Japanese-held islands named Florida, Tulagi, Tanambogo and Gavutu. A distance of about 15 miles now separated the two groups of ships, across a stretch of water the Americans were soon to dub Ironbottom Sound, for all the hulks it would hold.

At first light, the planes and naval guns of the armada began bombarding their targets. On the decks of the transports, nervous Marines laden with rifles and packs silently lined the rails to watch the diving planes, the yellow flashes of the cruisers' guns, the long red arcs of the shells and the black smoke that soon billowed up from the beaches.

Then came the order "Land the landing force," and the Marines started clambering down rope nets to the landing craft below. "Antlike they went over the side," wrote Leckie. "They stepped on the fingers of the men below them and felt their own hands squashed by men above. Rifles clanged against helmets. Men carrying heavy machine guns or mortar parts ground their teeth in the agony of descending to the waiting boats with 30 or 40 pounds of steel boring into their shoulders. And the boats rose and fell in the swells, now close in to the ships' sides, now three or four feet away. The men jumped, landing in clanking heaps, then crouched beneath the gunwales while the loaded boats churned to the assembly areas, forming rings and circling, finally fanning out in a broad line and speeding with hulls down and frothing wake straight for the shores of the enemy."

The date was August 7, 1942. The first American offensive of World War II was under way.

The planners of the assault could not foresee that Guadalcanal would prove to be the first of the island steppingstones on the road to Tokyo and ultimate victory in the war in the Pacific. All they had in mind was a limited operation aimed at rooting the Japanese out of the footholds they had recently seized on Guadalcanal and its smaller neighbors. These islands—part of the chain known as the Solomons—marked Japan's farthest advance to date toward the eastern half of the South Pacific. The Japanese had to be checked; any thrust they made still farther eastward would directly imperil the vital supply lines from the United States to Australia. Without American planes, tanks, arms and troops Australia could not hold, and without Australia the main line of defense against Japan would have to be moved back to the North American continent itself.

Thus far, in the eight months since Pearl Harbor, the Japanese had appeared to be unstoppable. The defeat they had suffered in the naval battle with the Americans off Midway Island in June of 1942 was not yet recognized as the turning point it in fact was; neither side could foretell that the Japanese Navy would never fully recover from the blows inflicted on it at Midway. But the Japanese Army, as of the summer of 1942, had tasted no defeat at all.

It had routed the Americans in the Philippines, the Dutch in the East Indies, the British in Burma, Malaya, Singapore and Hong Kong. Amid these successes, the Japanese had made a number of other moves to threaten the homeland of a fourth foe, the Australians.

North of Australia lay a host of islands traditionally regarded by the Australians as their outer ramparts against an aggressor. The nearest, New Guinea, was in itself enough to give a would-be invader pause. Next to Greenland, it is the largest island in the world, covering some 310,000 square miles, mostly jungle and swamp, ribbed by rugged mountain ranges that rise to 16,000 feet. Beyond New Guinea lay the smaller but still sizable island of New Britain, and beyond that the 900-mile-long Solomons chain.

Throughout the first half of 1942, the Japanese had methodically breached these supposed ramparts, one by one. In January they landed on New Britain and seized the port of Rabaul, easily overwhelming its meager Australian garrison. The invaders quickly built a huge air-and-sea base at Rabaul and quickly put it to use. From it, in February, their bombers hit at Port Moresby, the Australians' naval station on New Guinea's southeast coast. In March, Japanese seaborne troops landed on New Guinea's northeast shore and with little effort took the towns of Lae and Salamaua. At once Lae began to be turned into a forward air base; Salamaua was needed to make Lae secure. The threat to the Australian mainland was now more serious than ever.

In the same month, the Japanese began moving into the Solomons, meeting even less opposition than they had encountered in New Britain and New Guinea. Among the several hundred islands constituting the chain, they had a wide choice of those they deemed worth occupying. Neither the Australians, who controlled the islands at the western end under a League of Nations mandate, nor the British, who governed the rest of the chain as a protectorate, had done anything to fortify their holdings.

One prudent measure, however, had been taken—a precaution that would prove of immense value to the Allies. As far back as 1919, the Royal Australian Navy had set up a unique intelligence network of volunteer "coastwatchers," along Australia's own coastline, assigned to report instantly any suspicious or unusual happenings, including the sighting of a strange ship or plane. In 1939, studying reports of Japanese ship movements in the southwest Pacific, the Australians had concluded that Japan was displaying "an overkeen interest" in the area, and expanded the coastwatchers' network to include the islands to the north and east.

The activities of the members of the network were to continue even after the Japanese overran the islands. Included in the several hundred recruits were civil servants, coconut planters, missionaries and traders—each long resident in the Solomons, New Britain, New Guinea and other islands, and each man fluent in the me-fella-you-fella pidgin English that helped them enlist the support of the local population. Every coastwatcher was taught to use a code and to operate a radio fitted with a special crystal for broadcasting on a frequency that was continuously monitored at several headquarters.

With a touch of whimsy, the Australians gave the island coastwatchers the code name of "Ferdinand"—because, like the storybook bull that preferred smelling flowers to fighting matadors, they were to avoid combat and flee when in danger. Emergency stations to which they could retreat at first sign of a Japanese landing were set up well inland from the coastal strips. There, hidden by the jungle, they could continue to transmit their messages.

It was through this vigilant network that word first came, in May of 1942, of the Japanese seizure of Tulagi, the British administrative capital in the Solomons and site of one of the best ship anchorages in the entire island chain. A month later came a coastwatcher's report that a Japanese work party had crossed from Tulagi to Guadalcanal and was starting to build an airfield on a grassy plain at a place called Lunga Point, in the middle of the island's north coast.

The intent of the Japanese was now chillingly clear. An air base at Guadalcanal could be as pivotal as the one at

By August 6, 1942—the eve of the Guadalcanal campaign and the first major Allied offensive in the Pacific war—the Japanese had swept across the central and southwest Pacific and were in control of all of the areas marked in red on the map. In preparation for their counterthrust, the Allies divided this vast arena into two major commands, as indicated by the white line on the map, with General Douglas MacArthur in charge of the area enclosed by the line and Admiral Chester W. Nimitz responsible for operations east and north of it. Maps of specific campaigns and battles appear throughout the book: Guadalcanal, page 26; Papua, page 48; central Solomons, page 76; Tarawa, page 109; New Guinea, page 138; Guam, Tinian and Saipan, page 168; and Peleliu, page 178.

Japan

Tokyo

Pacific Ocean

Midway

Pearl Harbor

Hawaii

Mariana Islands

MICRONESIA

Ulithi Atoll

Caroline Islands

Truk Islands

Marshall Islands

Peleliu

Tarawa Atoll

Gilbert Islands

EQUATOR

MELANESIA

New Guinea

Rabaul

Solomon Islands

Ellice Islands

Papua

Bougainville

Choiseul

New Georgia

Santa Cruz Islands

Port
Moresby

Guadalcanal

Samoa Islands

Coral Sea

New Hebrides

Fiji Islands

Cook Islands

New
Caledonia

Noumèa

Australia

Brisbane

159th Meridian

Sydney

Canberra

Melbourne

0   500   1,000

Scale of Miles at the Equator

New Zealand

21

Rabaul—and 560 miles farther east in the Pacific. Planes flying from Guadalcanal would be within striking range of other islands still in Allied hands: the New Hebrides, New Caledonia, the Fijis, Samoa. If these fell, Japanese bombers—and Japanese battleships moving out of the anchorage at Tulagi—would be in a good position to hit at the main shipping routes from the United States to Australia. Guadalcanal and Tulagi had to be retaken, and quickly, before the Japanese finished building the airfield.

The operation, set to begin in early August, was planned as an American affair, with the United States Navy's ships and planes providing the cover, the Marines seizing and securing the beachheads, and Army infantry then coming in as relief. Australia was to furnish some warships, but it could spare no troops; those of its fighting men who were not guarding the homeland, or trying to hold the line against further Japanese inroads in New Guinea, had been dispatched to shore up British forces in the Middle East. Similar manpower problems beset New Zealand, Australia's closest neighbor in the British Commonwealth of Nations, which faced the same threat from the Japanese and had also supplied troops for the fighting in the Middle East.

Because the war in Europe and the Middle East had first call on all Allied resources—ships, troops, weapons, supplies—the planners of the Guadalcanal offensive would have to manage with strict economy. To Major General Alexander A. Vandegrift, whose 1st Marine Division was to bear the burden of the assault, the odds looked far from promising. As he later put it, he could have listed "a hundred reasons why this operation would fail."

Some of the reasons were apparent on the docks of Wellington, New Zealand's capital, throughout the frantic rush of July. Wellington was serving not only as the projected jump-off point for Guadalcanal but as the port of debarkation for troops arriving from the U.S. When the offensive was ordered, many of Vandegrift's men were still at sea; like those who had preceded them, they had been shipped overseas as part of the growing American military presence in the southwest Pacific, and had been scheduled for six months of training before going into combat anywhere in the area. Though the ships bringing them to New Zealand carried such essentials of battle as field rations, fuel, weap-

ons and ammunition, these had not been loaded in a way that would expedite their orderly unloading.

The scene on Wellington's waterfront bordered on chaos. Ships were simultaneously unloading and reloading. The docks were strewn with all sorts of items useless in combat but designed to make a soldier's life away from home more bearable. It rained constantly—July is midwinter in that hemisphere—causing the cardboard cartons to burst; mushy breakfast cereals and mashed cigarettes lay scattered about amid matériel bound for Guadalcanal. Pressed for time and desperate over the shortage of shipping space, Vandegrift ordered that only items "actually required to live and to fight" were to be put on the island-bound ships. Even those items were reduced. The ammunition supply was cut by a third; the 90-day supply of food and fuel theoretically regarded as necessary was cut to 60 days' worth.

Working round the clock in eight-hour shifts, forming human chains to pass cargo loads from hand to hand, Vandegrift's troops found time for a wry joke: the official code name for the operation, Watchtower, was informally supplanted by one deemed more apt—Shoestring. Otherwise there was little of the usual banter. Some of the Marines had just crossed the Pacific on a transport that had served spoiled food, and they were still suffering from diarrhea. Others had colds or the flu, induced by Wellington's relentless rains. On the eve of their first taste of battle, the Marines' vaunted morale was at a low ebb.

In the upper echelons, anxiety over the coming offensive was mixed with a sense of relief: a hard-fought behind-the-scenes dispute as to who was to wield ultimate authority over the operation had finally been settled. Geographically, the Solomons lay within General Douglas MacArthur's Southwest Pacific Area Command, which also encompassed Australia, the Philippines, New Guinea and its neighboring islands, and all of the Dutch East Indies except Sumatra. This vast domain had been placed in MacArthur's charge in April of 1942, after his arrival in Australia from the Philippines. At the same time, the rest of the Pacific—except for a broad band of ocean off Central and South America—had been designated as the Pacific Ocean Areas Command and assigned to Admiral Chester W. Nimitz, with headquarters in Hawaii. The South Pacific part of Nimitz' domain—including New Zealand, the Fijis, Samoa, New Caledonia, the New

Hebrides and a host of smaller islands—directly bordered on MacArthur's command.

MacArthur and Nimitz, coequal and each responsible only to the U.S. Joint Chiefs of Staff, were agreed that the threat to Australia would remain until the key Japanese base at Rabaul was retaken. The Navy's planners felt that this step was best preceded by seizure of Japan's holdings in the Solomons. MacArthur, typically, had a more dramatic idea. He proposed a direct assault on Rabaul—provided he was given the services of the amphibiously trained 1st Marine Division and two of Nimitz' carriers.

Nimitz and his admirals, no great admirers of the imperious MacArthur, were aghast at the prospect of entrusting their precious carriers to him. In an assault on Rabaul, the flattops would be easy targets for Japanese planes; moreover, the ships would have to maneuver in perilously reef-ridden waters. The Navy's strategists not only urged priority for the Solomons offensive but also argued that it be put in Nimitz' charge—even though the islands were in MacArthur's assigned area—since all the operational forces involved would be naval and Marine.

The decision arrived at by the Joint Chiefs of Staff in faraway Washington was what one military historian, with no pun intended, described as "Solomonic." The line of demarcation between MacArthur's and Nimitz' commands below the equator was moved westward from the 160th east meridian to the 159th east meridian, so that Guadalcanal and Tulagi lay within Nimitz' sphere.

In the same directive that ordered Nimitz to move ahead with Task One—the seizure of Guadalcanal and Tulagi—the Joint Chiefs assigned MacArthur to what they designated as Task Two and Task Three. He was to seize the more westerly Solomons that the Japanese had occupied, as well as Japanese-held Lae and Salamaua in northeast New Guinea. These operations were to be followed by the seizure of Rabaul in New Britain.

The assault on Guadalcanal and Tulagi caught the Japanese completely by surprise. As dawn on August 7 revealed the American armada offshore, an excited Japanese radio operator on Tulagi tapped out a message to Rabaul: "Large force of ships, unknown number or types, entering the sound. What can they be?" And a little later, just before American naval guns silenced the transmitter: "Enemy forces overwhelming. We will defend our posts to the death, praying for eternal victory."

That vow was kept. The Japanese on Tulagi held out for 31 hours of brave, bitter fighting. Some died in suicide charges across what had once been a cricket ground for the British administrators of the Solomons. Others holed up in deep caves in the hills back of the shore, pouring machine-gun fire on approaching Marines until they were killed by high-explosive charges tipped into the caves.

The Japanese use of such natural redoubts—a technique they were to employ again and again in the fighting in the Pacific—was a tactic new to the Americans, and one they also learned at considerable cost in the honeycombed hills of nearby Gavutu and Tanambogo. On these islets, linked by a causeway, the Japanese fought as fiercely as their comrades on Tulagi.

Just getting ashore on Gavutu posed enormous difficulties for the Marines. The islet was rimmed by coral reefs, and the only practicable place to land, a Japanese-built seaplane ramp, had been wrecked by the Americans' sea and air bombardment. Forced to go ashore on the exposed areas adjoining the ramp, the Marines proved to be an easy target for the defenders in the hills. The Tanambogo landing, which the Marines had delayed until after sunset on D-day, produced its own special disaster. Just as the men came ashore, one of the last shells from their support ships hit a fuel dump on the beach. Instead of the cover of darkness the attackers had hoped for, they were brightly silhouetted in the flaming oil and raked by fire from the hills.

The taking of the three islands cost the Marines 144 dead or missing and 194 wounded. But they had exacted a heavier toll from the Japanese: of an estimated 800 troops, all but about 100 were killed. About 70 escaped across to Florida Island; mopping up on Florida was to go on for several weeks. The few Japanese taken alive on Tulagi, Gavutu and Tanambogo—23 captured, of whom only three surrendered—proved as instructive to the Americans as the Japanese tactic of holing up in caves. They now knew that to all but a few Japanese soldiers, death was preferable to what was viewed, in the Japanese code, as eternal dishonor.

By contrast, the landing on Guadalcanal itself went easily. The Marines swarmed ashore, unopposed, on the level sands east of the airstrip the Japanese were building at Lunga Point; the Japanese construction workers and the sailors who had brought them across from Tulagi the month before fled into the jungle to the west. At least for a while, Guadalcanal, 90 miles long and about 35 wide, seemed big enough for both the invaded and the invaders. The first American casualty was a Marine who cut his hand with a machete while trying to open a coconut from a plantation along the beach, and the only moving targets the Americans found were some wild pigs galloping through the underbrush back of the shore.

But in the waters off Guadalcanal the action came soon enough. The first wave of Marines had been on the island barely two hours when the emergency "Bells" radio frequency that was monitored by every combat ship in the fleet beeped with a message in code: FROM STO: 24 TORPEDO BOMBERS HEADED YOURS.

STO was the call sign of Paul Mason, a coastwatcher hidden on the Japanese-held island of Bougainville, 350 miles away on the air route between Guadalcanal and the Japanese base at Rabaul. Mason was wrong about the number of planes he saw; actually there were 27. But his warning, the first of many that the daring and resourceful Australian coastwatchers would flash to Guadalcanal in the weeks ahead, gave the American invasion fleet one vital hour to prepare for the enemy raid. Unloading operations ceased; the ships raised anchor and got under way; antiaircraft gunners donned helmets and scanned the skies. From the carriers *Enterprise* and *Saratoga,* cruising with the carrier *Wasp* south of Guadalcanal, squadrons of stubby Grumman Wildcat fighters rose to take station over the fleet.

Fortunately for the Americans, the two-engine Mitsubishi "Bettys" spotted by Mason had been fitted with bombs for a raid on an Allied airfield at Milne Bay, on New Guinea's southeast coast, when they received urgent orders to head for Guadalcanal and "drive back the American invasion forces at any cost." They had zoomed off without exchanging the bombs for the torpedoes that would have been more effective against the ships; high-level bombing could do little damage to alerted vessels maneuvering at high speed. The circling Wildcats and the ships' antiaircraft guns downed a number of the attacking bombers and their fighter escorts. More of the Japanese planes ran out of fuel on the way back to Rabaul and had to be ditched; the 650-mile distance to Guadalcanal was just too far for effective air strikes from Rabaul. Nevertheless, other raids followed in the next two days. All told, these cost the Japanese naval air arm at Rabaul 42 planes and, worse, 42 expert pilots. The Americans lost a transport and a destroyer, and had to delay the unloading of supplies, already behind schedule.

Meanwhile, the Marines on Guadalcanal were trying to adjust to an environment they found strange and unnerving. At night jungle birds screeched from the trees and huge land crabs crunched away under the sand, making a noise that sounded to one Marine like "tunneling operations with a hacksaw blade, or the chewing of pecans, shell and all." At every unfamiliar sound, jittery men on guard—aware from their know-your-enemy lectures that the Japanese of-

Bearing bad news, Rear Admiral Richmond Kelly Turner (left) tells Major General Alexander A. Vandegrift, commander of the Marines on Guadalcanal, that American transports must be pulled out of the landing area, even though men and supplies needed by Vandegrift were still on board. The decision was forced on Turner when Vice Admiral Frank Jack Fletcher, commander of Task Force 61, withdrew his carriers after heavy losses of his planes and under pressure of enemy bomber attacks, thereby leaving the transports with no protective air cover. The withdrawal left the Marines undefended against air and sea bombardment.

ten attacked at night—opened fire, and every time one Marine pulled his trigger another down the line would also shoot into the dark. But the Japanese were far away, lying low, and they wondered what the Americans were firing at.

The Marines' passwords had been chosen in the knowledge that the Japanese had trouble pronouncing the letter "l," and would surely stumble over words like "lollipop" or "lallygag." The first night a jeep without its lights on approached a Marine position from the beach. "Halt!" a sentry shouted. The jeep moved on. "Halt, damn you, give the password!" Still the jeep failed to stop. The sentry fired and the bullet "thwangged" off the vehicle's side. The driver then jammed on the brake and, in a Tennessee drawl that conveyed all the fervor of a revival meeting, called out: "Hallelujah, brother, Hallelujah!"

Next morning the Marines moved west through the coconut plantations and after a few brief skirmishes captured the airfield and installations the Japanese had been laboriously constructing at Lunga Point. The 2,600-foot runway was nearly completed; revetments, repair sheds and blast pens were already finished. In just a few days the Japanese would have brought in their first planes.

Wharves and machine shops, only slightly damaged by the prelanding bombardment, could quickly be utilized. More than 100 trucks and nine road rollers stood where the Japanese had left them. The Japanese had also abandoned quantities of gas, oil, kerosene, cement, many kinds of machinery and, to the delight of the division's doctor, surgical instruments that he pronounced better than his own. Other items seemed certain to ease the rigors of Operation *Shoestring*: hundreds of cases of canned meat, fish and fruit, tons of rice and—especially welcome in the humid climate—a machine for making ice. The shed housing the machine soon bore a gaudily painted sign crediting the Premier of Japan for the gift. "TOJO ICE COMPANY," it read. "Under New Management."

All in all, the Marines had captured a rich prize. But there was one flaw: seizing the airfield was not the same as holding on to it.

Shortly before 11 p.m. on August 8, General Vandegrift left the island and sped by small boat to the flagship *McCawley* to confer with Rear Admiral Richmond Kelly Turner, commander of the amphibious force. Turner had summoned Vandegrift on short notice; also present was Rear-Admiral Victor A. C. Crutchley, the Englishman in charge of the escort force of American and Australian cruisers and destroyers whose function was to protect the invasion armada from attack by sea.

Turner had three pieces of bad news to report. The first was that a Japanese naval force had been sighted en route from Rabaul. The second was that Vice Admiral Frank Jack Fletcher, commander of the entire Task Force 61, was removing the three carriers from the scene. Fletcher was concerned about the flattops' safety; a number of enemy planes had already appeared in the area. Permission to withdraw the carriers had been sought and obtained by Fletcher from the top American commander in the South Pacific, Vice Admiral Robert L. Ghormley. The third piece of news was related to the second. Turner himself, now deprived of the carriers' air cover, felt compelled to take away the vulnerable transports the next day, even though some 1,400 Marines had not debarked and more than half of Vandegrift's supplies was still in the ships' holds.

Vandegrift was stunned at Fletcher's decision to depart. Privately, he felt that the admiral was "running away." But the decision had been made. All he could do was to hurry and keep his troops unloading through the night, and hope that the Marines could get by for the few days it was expected to take the carriers to refuel and return.

But even as Vandegrift and Crutchley were leaving the *McCawley* about midnight, the stage was being set for a battle that would deprive the Marines of their lifeline for much longer than a few days.

Six cruisers and six destroyers of Crutchley's force were patrolling off tiny Savo Island, at the western entrance of Ironbottom Sound, leading to Guadalcanal. But Crutchley had taken his flagship, the cruiser *Australia*, out of the line to attend Turner's conference 25 miles away, and he had not told all of his captains that he was leaving. His ships not only lacked a battle plan, but were patrolling in two separate groups, out of touch with each other.

When small floatplanes appeared overhead at about 11 p.m. the ships' officers thought they were friendly, because their running lights were on and no alert had been received. Poor communications and bungled command responsibility prevented word of the floatplanes' appearance from reaching the flagship *McCawley*. Crutchley and Turner, knowing that the American carriers and their aircraft were on their way out of the area, would have realized that these were planes from an approaching enemy force.

This was the Japanese naval force that Turner had mentioned at the conference, but it was much larger—and nearer—than he thought. Commanded by Vice Admiral Gunichi Mikawa, one of the Japanese Navy's boldest tacticians, seven cruisers and a destroyer swept unchallenged into the channel between Savo and Guadalcanal. Shortly before 1 a.m., a Japanese lookout spotted a lone American destroyer, the *Blue*, on picket duty. On the bridge of the cruiser *Chokai*, Mikawa's flagship, the admiral and his staff froze. From the destroyer's "deliberate, unconcerned progress," one Japanese officer recalled, "it was plain that she was unaware of us—or of being watched—and of the fact that every gun in our force was trained directly on her.

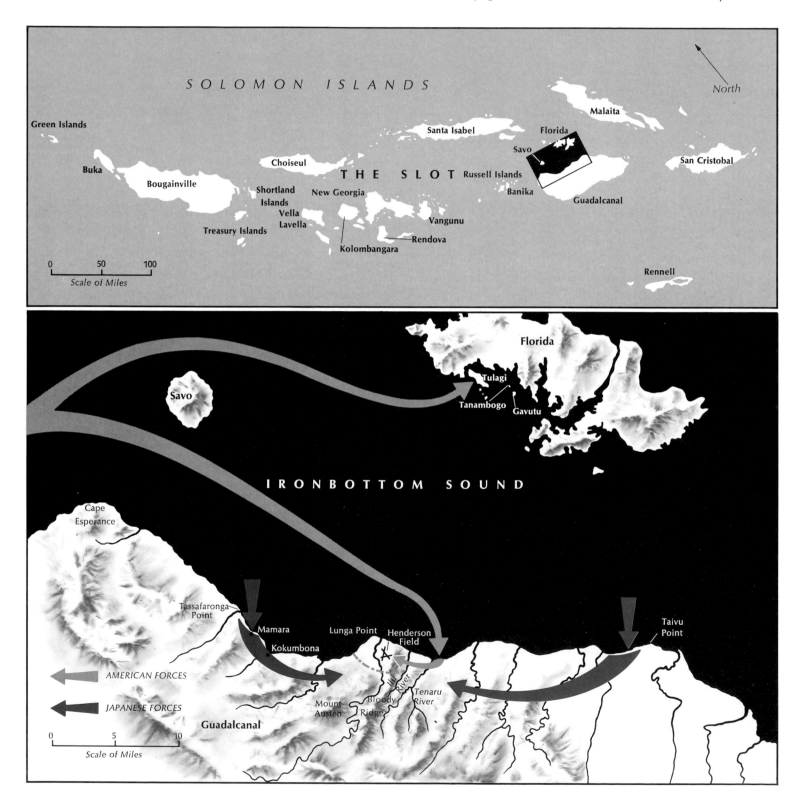

Mount Austen

Henderson Field

Ilu River

The first U.S. offensive in the southwest Pacific got under way on the 7th of August, 1942, in the Solomon Islands (top map at left) with an assault on Japanese-held Tulagi and Guadalcanal (highlighted area). U.S. Marine amphibious forces, rounding Cape Esperance (bottom map), split into elements for the landings. One secured Tulagi, Tanambogo and Gavutu after stiff initial resistance from Japanese manning cave and dugout emplacements. The other landed to the east of the Tenaru River on Guadalcanal and advanced along the coast, capturing a partially built airstrip on Lunga Point. Waves of Japanese counterattackers came ashore near Mamara, Kokumbona and Taivu Point from late August through October, and staged several unsuccessful attempts to penetrate the U.S. defensive perimeter (broken line) and regain the airfield. The most crucial fighting resulted in an American victory at Bloody Ridge.

The north coast of Guadalcanal, where the heaviest fighting of the bitter campaign took place, is seen in a labeled photograph taken from a Navy reconnaissance plane in late August, 1942. In two days of combat along the Ilu River (foreground), some 800 Japanese soldiers were killed. In the background is Henderson Field, site of the American headquarters and base for U.S. planes. Overlooking the airstrip is Mount Austen, a strategic 1,500-foot ridge that was held by the Japanese until January 1943.

Seconds strained by while we waited for the inevitable moment when she must sight us—and then the enemy destroyer reversed course."

Mikawa, incredulous at his good fortune, held his fire and steamed through the open picket fence. Not until 1:43 a.m., when his battle line was within two miles of the southern part of Crutchley's force, did an American destroyer, the *Patterson*, radio an alarm. It was too late. Torpedoes from Mikawa's cruisers were already in the water; within seconds brilliant flares dropped by his scout planes lighted up the scene and his guns began firing. Some Allied ships were hit while the general alarm was still sounding. With Crutchley absent, no orders were issued between ships, and no warnings were sent after the first one—which not all the ships had heard.

In 40 minutes the Battle of Savo Island was over. Two Allied cruisers were sunk and another two were so badly damaged that they were later abandoned. Floatplanes aboard the cruisers, intended to be used to scout for the 1st Marine Division, were also lost. The fifth cruiser was put out of action and required extensive repairs. One of the destroyers was also heavily damaged. The Japanese emerged unhurt except for the destruction of Mikawa's chart room on the *Chokai,* which had taken a salvo from the cruiser *Quincy.* Not wishing to press his luck, believing that American carriers were still in the area and that their planes would find him in the morning, Mikawa ignored the now unprotected transports and sped homeward. His superiors later chastised him for not attacking the transports. But behind him he left 1,023 Australian and American sailors dead—a loss greater than the total number of Marines who were to die on Guadalcanal—and another 709 wounded, burned and exhausted men floundering in the oil-covered, shark-infested waters of Ironbottom Sound.

Now the Marines stood alone. With the carriers gone, Japanese planes raided every day around noon—"Tojo Time," the Marines began to call it. Turner's transports had left after picking up survivors of the Savo battle, and no one knew when his ships would be able to return. Almost daily, a Japanese cruiser or destroyer appeared in plain view of the cursing Marines, but out of range of their guns, and shelled the exposed four-mile expanse of the Lunga Point beachhead. Then the threat from the land side took on new urgency. On August 12 the 1st Marine Division's intelligence officer led a patrol by boat to follow up a Japanese prisoner's hint that some of his comrades on a beach to the west might want to surrender. The patrol was virtually annihilated on the beach: only three of its 26 members returned, swimming. Imprinted in the mind of one of them was the memory of "sabers flashing in the sun." For the first time, the Marines had some measure of the toughness of the foe they faced.

The shoestring of supply had been cut by the departure of the transports. The amount of food on hand was enough for only 30 days—counting 10 days' worth of captured Japanese rice and fish—and the Marines would have to be put on short rations. Less than one half of the ammunition, and only 18 spools of barbed wire, had been brought ashore. Thousands of sandbags and such elementary tools as shovels, axes and saws had been left aboard, as had radar sets, 155mm howitzers and coastal defense guns. All of the Marines' heavy equipment, with the exception of one bulldozer, was still in the ships' holds and now en route south to New Caledonia, the nearest big island that was under Allied control.

The lone bulldozer soon became a legend. It belonged to the Marine 1st Pioneer Battalion, an engineer unit, and only its regular operator, Private Roy F. Cate, was allowed to touch it. Cate drove it from morning to night on every conceivable sort of tugging and towing job until finally it fell apart, as one officer recalled, "like the one hoss shay, never to run again."

Yet the airfield had to be completed, defenses had to be dug. The equipment left behind by the Japanese proved to be the answer to the problem—indeed, to many problems. Lieut. Colonel Samuel B. Griffith later described the way it went: "Daily the engineers extended the runway. With Japanese dynamite they cleared obstructing trees from the north end, and with three earth tampers operated by Japanese air compressors laboriously packed new fill excavated by Marine-powered Japanese picks and shovels, and brought to the site in Japanese trucks fueled with Japanese gasoline. . . . Marines queued up to use latrines built of Japanese lumber and protected from flies by Japanese screen. When the Japanese siren announced the approach of Japanese planes, Marines dove into holes dug and roofed by the Japanese."

The airstrip was completed within two weeks. It was named Henderson Field, in honor of Major Lofton R. Henderson, a Marine dive-bomber squadron leader who had died in air combat during the Battle of Midway. The field was now ready for U.S. planes, and on the evening of August 20—13 days after the Marines had landed—General Vandegrift was standing by the side of the strip when he happened to look up at the sky. "From the east," he recalled, "flying into the evening sun came one of the most beautiful sights of my life—a flight of 12 SBD dive bombers." The flight leader was Marine Major Richard D. Mangrum, and his arrival stirred deep emotion. "I was close to tears and I was not alone," Vandegrift later wrote, "when the first SBD taxied up and this handsome and dashing aviator jumped to the ground. 'Thank God you have come,' I told him." Then 19 Wildcats arrived, led by Marine Captain John L. Smith. The planes had flown in from the carrier *Long Island,* stationed about 200 miles southeast of Guadalcanal.

The "Cactus Air Force," so called for the code name of Guadalcanal, was in business. And just in time: a Japanese attempt to retake the Marines' beachhead was under way.

Vandegrift had some 10,000 men on Guadalcanal, 6,000 on Tulagi—and an advantage he was not aware of: the Japanese had underestimated his strength. They believed that no more than 2,000 Marines had gone ashore, and when they saw that the beachhead had been left unprotected they concluded that Vandegrift had been abandoned. Eager to "recapture these areas promptly," Imperial General Headquarters had on August 13 authorized an immediate attack. No more than about 2,000 men seemed needed to retake the beachhead. The Japanese still regarded the New Guinea campaign as their major effort and considered the Marines on Guadalcanal as no more than a nuisance.

The crack Army regiment assigned to eliminate the nuisance was led by Colonel Kiyono Ichiki. On the night of August 18, destroyers from Rabaul slipped through the waters off Guadalcanal, past Lunga Point, and deposited Ichiki and 1,000 of his men 20 miles to the east, at a place called Taivu Point. Marines at Lunga heard the wash of ships going in that direction; next day a patrol ambushed some Japa-

nese who were stringing telephone wire and brought back grim confirmation that fresh Japanese troops had landed.

Among the many small rivers and streams that flowed from the mountains back of the shore, one that separated the Japanese and American positions was the Ilu River. Because it was mis-marked on the Americans' maps as the Tenaru, the savage confrontation that took place there was to go down in Marine annals as the Battle of the Tenaru River. The Marines dug in along the creek and waited.

Either out of supreme self-assurance or because he knew his presence had been detected, Ichiki impetuously decided to attack at once with his 1,000 men instead of waiting, as ordered, for the rest of his regiment to arrive. So confident was he of success that he postdated an entry in his diary: "21 August. Enjoyment of the fruits of victory." As night fell on the 20th he moved his small force westward, passed along the beach area where the Marines had first landed and at about 3 a.m. gave the signal to attack. Japanese mortar shells exploded on the Marine line along the west bank of the creek and some 200 of Ichiki's men charged across a narrow sandspit at its mouth. In the sickly green light of flares the Marines saw a closely packed throng of Japanese trotting through the shallows, their bayonets fixed.

Lieut. Colonel Edwin A. Pollock's 2nd Battalion, 1st Marine Regiment, was ready. Point-blank fire from an antitank gun loaded with canister shells cut down the attacking soldiers in clumps. Those who made it across the creek got caught on a line of barbed wire; Marine machine guns farther up the stream picked them off from the flank.

But a few spots were unprotected by wire, and some of Ichiki's men got through. Three rushed at Corporal Dean Wilson in his foxhole. Wilson's automatic rifle jammed. The Japanese came on, screaming "Marine, you die!" and one leaped into the foxhole. Wilson lunged for his machete and slashed, and the attacker clutched his oozing middle. Wilson then jumped out of the hole and hacked the other two to death. Other Marines were not so quick. In a wild melee of knives, bayonets and rifle butts, the Japanese overran some Marine positions. But not enough had come through to hold when Pollock threw in a reserve platoon.

One Marine machine gunner who was firing tracers was spotted by a Japanese gunner across the creek; the Marine was fatally hit, but his finger froze on the trigger and 200 more rounds went off. Private Albert Schmid took over the gun; another Marine helped him spot targets, punching Schmid on the arm and pointing when he found one, for the noise made talking impossible. Schmid heard one Japanese officer "screeching and barking commands at the others; he had a nasty shrill voice that stood out over all the firing." Schmid let off a burst in the direction of the voice but failed to silence it; it was to haunt him for years. Then Schmid's buddy was hit and there was no one to load for him. Schmid kept firing at shadowy waves of Japanese in the river and at flashes he could see in the coconut palms on the other side. Then a grenade sailed into his position; there was an explosion and Al Schmid could see no more. (Almost totally blinded, he was to win the Navy Cross and help Hollywood make a movie about his life.)

All night Ichiki continued his assault. All night the Marines' antitank guns, machine guns and artillery cut his men down. At dawn, when it was clear the position would hold, Vandegrift sent a reserve battalion to cross the creek upstream and move down on the Japanese survivors from their flank and rear. The Japanese panicked. Some ran into the sea. Others fled eastward along the shore, where they were strafed and bombed by Vandegrift's newly arrived planes. Meanwhile, Marine tanks crossed the sandbar spitting canister and flushing out Japanese still hiding in a coconut grove. The steel treads crushed and mangled the Japanese—living, dead and dying—until, as Vandegrift put it, "the rear of the tanks looked like meat grinders."

Some 800 elite Japanese soldiers had been killed. Their torn bodies lay on the sandspit and clogged the mouth of the creek. Ichiki escaped with a handful of men. At the spot where the destroyers from Rabaul had put him ashore, he burned his regimental colors and committed hara-kiri.

There was an ironic postscript to Ichiki's failure to heed orders to attack only after the rest of his men had landed: the additional troops never did arrive. Instead they found themselves in the middle of a naval battle. To deliver them to the island, an especially large fleet had been put together by Admiral Isoroku Yamamoto, the Japanese Navy's commander in chief. The acclaim accorded Yamamoto as the hero of the Pearl Harbor attack had been distinctly muted as a result of his crushing defeat in the Battle of Midway. Thirsting for revenge on the American carriers, he assigned

Japanese soldiers, killed by U.S. Marines on Guadalcanal, lie half-buried in a sand bar near the mouth of the Ilu River in August of 1942. Members of Colonel Kiyono Ichiki's crack 28th Infantry Regiment, they made a futile attempt to overrun positions held by the 2nd Battalion, 1st Marine Regiment, and were mowed down by rifles, machine guns and 37mm guns.

a cruiser and three destroyers to escort the transports taking the troops to Guadalcanal. Yamamoto also dispatched three carriers, two battleships, 11 cruisers and 19 destroyers to range farther east in search of the American fleet.

Contact was made on August 24, and the result was the battle of the eastern Solomons, a two-day encounter without a clear-cut decision for either side. The Japanese lost one carrier, the *Ryujo,* and 90 planes. The American carrier *Enterprise* was damaged and 20 planes lost. While the big ships of both sides were withdrawing, the Japanese troop convoy was spotted 100 miles west of Guadalcanal and racing toward it. Dive bombers from Henderson Field, including a carrier squadron that had transferred there when the *Enterprise* was hit, attacked the enemy convoy first; they sank one transport and forced the convoy's commander, Rear Admiral Raizo Tanaka, to abandon his damaged flagship, the cruiser *Jintsu,* and send it back to base. Minutes later land-based B-17s from the Allied-controlled New Hebrides appeared and sank one of Tanaka's destroyers. The rest of the Japanese warships and transports took off, their mission unfulfilled.

After the battle was over, supplies began to arrive again on Guadalcanal, but the Marines were less than jubilant. The island itself was taking its toll.

From the landing craft that had brought the men ashore in early August, many had thought Guadalcanal beautiful—green, lush, mountainous, barely touched by civilization. The admiration was fleeting. By now the Marines were all too familiar with Guadalcanal's other faces: the heavy rains that kept everything soggy, the patches of *kunai* grass—taller than a man—with edges that cut like hack saws when patrols tried to get through. And there was still worse, later vividly described by the perceptive Private Leckie.

Beneath Guadalcanal's loveliness, he wrote, "she was a mass of slops and stinks and pestilence; of scum-crested lagoons and vile swamps inhabited by giant crocodiles; a place of spiders as big as your fist and wasps as long as your finger, of lizards . . . tree-leeches . . . scorpions . . . centipedes whose foul scurrying across human skin leaves a track of inflamed flesh. . . . By night, mosquitoes come in clouds—bringing malaria, dengue or any one of a dozen filthy exotic fevers. . . . And Guadalcanal stank. She was sour

with the odor of her own decay, her breath so hot and humid, so sullen and so still, that the Marines cursed and swore to feel the vitality oozing from them in a steady stream of enervating sweat."

Just about everyone's health suffered. Dysentery raged, crippling the men. The affliction was spread by the swarms of flies that settled on food whenever a ration can was opened. The men developed a twitching flick-bite habit of eating, shaking the flies off with one motion of the spoon, then quickly bringing the spoon to the mouth with another. Feverish troops began turning up at the sick bays; in the end malaria was to account for more Marine casualties than enemy bullets did. Many who showed no outward signs of the disease nevertheless grew listless; they would collapse on patrol and refuse to go on until threatened with abandonment. Some balked at taking Atabrine—which would have helped—believing that it would make them impotent; medics were posted at the chow lines with orders to watch each man swallow a pill before allowing him to eat.

"Day by day," wrote Vandegrift, "I watched my Marines deteriorate in the flesh. Although lean Marines are better than fat Marines, these troops were becoming too lean."

The arrival of the Cactus Air Force had strengthened Vandegrift's beachhead and at the same time had made it a more critical target. Planes from Rabaul pounded Henderson Field continuously, and in mid-September the Japanese launched another drive to take it from the ground. Colonel Ichiki's ill-fated earlier attempt was not repeated. This time there were many more men—including Ichiki's second echelon of elite soldiers.

The troops, led by Major General Kiyotake Kawaguchi, were brought to Guadalcanal in ships commanded by Admiral Tanaka. After losing one of his transports in the wake of the eastern Solomons battle, Tanaka had concluded that the only way to bring troops to Guadalcanal was in fast destroyer runs at night. General Kawaguchi objected; he wanted his force to travel by barges, which could carry artillery and more supplies. The dispute was resolved by compromise; both means were used—and the barges were promptly sunk by planes from Henderson. But meanwhile, in six night runs, Tanaka's destroyers landed Kawaguchi himself and 6,000 of his men. The runs were made through the main channel dividing the Solomons to the north from

Japanese troops on Shortland Island in the Solomons prepare to board barges that will carry them south through "The Slot" and deposit them on Guadalcanal. Barges, cruisers and destroyers delivered troops and supplies at night in order to avoid American planes and ships; Marines nicknamed the clandestine nocturnal runs "The Tokyo Express."

those to the south; the islands were, in fact, a double chain. The Marines called the channel "The Slot," and dubbed Tanaka's nightly sorties the "Tokyo Express." The Japanese had their own rueful name for them—"rat" runs.

Incredibly, Kawaguchi repeated Ichiki's mistake. He decided he could take Lunga Point with the forces he had on hand, even though his more prudent superiors had ordered him to reconnoiter and see if more men were needed. He planned to accept Vandegrift's surrender personally—he had even decided the very spot where it would take place.

Kawaguchi's main force had landed to the east of Henderson, near Ichiki's original base in the Taivu Point area, and the general planned to lead it around through the jungle to strike at the field from inland. Simultaneously another part of Kawaguchi's force was to attack from the east across the same creek where Ichiki's men had fought, while a third part, landed near the village of Kokumbona to the west of the Marines, would come in from that side. Japanese cruisers and bombers stood by to support the attack from sea and air. Once Henderson was captured, other air units from Rabaul were to land on the field and take it over. Even the date had been set: September 13.

Things went wrong for the Japanese from the outset. As Kawaguchi started westward through the jungle, the 1st Marine Raider Battalion under Lieut. Colonel Merritt A. Edson raided his base camp, destroyed his big guns and his radio, and ruined his food supply by what one report called "unorthodox but effective means" (the Marines relieved themselves on it). Having set out through the jungle without native guides or reliable maps, the Japanese force bogged down in mud and rain, and quickly became disorganized

and dispersed. Without dependable radio communication, Kawaguchi could not coordinate the complex operation he had planned.

Vandegrift and his staff guessed that the enemy attack, when it materialized, would come along a low, grassy ridge about a mile south of the airstrip, roughly parallel to the Lunga River. Edson's battalion was assigned to defend the ridge, and was deployed along its lower slopes, leading down to the Lunga's east bank. Edson knew he was in the right place when a Japanese Betty, ignoring the airfield, neatly laid a stick of bombs along the top of the ridge.

At dusk on September 12 the atmosphere at Vandegrift's headquarters was especially tense. More planes had arrived at the field, but many others had been lost to enemy action, accidents and the bomb-cratered runway. Shortages of gasoline, bombs and oxygen limited the effectiveness of those that could fly. Vandegrift had only one battalion of troops in reserve; the rest of his "too lean" Marines were on the line. And Admiral Ghormley had sent word that because of a major Japanese build-up at Rabaul, the Marines at Guadalcanal could no longer count on sea or air support. Quietly, the division's operations officer was told to draw up a secret contingency plan for withdrawal into the hills.

The battle of Bloody Ridge began that night at nine, with a barrage of shells from Japanese warships offshore, followed by an outbreak of rifle and mortar fire. Japanese soldiers wriggled forward through the underbrush on the lower slopes, probing the Marines' positions.

Next day Edson pulled back to higher ground, leaving an open, grassy no man's land between his lines and the Japanese. "This is it," he told his men. "There is only us between

the airfield and the Japs. If we don't hold, we will lose Guadalcanal." That night Kawaguchi's battalions, moving in from south of the ridge, came double-timing along the east bank of the Lunga, wheeled up to the ridge and cut an entire Marine company into small pockets while chanting "U.S. Marine be dead tomorrow." They crossed the grassy area, retreated under artillery fire, and then regrouped and came on again. Edson picked up his field phone to order the company captain to withdraw as many of his men as possible. The voice on the other end spoke to him formally, in clipped tones: "Our situation here, Colonel Edson, is excellent. Thank you, sir." Edson knew none of his officers talked like that; the enemy was on the line. He found a leather-lunged corporal and had him bellow toward the company's position: "Red Mike says it's okay to pull back." The use of Edson's nickname made clear that the message was genuine, and the company fought its way back up the ridge.

The Japanese drove Edson's men to the last knoll on the ridge, to within 1,000 yards of the airfield. But reserve companies of Marines moved in to bolster Edson's lines, and the division's artillery was firing from the top of the ridge. By dawn Kawaguchi's attack was running out of bodies to carry it forward; then, at first light, those Japanese who were still on the ridge were strafed by Henderson Field's Army P-39 fighters. Kawaguchi ordered retreat.

His other two forces, attacking along the coast from the east and the west of Henderson, fared no better. They were unable to penetrate the Marines' positions, and were driven back. Out at sea the Japanese fleet had confidently awaited word of Henderson's capture. When Kawaguchi signaled that he had failed, one Japanese captain recalled, "We stamped our feet in bitter anger." At his headquarters on the Japanese island of Truk 1,200 miles to the north, Admiral Yamamoto decided it would take a full division to recapture Guadalcanal. At his headquarters in Nouméa, 800 miles to the southeast in New Caledonia, Admiral Ghormley reassessed the situation and decided he could send more troops to Guadalcanal after all.

For 600 of Kawaguchi's men the ordeal was over. For the rest of his troops, wounded or not, worse was to come. They had expected to be eating Marine rations at Henderson Field on September 14. Now they had to make their way through the mountains to the Japanese-held areas to the west, and they had nothing to eat. They clawed at the bark of trees, gnawed at their leather rifle straps, dug up roots and struggled on. They passed bodies of their comrades, arms upraised as if reaching for something. Noncoms had to lash the younger soldiers to keep them going. "We are nothing but skin and bones, pale wild men," noted one Japanese who managed to hang on to his diary. "I have become like a primitive man."

In October, a full division of the Japanese Seventeenth Army under Lieut. General Haruyoshi Hyakutake was sent in against the Marines. A month earlier Hyakutake would probably have prevailed, but by October, General Vandegrift had been reinforced too, with more Marines, more planes and the vanguard of the Army troops that had been projected as replacements when the Guadalcanal offensive was planned; moreover, a second runway had been built to supplement the main runway at Henderson Field.

The Japanese division jumped off from Kokumbona, the same area used by part of Kawaguchi's ill-fated force in September, and launched an attack that was almost a replica of Kawaguchi's operation, on a larger scale: a debilitating, poorly planned march through the jungle, from the west this time, a night assault on a strong Marine defense line within rifleshot of Bloody Ridge, diversionary attacks that failed to coordinate and ignominious defeat. Thereafter Hyakutake concentrated on defending the western end of the island against larger and larger American forays, expecting the Japanese Navy to provide his ultimate salvation.

The Japanese Navy had every intention of doing so. As October ended, it moved to seize full and final control of the waters around Guadalcanal. The campaign lasted through the month of November and was to be what one American historian described as "a rough school for the U.S. Navy." Supervising the American effort was bluff, tough Vice Admiral William F. "Bull" Halsey Jr., who had just replaced Ghormley as chief of the South Pacific command.

The campaign took the form of a series of naval engagements at widely separated points around Guadalcanal. On October 26 a one-day battle off the Santa Cruz Islands to the east caused heavy damage to two Japanese carriers and a cruiser, and the loss of 100 planes. The American force, smaller than the enemy's, came off worse. The carrier *Hor-*

net and a destroyer were sunk, 74 carrier planes were lost, and the carrier *Enterprise,* the new battleship *South Dakota,* a cruiser and a destroyer were damaged.

In mid-November three days of encounters, collectively known in American Navy annals as the Battle of Guadalcanal, took place closer to the island itself, off Cape Esperance and Tassafaronga Point. The Americans suffered the loss of two light cruisers and seven destroyers, and damage to seven other ships; in addition, the commanders of two of the three American groups, Rear Admirals Daniel J. Callaghan and Norman Scott, were killed. The toll taken of the Japanese came to 13 ships sunk—including two battleships, a heavy cruiser, three destroyers and seven transports—and nine ships damaged. Another four transports were destroyed by planes from Henderson Field after they had been run aground at Tassafaronga Point; more than 6,000 Japanese reinforcements intended for General Hyakutake were killed.

The final encounter, off Tassafaronga on the night of November 30, cost the Americans one cruiser, while three others were badly damaged. The Japanese lost only one of the eight destroyers that made up their force. Despite the drubbing they gave the Americans, the Japanese were repulsed and withdrew—taking with them the troops and supplies they had proposed to land on Guadalcanal. Thereafter they succeeded in sending in only trickles of supplies and troop reinforcements, no more than 1,000 men in all.

For the Americans, the seas off Guadalcanal were now, for all intents and purposes, clear of the enemy threat. By early December, more and more ships, bearing new supplies and fresh fighting men, began arriving on the island.

On December 9, General Vandegrift and his 1st Marine Division left Guadalcanal for a richly deserved rest in Australia. They had stood their ground far longer than the planners of the offensive had counted on, taking Japanese air raids and naval bombardments and infantry attacks, subsisting on skimpy rations, enduring sickness and disease. A Presidential Unit Citation for the entire 1st Marine Division acclaimed its achievement.

Taking the 1st's place on Guadalcanal were the 2nd Marine Division and two Army divisions—the Americal and 25th—with Major General Alexander M. Patch as commander of the newly activated XIV Corps. For much of January, Patch devoted his attention to Mount Austen, a 1,500-foot peak where a number of Japanese had dug in. It lay about six miles southwest of Henderson Field and afforded a clear view of the field—and of ship unloadings and troop movements everywhere in the Lunga Point area.

General Vandegrift had intended to take Mount Austen when his troops first landed, but had dropped the plan upon discovering that it was much farther from Lunga Point than his maps indicated; he had enough to do to hang on to the beachhead. General Patch now concluded that taking the mountain was an essential prelude to a major offensive against General Hyakutake's main force to the west.

Actually, the mountain was not a single peak but a jumble of ridges, steep and rocky, with grassy areas amid dense jungle. Supplies had to be hand carried; the wounded had to be evacuated over rough tracks. The fighting was savage and often close up; the Japanese had entrenched themselves in caves and man-made dugouts, and had to be blasted out with grenades and mortars.

In time, the 132nd Infantry Regiment of the Americal Division gained control of a strong point called the Gifu. Its occupation by the Americans deprived the Japanese of a crucial overlook; they could no longer observe the comings and goings at the Lunga beachhead. In the end, they were simply isolated. Patch had changed his tactics; part of Mount Austen remained in Japanese hands, but Patch decided to send his troops around it, and they headed toward Hyakutake's main force.

Hyakutake himself, along with his staff, had already departed for the big Japanese-held island of Bougainville in the western Solomons, closer to Rabaul. Some of his senior commanders also decamped, deserting their troops.

On three dark nights in early February of 1943, while American soldiers approached Hyakutake's force from two sides, the last Tokyo Expresses raced down The Slot. They evacuated Hyakutake's 13,000 sick, wounded and starving survivors—all that was left of 36,000 Japanese who had come to fight on what they now called the Island of Death.

After their departure a Japanese report written during the battle was found. It contained these prophetic words: "It must be said that success or failure in recapturing Guadalcanal, and the results of the final naval battle related to it, is the fork in the road that leads to victory for them or for us."

THE ALLIES' EYES AND EARS

Behind enemy lines, coastwatcher scouts paddle to a U.S. rescue seaplane to deliver a Marine pilot shot down over Segi Point, New Georgia, in April 1943.

ISLAND NETWORKS OF SCOUTS AND SPIES

Chief of the coastwatchers, Australian Lieut. Commander Eric Feldt (middle row, second from left) is pictured with his men late in the War.

While the Japanese swept through the southwest Pacific, an intrepid band of Allied coastwatchers manned more than 100 lonely, radio-equipped lookout posts on enemy-occupied islands. Recruited by the Australian Navy, these former traders, planters, prospectors and government officers monitored Japanese naval, troop and air movements across a 2,500-mile crescent of ocean, stretching from New Guinea to the New Hebrides, and radioed the intelligence they gathered to Allied headquarters. On one occasion, a radio flash from coastwatcher Jack Read on Bougainville in the Solomon Islands alerted American fliers, who subsequently shot down 36 of 44 Japanese planes that were heading for Guadalcanal.

In addition to their intelligence-gathering activities, the coastwatchers rescued downed Allied airmen and saved hundreds of survivors of ships and boats destroyed by the Japanese, including the crew of Lieutenant (jg.) John F. Kennedy's PT 109.

The success of the network depended heavily on the good will—and oftentimes the extraordinary bravery—of many local inhabitants, some of whom risked their lives serving the Allies as scouts, guides, porters and spies. One scout, Jacob Vouza (right), was captured by a Japanese patrol as he returned from a mission on Guadalcanal in August of 1942. The Japanese soon discovered that he was carrying a small American flag that had been given to him by a Marine. When Vouza refused to answer their questions, they tied him to a tree and pummeled him with rifle butts. When he still refused to talk, his captors bayoneted him in the chest five times, slashed his throat with a sword and left him for dead. But Vouza gnawed through his bonds and half-crawled, half-staggered three miles to a Marine post. There, before collapsing from loss of blood, he managed to give the best report yet received of enemy strength on the island.

"The coastwatchers saved Guadalcanal," said Admiral William F. Halsey Jr., commander in chief of the South Pacific area, "and Guadalcanal saved the Pacific."

Island scout Jacob Vouza, in Marine fatigues, wields a captured Japanese sword. After delivering vital intelligence, Vouza was awarded the U.S. Silver Star.

SURVEYING THE SCENE FROM HIDDEN LOOKOUTS

From their meticulously camouflaged vantage points on beaches, ridges and mountaintops, the coastwatchers passed long, tension-filled days scanning the horizon for signs of Japanese activity. When there was information to report, they transmitted it by teleradio, which could send messages 400 miles by voice and 600 by Morse key. Allied control stations continuously monitored the network's emergency "X" frequency, and news of Japanese troop, naval and air movements could be beamed across the entire Pacific within minutes.

While the Japanese found it almost impossible to spot the coastwatchers' hideaways from the air, they did intercept the coastwatchers' signals, and they employed radio direction-finding equipment to pinpoint the source. Japanese patrols fanned out over islands where the coastwatchers were operating. Alerted to the enemy's approach by local inhabitants, the Allied lookouts fled on foot or by boat to secluded areas where caches of supplies had been carefully hidden. At one fallback position on Guadalcanal were 110 cases of food, 93 bags of rice, 200 cases of kerosene—and 50 cases of whiskey.

The hideaways of the coastwatchers—often clusters of leaf huts—were supplied by airdrops or, less frequently, by submarine. But airdrops could not always be arranged and were often inaccurate. When the supply efforts failed, the coastwatchers had to rely on food that grew wild or that could be provided by their island friends—potatoes, taro root, coconuts, bananas, a melon-like fruit called *pau-pau* and, on occasion, pumpkins.

Some of the coastwatchers were lucky enough to occupy outposts so remote—and therefore so secure—that they could enjoy a fairly comfortable life style. Donald G. Kennedy (*right, bottom*) took over a plantation house at Segi Point, New Georgia, and turned it into an efficient tropical camp. When he had visitors, Kennedy liked to serve cocktails on the veranda, and would have his table set with silver, china and clean linen. Houseboys wearing jackets served the meals, while outside, sentries patrolled the perimeter and guarded a stockade where Japanese prisoners who had come dangerously close to the compound were kept.

Atop a tree, coastwatchers keep a lookout for Japanese activity near Salamaua, New Guinea, in 1942.

Heavily camouflaged coastwatchers man a secret observation post hidden by thick jungle growth.

The Waiai, used by Donald Kennedy in his coastwatching work, sits at anchor in a remote cove.

Sweltering in an earthen dugout on Guadalcanal, a teleradio operator and his assistant monitor the control station for all coastwatchers in the Solomons.

In the dining room of his hideaway on New Georgia, Donald Kennedy (center) takes tea with military personnel who had come to discuss invasion plans.

Pipe-smoking Jack Read saved American nuns.

The four nuns rescued on Bougainville stand with their mother superior, M. Francis (second from left).

The United States submarine Nautilus, which transported nuns and civilians away from Bougainville on December 31, 1942, heads out on another mission.

THE COASTWATCHERS' DANGEROUS MISSIONS

Maintaining their cover was key to the survival of the coastwatchers, yet there were times when they risked everything to help or rescue people in trouble—going so far as to scoop out of the open sea downed airmen or shipwrecked sailors. Though the coastwatchers grumbled about the intrusion of the people they called "boarders," they did their best to make them feel at home. Nick Waddell, a coastwatcher on Choiseul in the Solomons, kept a guest register and formed the "Rubber Rafters Association," a club composed of rescued Allied pilots. Each member received a certificate, and promised to get drunk annually on the anniversary of his rescue.

Coastwatchers were also responsible for saving many island residents, landowners, prospectors and missionaries who believed that they could remain on the Japanese-occupied islands as neutrals. Among those reluctant to leave were four nuns who had been sent to Bougainville in 1940 by the Sisters of Saint Joseph of Orange, California. Bougainville coastwatcher Jack Read, aware of atrocities committed by the Japanese elsewhere in the Solomons, knew their likely fate if the nuns were to stay on to continue their missionary work. He radioed an appeal direct to Admiral Halsey requesting the evacuation of the nuns and 25 other civilians.

On a pitch-dark night in December of 1942, the U.S. submarine *Nautilus* hovered outside Teop Harbor, Bougainville. Waiting on the beach, signaling by fires and a white sheet, was Jack Read's party of refugees. In a race against the dawn—and possible snooping Japanese patrol boats—the *Nautilus*' launch made two trips ashore and ferried the entire group to safety.

His hands lashed together, a 19-year-old Japanese Zero pilot, who was captured when engine trouble caused his plane to crash, grimaces with terror as he is held in custody by scouts on New Georgia in 1942. The chief tribesman of the island (holding lantern) supervises the detention. Islanders like these were frequently awarded one bag of rice each for the rescue and return of downed Allied and enemy airmen.

Accompanied by an oarsman, Marine Lieutenant Milton N. Vedder watches in a boat for the seaplane that will fly him out of Japanese-occupied New Georgia in April 1943. Vedder bailed out at 300 feet after his plane was hit during a dogfight. He paddled seven miles in a rubber boat to New Georgia, where he won over unfriendly inhabitants by blowing smoke rings, before coastwatchers at Segi Point arranged for his rescue.

With stripes taped to his bare arm to indicate his rank in the New Guinea Native Constabulary, Sergeant Yauwika, chief coastwatching scout on Bougainville, is awarded the Loyal Service Medal by an Australian Navy officer in 1945. Other scouts and Australian officers witness the ceremony.

2

Shortly after dark on the evening of July 21, 1942, Japanese troops began landing on the northern coast of that part of New Guinea known as Papua. The following day, Allied airmen tried to halt the build-up of the invasion forces, flying 81 sorties, dropping 48 tons of bombs and using up more than 15,000 rounds of ammunition on the landing area. But hampered by haze, they sank only one transport, one landing barge and one floatplane. By 9:15 a.m. the invasion fleet had disgorged the attacking force and was on its way back to Rabaul to load up with reinforcements. Japanese troops, safely landed on the beach to the east of the village of Gona, with its small Anglican mission, now scooped up their supplies and hurried toward the jungle, shielded at first by the thickening haze and then by the luxuriant growth. Quickly, silently, they filtered inland.

Their ultimate objective was Port Moresby, a little coastal town over the Owen Stanley Range in southern Papua. Only 300 miles across Torres Strait from the Australian mainland, Port Moresby had grown in six months into a major Allied base, a bulwark against a Japanese onslaught on Australia and a vital launching platform for air attacks on enemy-occupied Lae and Salamaua in eastern New Guinea.

The Japanese had been planning an offensive against Port Moresby for several months. They wanted the Allied base as a springboard for attacks on Australia and a link with their bases at Lae and Salamaua.

But wanting it was one thing, taking it another. Any approach over water would be barred by Allied warships—as the Japanese had learned to their sorrow two months earlier, when their seaborne thrust was parried by carriers of the U.S. Pacific Fleet in the Battle of the Coral Sea.

Thwarted in their attempt to capture Port Moresby by sea and unsuccessful in their efforts to breach its steadily improving defenses by air, the Japanese had decided up-on a daring alternative. They would land an army on the northern coast of Papua and attempt to advance overland through the towering Owen Stanley mountains and strike Port Moresby from the rear.

Although Port Moresby was protected from sea attack—and now also from air attack by new airfields from which fighters and bombers could take off at a moment's no-tice—there was one small loophole in its defenses. From Buna, the administrative headquarters of northern Papua

TREADMILL IN PAPUA

10 miles from Gona, a jungle trail led over the mountains.

For 50 miles, from Buna to Kokoda, a small village in the foothills, the trail followed a relatively easy route through undulating jungle country and over the great gorge of the torrential Kumusi River at a place known as Wairopi—so named, in pidgin English, for the wire-rope cables of the narrow footbridge spanning the river. At Kokoda was a small airfield on a plateau, with possibilities as a supply base. Then the trail narrowed to become no more than a shoulder-wide footpath running along precipitous slopes that led from one precariously perched village to another through a nightmarish jungle landscape. The path tunneled between trees so overgrown with moss and creepers that sunlight could barely filter through to the rotting leaves and mud underfoot. One misstep, one misplaced grasp, could mean a slide down to oblivion on sharp rocks or into a turbulent mountain stream.

Forbidding as it was, the Kokoda Track could not be ignored as an overland route to Port Moresby. On June 9, General MacArthur had written to General Sir Thomas Blamey, commander of the Allied Land Forces, advising him that intelligence sources had turned up "increasing evidence that the Japanese are displaying interest in the development of a route from Buna on the north coast . . . through Kokoda to Port Moresby." Whatever the enemy's intentions, he told Blamey, it was vitally important "that the route from Kokoda westward be controlled by Allied Forces, particularly the Kokoda area."

General Blamey, in turn, flashed an urgent radio message to Major-General Basil Morris, commander of all Australian forces in New Guinea, ordering him to take immediate steps to prevent a Japanese landing in the Buna area and to command the tortuous pass.

General Morris had only limited means at his disposal, but by June 25 he had managed to establish a special unit, the Maroubra Force, for the purpose of holding Kokoda. The force consisted of a light reconnaissance unit known as the Papuan Infantry Battalion (PIB)—280 indigenous soldiers and 20 Australian officers—plus all five companies of the 39th Australian Infantry Battalion. Company B of the 39th started for Kokoda on the 7th of July, while the rest of the battalion stayed at Port Moresby for more training.

As this modest shuffling of troops indicates, the Japanese invasion was not viewed as a serious threat. Indeed, news of the landing at Gona had been received with equanimity. Australian war correspondent George H. Johnston reported the event laconically. "At dawn today, July 22," he wrote, "a Japanese invasion force, very tentatively estimated to number between 4,000 and 6,000 troops, made a successful landing near Gona Mission." Johnston saw no danger to Port Moresby from the Kokoda Track. "With the exception of a small stretch between Buna and the Kumusi River," he noted, "the track is impossible for mechanized transport, and so it seems unlikely that the Japs can hope to attempt any overland invasion of Moresby by pushing southward through the mountains."

General Morris also considered an overland invasion unlikely. He was convinced that the Owen Stanleys, towering to 13,000 feet above sea level at their highest point, were an impenetrable barrier for an invasion force. Even the mountain pass called "the Gap" through the central range was traversable only by men walking in single file. What the Japanese intended, he believed, was to establish an air base in the Buna-Gona area.

Morris was partially right. The Kokoda Track was indeed impassable for large-scale, mechanized military movements, but not for a stripped-down infantry force trained in jungle warfare and using porters to carry supplies. Furthermore, the Japanese Army operated on the assumption that no terrain was impassable. The crossing of the Owen Stanleys was entrusted to crack troops of Major General Tomitaro Horii's South Seas Detachment. They had every intention of achieving their objective.

The first phase of the operation was to be carried out by Colonel Yosuke Yokoyama's advance force of nearly 2,000 troops. Supported by 1,200 inhabitants of New Britain who had been impressed to serve as laborers and carriers, they were assigned the task of securing a foothold between Buna and Kokoda and reconnoitering the mountain track. Once that was done, the main body of the South Seas Detachment, plus the 41st Infantry Regiment under the command of Colonel Kiyomi Yazawa—blooded veterans of the Malayan campaign—would follow and complete the thrust to Port Moresby.

As Yokoyama's force moved inland, it encountered only light opposition. Company B of the 39th Australian Battal-

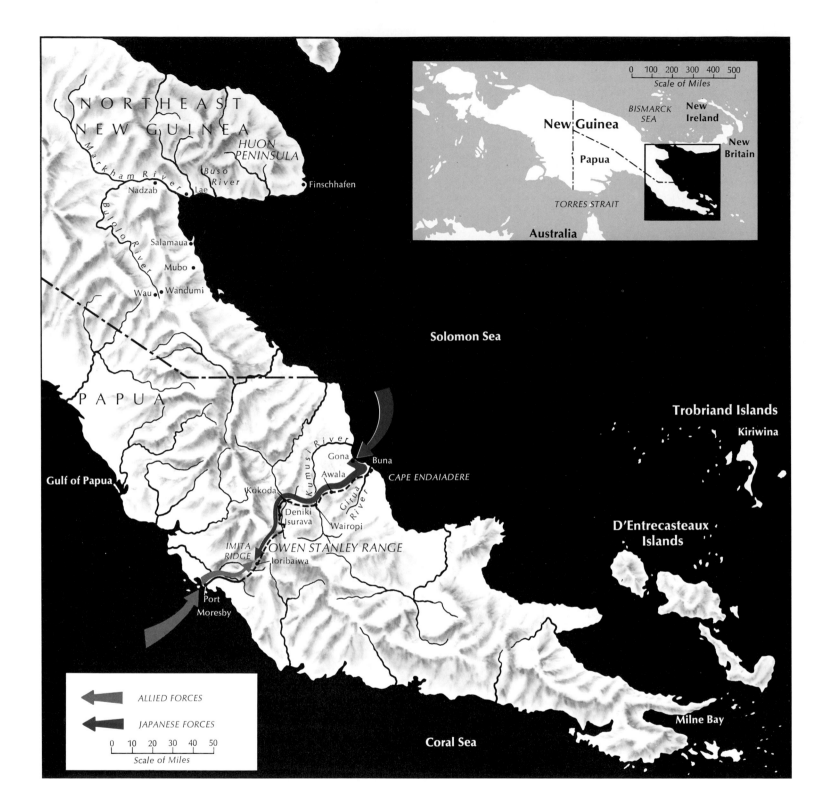

The Kokoda Track (dashed line)—100 miles of hills and gorges for the men who fought on it—led from Buna on New Guinea's east coast to Port Moresby, the Allied base on its southeast coast. In July and August of 1942, the Japanese landed 11,430 troops near Buna and Gona on the Papuan peninsula (inset) and set out across the Owen Stanley Range toward Port Moresby. After six weeks they reached Ioribaiwa, just 32 miles from Port Moresby, then were forced by lack of supplies to retreat.

ion, 129 men at full strength, stood alone at Kokoda, and members of the PIB constituted the sole defense at Awala, about 25 miles up the track in the direction of Buna.

General Morris was caught at a grave disadvantage. There were no suitable aircraft at Port Moresby to carry the remaining companies of the Maroubra Force over the mountains and there was no way of sending in supplies except on the backs of porters. All Morris could do was order the commander of the 39th Battalion, Lieut. Colonel William T. Owen, to fly to Kokoda in the only plane capable of making a landing in the mountains, there to be joined by Company C, now on exercises in the foothills. But the march up the Kokoda Track would take Company C at least eight days, and in the meantime Owen would have to make his stand at Kokoda as best he could.

Late in the afternoon of July 22, before Owen could get to Kokoda to take command, members of a PIB patrol caught sight of the Japanese coming down the track. Some were on bicycles; all wore green jungle uniforms that blended with the foliage, steel helmets festooned with leaves, and green dye daubed on hands and faces. Each man carried a mess kit of cooked rice to avoid having to light fires that might give away his position, a machete for cutting through jungle growth and a sharp-edged shovel specially designed for jungle digging, with holes in the blade to prevent the moist soil from clinging to it by suction.

Alerted by the patrol, a platoon of Company B rushed from Kokoda to Awala, and together the Australians and Papuans clashed with the enemy the next day. The Japanese spread out in a flanking maneuver and blazed away with mortars and machine guns. The bewildered Papuans scattered into the jungle—"went bush," as the Australians put it—and the men from Company B were forced back across the swiftly rushing Kumusi River. There they destroyed the Wairopi bridge by ripping out the lock nuts that secured its steel cables.

The Japanese wasted no time in throwing a bridge of their own across the river and advancing on Kokoda. By the time Colonel Owen arrived on the scene on July 24, it was clear that the Australian force on hand was no match for the superior numbers of the enemy. At dawn on the 29th, the Japanese pounced. After two hours of fighting, in which Colonel Owen was killed in the act of pitching a grenade,

the enemy broke through the defenses and drove the Australians out to prepared positions at Deniki, a small village southwest of Kokoda.

In the meantime, Australian reinforcements had been arriving in the forward area on foot. By August 7, all five companies of the 39th Battalion were assembled in the vicinity of Deniki. Added to the battalion's strength was a small force of Papuan soldiers. The Maroubra Force—temporarily commanded by Major Alan Cameron—now came to a grand total of 533.

Major Cameron quickly drew up plans to recapture Kokoda. In the early morning of August 8, three companies of the 39th moved out for the attack, leaving the balance of the battalion to defend Deniki. Two of the advancing companies were held up by intense Japanese fire, but the third company filtered unseen through a rubber plantation and took possession of the Kokoda airfield without incurring a single casualty.

Heavy rain fell through the night and into the morning. At midmorning an Australian platoon spotted Japanese soldiers, smeared with mud, stealthily making their way toward the airfield. The Australians drove them back with heavy fire, but the Japanese returned again and again in increasing strength throughout the day and into the night. Casualties were heavy on both sides.

Two more Japanese attacks were beaten off the following morning, but the Australians, running low on food and ammunition, could not hold out much longer. Late in the afternoon a strange chant rose from the Japanese position. As the weird chorus faded, a Japanese voice called out in English: "You don't fancy that, do you?" The Australians roared back, "Never heard worse!" and added some well-chosen epithets. Then a furious bombardment from mortars, machine guns, rifles and exploding grenades deluged the Australians. Lacking heavy weapons of their own and unable to withstand the vehemence of the attack, they fell back slowly, and under cover of darkness and rain, struggled through an overgrown track back toward Deniki.

As they approached Deniki, they found the Australian position at the little village under heavy attack by the main body of Colonel Yokoyama's force. Outnumbered 3 to 1, the 39th Battalion was forced to withdraw to Isurava, five miles down the Kokoda Track. So hasty was the retreat that the men left most of their equipment behind. In the pouring rain they used their bayonets, helmets and bully-beef tins to dig out a perimeter of crude foxholes from which to make a stand.

When Lieut. Colonel Ralph Honner arrived at Isurava on the 16th of August to take over command from Major Cameron, he was dismayed by the men's appearance. "Physically the pathetically young warriors of the 39th were in poor shape," he later wrote. "Worn out by strenuous fighting and exhausting movement, and weakened by lack of food and sleep and shelter, many of them had literally come to a standstill."

The Japanese onslaught on Isurava began on August 26. The Australians had received only light reinforcements that consisted of a few elements of the 7th Australian Division, which had been trained in desert warfare and which had fought in North Africa. Moreover, there would be no further reinforcements: only the day before, the Japanese had landed at Milne Bay, on the easternmost tip of New Guinea, and were attempting to seize the airfield there, which would give them a chance to strike at Port Moresby from the southeast. This forced the Australians to keep any men originally intended for the Kokoda Track at the Allied base to fend off a possible frontal attack.

The defenses at Isurava held until the morning of August 29, then began to crack. Australian war correspondent Osmar White was struck by the surreal quality of the fighting: "It was seldom that anyone got a glimpse of the enemy," he noted. "I must have heard the remark 'You can't *see* the little bastards!' hundreds of times in the course of a day." White noted the ease with which the Japanese infiltrated the Australian positions. "Their patrols had penetrated far into the hills on the flanks of the trail positions. Indeed, they ignored the positions we were anxious to defend, and were striking out boldly into the trailless forest of the high hills."

By September, Isurava had fallen and the Australians were in retreat. At Milne Bay, however, things had not gone well for the Japanese. General MacArthur had anticipated the invasion and dispatched the 18th Australian Infantry Brigade to bolster forces already there, including two Royal Austra-

lian Air Force fighter squadrons and about 1,300 American service and combat troops. Thus Major-General Cyril A. Clowes, commander of the Milne Force, had at his disposal more than 9,000 men. The Japanese, as they often did, attacked with too small a force—only 1,900 men.

A violent rain squall screened the Japanese amphibious landings from air attack on two successive nights. Once the troops were safely ashore, tanks crossed the narrow coastal strip and lumbered through the muddy undergrowth toward their objectives—the airfields and the wharf at the head of Milne Bay.

The Australians, in spite of all their preparations, were taken aback when brilliant headlights suddenly stabbed at their eyes through the darkness. As one of the forward tanks approached a defensive position with its engine roaring and its headlights blazing, a young Australian soldier yelled: "Put out that —— light!" The answer, as later reported in the history of his battalion, was "a high-pitched voice chanting in Japanese from the depths of the jungle." The solo soon swelled into a chorus of hundreds of voices that drew steadily closer to the defenders; then the chanting died away, and the Japanese forces, cloaked in darkness, fired at the Australians down the dazzling beams of their tank headlights.

In one position after another, fighting back with rifle fire and grenades that failed to explode because jungle mold had grown inside them, the Australians were assailed by Japanese voices offering them advice in labored English, by the blinding glare of the headlights and by deadly tank fire.

But the massive manpower of the Milne Force was too much for the Japanese; at one of the three Milne Bay airstrips an aggressive assault met such a solid wall of fire that not a single Japanese succeeded in crossing the strip. With their casualties mounting alarmingly and their tanks bogged down in mud, the attackers began to yield. The Australians counterattacked, smashing pockets of resistance with air strafing and heavy concentrations of artillery fire. By September 5 the bulk of the surviving invading force was back on the beach, piling hastily into ships that had arrived to evacuate them.

The battle of Milne Bay gave the Allies their first victory in Papua and—coming as it did before the Guadalcanal campaign had been decided—their first large-scale land victory over the Japanese since the beginning of the war in the Pacific. With it, the southern prong of the Japanese drive on Port Moresby was eliminated. The Japanese plan now depended solely on General Horii's pressing successfully overland along the Kokoda Track.

After the fall of Isurava, the Australians, outflanked, outnumbered, and running out of food and equipment, were pushed back along the track. Most supplies dropped from the air either smashed on impact, fell wildly off the mark or were swallowed up in the jungle. The Australians could do no more than put up a gallant delaying action.

Inexorably, General Horii's troops thrust their way up the northern slopes of the Owen Stanleys toward the Gap. But their progress was becoming increasingly difficult as they pushed deeper into the mountains. A soldier recorded their ordeal in his diary: "The road gets gradually steeper. The sun is fierce here. We make our way through a jungle where there are no roads. The jungle is beyond description. Thirst for water, stomach empty. The pack on the back is heavy. My arm is numb like a stick. 'Water, water.' We reach for the canteens at our hips from force of habit, but they do not contain a drop of water."

In spite of their problems along the way, the Japanese reached the Gap on September 5. They then began a relentless drive down the southern slope of the range toward Ioribaiwa, one of the last villages before Port Moresby; on September 17 they seized it. But by now their supply situation had become desperate, in part because of the indefatigable efforts of Major General George C. Kenney's Fifth Air Force. Planes ranged over the area, destroying Japanese supplies and communications, and knocking out the bridge built by the Japanese at Wairopi.

Ioribaiwa was only some 30 miles from the Japanese goal. But Horii's men were ill with malaria and dysentery, and their rations were exhausted. "Not a grain of rice left," an officer wrote. "In another few days we will have to eat roots or tree bark. No medicines have arrived. Patients will die, and we will soon starve. How can we fight against this?"

Still, Horii himself saw no reason to be discouraged. "Today we stand firmly on the heights," he proclaimed triumphantly. "The Detachment will stay here and firmly hold its position in order to perfect its organization and replenish its fighting strength. We will strike a hammer blow at the stronghold of Port Moresby."

But the drive was over. Because of the reverses suffered by the Japanese at Milne Bay and Guadalcanal, no reinforcements were available. Moreover, the Australians who were facing Horii's men on Imita Ridge, opposite Ioribaiwa, had been reinforced by fresh troops from units of the 7th Division. At last Imperial General Headquarters ordered Horii to withdraw to the Buna-Gona area and hold on there until forces committed to Guadalcanal could be freed to assist in the seizure of Port Moresby. Reluctantly Horii prepared to pull his troops back.

On September 26 the 7th Australian Infantry Division assaulted Ioribaiwa and encountered only minimal resistance from a Japanese rear guard. The main body had moved back up the track, occupying a series of defensive positions on high ground overlooking the trail.

The 7th pressed its advance, driving Horii's troops out of one strong point after another, while bombers and fighter planes of the Fifth Air Force hammered away at the Japanese supply lines. Their plight was getting desperate. Many were sick. "Because of the food shortage," an officer ob-

Lieut. General Haruyoshi Hyakutake, commander of Japan's Seventeenth Army, stands at attention in front of his headquarters at Rabaul. While directing the Papuan and Guadalcanal campaigns, Hyakutake faced a cruel dilemma: either rob his Papuan forces of vital supplies to strengthen his Guadalcanal counteroffensive or risk defeat on Guadalcanal. He sent warships, planes and troops to Guadalcanal—and lost both battles.

served, "some companies have been eating human flesh"; it came from the bodies of dead Australians.

In order to cover the withdrawal and delay the Australian advance on Kokoda, Horii directed one of his retreating battalions to establish a holding position at Eora Creek in a deep ravine north of Myola, in the heart of the Owen Stanley Range. Climbing to the heights on either side of the trail through the ravine, the Japanese dug themselves into an elaborate complex of concealed weapon pits, many of which were strengthened and roofed with logs. Here they planned to remain and block the Australians while General Horii prepared his last line of defense at Oivi, on the road from Kokoda to Buna.

Australians entered the ravine and overran the Japanese outposts. But every attempt to crawl up the slopes and assault the bunkers was met by heavy artillery fire, and in a week of persistent effort the Australians could not reach the Japanese fortifications. Then, on October 28, the bombardment from the heights suddenly increased in ferocity. That night, under this covering fire, Horii and his garrison withdrew toward their prepared positions at Oivi.

The pursuing Australians pushed on to Kokoda—and discovered that it had been abandoned two days earlier. On November 23, joined by the new commander of the 7th Division, Major General George A. "Bloody George" Vasey (who had earned his nickname by frequent use of the adjective most favored by Australian troops), they raised their flag over Kokoda. Leaving a detachment of engineers to ready the airstrip for landings, the 7th advanced to Oivi.

There they came up against Colonel Yazawa's troops. By now, Imperial General Headquarters had changed its mind about the situation, and had ordered him to hold out until reinforcements could be found to relieve him. Temporarily stalled but still attacking, the Australians sent a battalion around by a parallel track to hit the Japanese from the rear at Gorari, about three miles east of Oivi. With the Australian trap closing around them, Yazawa's men fought back savagely, determined to block the advance at least until Horii and the main body of the retreating force could cross the Kumusi River and rejoin the men at Buna-Gona. But the defenses at Gorari and Oivi collapsed under the weight of the Australian attack; both villages were overrun by the 11th of November, and Yazawa was forced to withdraw to

the Kumusi. In the meantime, the advance contingent had already managed to cross the turbulent water in boats and on rafts. But many drowned, including General Horii, whose log raft overturned.

On the far side of the Kumusi River, the surviving Japanese slogged wearily toward the coast. Japanese war correspondent Seizo Okada walked along with the bedraggled men. "Their uniforms were soiled with blood and mud and sweat, and torn to pieces," he wrote. "There were infantrymen without rifles, men walking on bare feet, men wearing blankets of straw rice bags instead of uniforms, men reduced to skin and bones plodding along with the help of a stick, men gasping and crawling on the ground." Many dropped from exhaustion, "some of them lying there for a while and struggling to their feet again, while others stirred no more."

With their overland thrust smashed, the Japanese were now more determined than ever to hang on to their positions in the Buna-Gona area and to attempt another assault upon Port Moresby. They dug themselves in, and Imperial General Headquarters scraped together 2,000 troops from China, Hong Kong, Java and Formosa. When reinforcements started arriving on the 17th of November, they had only to rush straight for the waiting fortifications and prepare for a do-or-die stand.

The Allies were now rapidly building up their forces for an attack on Buna-Gona. As far back as September, while Horii's troops were advancing on Ioribaiwa, General MacArthur had ordered all available forces from the Australian mainland to New Guinea. Among them were the 126th and 128th infantry combat teams of the United States 32nd Division, part of the I Corps then in training under Major General Robert L. Eichelberger. The bulk of the 32nd Division troops arrived at Port Moresby on September 28, fatigues newly dyed mottled-green for camouflage.

Reconnaissance units had located several level fields near the coast in the vicinity of Buna-Gona suitable for aircraft landings; and early in October the Fifth Air Force began transporting Allied troops to these fields. Since the men could carry only a small part of their equipment with them, supplies had to be brought in by sea.

By the third week in November the Allied forces were

ready to attack. The 7th Australian Division, under General Vasey, was to operate west of the Girua River and destroy the enemy at Gona and Sanananda to the east; the U.S. 32nd Division, under Major General Edwin F. Harding, would attack toward Buna.

Ground and air reconnaissance reports indicated that Buna, Gona and Sanananda all were lightly held. In fact there were about 3,000 Japanese troops entrenched on the Gona-Sanananda side of the river, and more than 2,500 at Buna—not counting the 2,000 reinforcements that came ashore in mid-November.

Despite the fact that the 32nd Division at Buna was inadequately equipped (the bulk of its supplies had been sent to the bottom of the sea by a Japanese bomber), General Harding believed Buna would be "easy pickings" and prepared to move the 32nd forward. Two improvised units would be involved: the Urbana Force, named after General Eichelberger's hometown in Ohio, and the Warren Force, named for another Ohio town.

On the 19th of November, in drenching rain, the Warren Force, consisting of two battalions of the 128th Infantry, launched an attack on the Japanese positions at Cape Endaiadere, east of Buna. To the consternation of the Americans, the jungle around them erupted with machine-gun and rifle fire from scores of unseen bunkers. Every movement drew a fresh fusillade, but the camouflage and flashless powder used by the Japanese and the reverberation of gunfire in the jungle made it impossible to pinpoint the location of enemy fortifications. Harding's men withdrew in confusion, badly shaken by their first encounter with the hidden enemy.

Two days later division headquarters ordered an all-out attack along the entire Buna front—even though Harding's artillery and additional mortars had not yet arrived and his men were ill equipped to deal with the bunkers. "Take Buna today at all costs" was MacArthur's message.

Harding attacked, and again his men were stopped cold. The Warren Force was flung back by heavy fire from the hidden bunkers at Cape Endaiadere. Air strikes intended to rip open the enemy positions proved disastrous: bombs fell on the advancing troops, killing 10 American soldiers and wounding 14. Meanwhile, the Urbana Force, composed of the 2nd Battalion of the 128th Infantry and the 2nd Battalion

of the 126th, was hit by withering Japanese fire from concealed weapon pits as it moved through an area called "the Triangle." When the Americans tried to outflank these emplacements, they became bogged down in mud.

Vasey's troops, to the west of the Girua River, fared only slightly better. The 7th Australian Division, temporarily reinforced by two battalions borrowed from Harding's forces, launched an attack against Gona and the approaches to Sanananda. The Australians, veterans of the bone-wearying Kokoda pursuit, were not able to make a dent in the enemy's defenses; but the American units did manage to work their way around the Japanese and establish a roadblock that would prevent supplies from reaching the Japanese forward units.

On November 30 the Urbana Force launched an attack on the outskirts of Buna. Creeping silently through the pitch-black night, each man gripping the shoulder of the man in front of him, the soldiers moved forward with bayonets fixed, holding their fire until they reached a line of enemy machine-gun posts. Then "all hell broke loose," according to Lieutenant Robert H. Odell, a platoon leader in Company F of the 126th Infantry. "Machine gun tracers lit the entire area, and our own rifle fire made a solid sheet of flame. Everywhere men cursed, shouted or screamed. Order followed on order. Brave men led and others followed. Cowards crouched in the grass frightened out of their skins."

The Americans overran the enemy outposts and crossed an open field of kunai grass to reach a cluster of buildings that had served as a Japanese field headquarters. Two main structures, built of timber and canvas, were strewn with military documents and officers' diaries, and one building housed a highly sophisticated radio. Tunnels from the main structures led directly to covered bunkers in the rear. In thatch-roofed huts close by, the soldiers found food, medicines, weapons and ammunition.

In spite of such gains, MacArthur was not satisfied with the progress of the 32nd. Moreover, he had heard Australian reports that American troops were reluctant to fight. On the 30th of November, in response to an abrupt summons from headquarters, Eichelberger, who had recently been made a lieutenant general, flew from Australia to Port Moresby. He was conducted immediately to the veranda of

Government House, where MacArthur was waiting for him.

Recalling the episode later, Eichelberger wrote: "General MacArthur was striding up and down the long veranda. General Kenney, whose planes were to do so much to make the ultimate victory possible, was the only man who greeted me with a smile. There were no preliminaries.

" 'Bob,' said General MacArthur in a grim voice, 'I'm putting you in command at Buna. Relieve Harding. I am sending you in, Bob, and I want you to relieve all officers who won't fight. Relieve regimental and battalion commanders; if necessary, put sergeants in charge of battalions and corporals in charge of companies—anyone who will fight. Time is of the essence; the Japs may land reinforcements any night.' "

Continuing his restless pacing, MacArthur pointed his finger emphatically as he spoke. "Bob," he said, "I want you to take Buna, or not come back alive."

Eichelberger arrived at the front on December 1 and was appalled by what he found. Communications between the Urbana Force and the Warren Force, and between them and Harding's headquarters, were in such disarray that none of the units appeared to know where it was supposed to be or what the others were doing. According to Eichelberger, "companies and platoons were as scrambled as pied type on the floor of a printing office. There were breaks in the chain of command, and any assay of the situation added up to confusion. I stopped all fighting, and it took two days to effect the unscrambling of the units and an orderly chain of command."

In a complete shake-up, Eichelberger relieved Harding, gave command of the 32nd Division to Brigadier General Albert W. Waldron, who had been Harding's artillery commander, and replaced the leaders of the Warren and Urbana forces with officers from his own staff.

Eichelberger soon discovered that the American troops were discouraged for good reason. They did not have the proper heavy weapons needed to dislodge the Japanese from their formidable bunkers. The soggy, overpowering heat had worn them down, and they lacked enough tents to shield them from the endless rains. Moreover, they were afflicted with all the illnesses that had plagued the Japanese on the Kokoda Track—malaria, dysentery, skin ulcers, dengue fever. And making things even worse, most had been living on short rations since the start of the campaign.

Coincident with Eichelberger's arrival, supplies ordered many days before by General Harding and delayed by the disruption of the Allies' coastal supply route now began to come through—food and weapons, including an American 105mm howitzer and five armored vehicles mounted with Bren machine guns manned by Australian crews. On December 3 the men on the Buna front had their first hot meal in 10 days.

Preparations were now begun for a general assault, to be launched on December 5. The Warren Force and the Bren-gun carriers, supported by elements of the Fifth Air Force, were to attack Japanese positions along the coast, while the Urbana Force attempted to take Buna.

The assault began inauspiciously. The Warren Force, leading the way, ran immediately into pulverizing fire from log barricades near the coast and concealed strong points in a coconut plantation. The Bren machine guns were knocked out of action within 30 minutes, and the infantry gained only a few yards against searing enemy fire from bunkers and pillboxes. "We have hit them and bounced off," report-

General Sir Thomas Blamey (left), commander of Allied land forces in the southwest Pacific, and Lieut. General Robert L. Eichelberger, leader of U.S. ground troops on New Guinea, pause at the entrance of a captured Japanese pillbox during the campaign for Papua.

ed Warren Force commander Colonel Clarence A. Martin as he withdrew his troops that night.

The Urbana Force opened its attack with an aerial bombardment of the headquarters building at Buna Government Station and an artillery and mortar barrage on Buna itself. Elements of both the 126th and 128th infantry regiments swarmed out of the jungle and were pinned to the ground by heavy enemy machine-gun and mortar fire. In hours of hard fighting, men approached within 50 yards of the main Japanese line and for their effort earned nothing but heavy casualties.

But there was one important success in that day's fighting. Staff Sergeant Herman J. F. Bottcher, leading an undersized platoon of 18 men armed with rifles and one machine gun, diverted his men from a direct attack on Buna, pushed northward through jungle mud, crossed a creek under fire, and reached a stretch of beach between the village and the Buna Government Station. There he emplaced his single machine gun and braced himself for attacks from both sides.

The Japanese attacked Bottcher's position on the following morning. "With his hand on the hot machine gun," Eichelberger wrote later, "Bottcher was able to mow them down like wheat in a field." The beach on either side of his gun—which became known as Bottcher's Corner—was piled with corpses before the Japanese gave up the attempt to dislodge him.

Meanwhile on the Gona front, after nearly two weeks of fighting, the Australians were still battling to breach the Japanese perimeter. The 25th Brigade of the 7th Division had suffered so many casualties that it was no longer in shape to attack. When the 21st Brigade, composed of veterans of the Kokoda Track, took over, it had no better luck. The Japanese themselves had suffered such heavy losses that they had gradually drawn in their lines to concentrate their defenses at the Gona Mission and a small area immediately around it. The mission grounds and the surrounding village were a labyrinth of camouflaged trenches, firing pits and bunkers, and the Australians, after several determined attacks, could not pry the Japanese out of their positions.

Lieut. Colonel Honner's 39th Battalion—composed also of veterans of the Kokoda Track—reached the front on December 3. Honner's unit, destined for Sanananda, was thrown instead into action in the Gona area. A fresh wave of assaults on the mission by the reinforced Australians brought only heavy casualties and minuscule advances.

A massive artillery-supported assault was planned for December 8, and General Vasey warned the 21st Brigade commander, Brigadier Ivan N. Dougherty, that if the attack failed, Gona would have to be contained while the main body of the Australian forces concentrated on smashing the Japanese positions at Sanananda. In view of the failures of the previous weeks, it seemed unlikely that the blow would shatter the Japanese defenses. But the enemy had taken a greater pounding than the Australians realized. There were only a few hundred of them left in their bunkers, and the holdouts were near the end of their tether.

The knockout punch at Gona was launched at midday on December 8 with a concentrated artillery and mortar bombardment. Shells with delayed-action fuses rained down on the grounds of the Gona Mission, boring into the dug-in positions. Even before the guns stopped firing, Honner's 39th Battalion broke into the mission area and advanced on the enemy positions while the Japanese were still reeling from the explosions. With considerably less difficulty than they had anticipated, the attacking troops swarmed over one position after another. By evening the heart of the garrison area was in Australian hands, and Japanese defenders, attempting to steal away in the darkness, perished in hand-to-hand combat or were cut down by Bren-gun fire.

Early next morning, Australian troops moving through the mission area to clear out the last pockets of defenders found ghastly evidence of the Japanese resistance. "Rotting bodies, sometimes weeks old," wrote British war correspondent Ian Morrison, "formed part of the fortifications. The living fired·over the bodies of the dead, slept side by side with them." Corpses were stacked on the barricades like sandbags, and piled one on top of the other inside the bunkers to serve as firing positions for the defenders. "Everywhere, pervading everything, was the stench of putrescent flesh," Morrison reported. Before the siege ended, the odor became so overpowering that the survivors had to fight in gas masks.

It was a gruesome and costly defeat for the Japanese, who left 638 dead. The Australians themselves also suffered heavily, losing more than 740 men, killed, wounded and missing; but after weeks of bloody fighting and frustration they had the satisfaction of relaying electrifying news to headquarters: "Gona's gone!"

Five days later, the Americans were able to report good news of their own. Every day since Bottcher's breakthrough to the Buna beach they had subjected the enemy at Buna to probing attacks by infantry and relentless pounding by artillery and mortars. On December 14, the Japanese defenses at Buna finally collapsed. Troops of the newly arrived 127th Infantry Regiment moved cautiously into the village and found it a deserted shambles.

Coupled with the more spectacular Australian triumph at Gona, the victory was the turning point in the Allied effort to rout the enemy from Papua.

The final effort to drive the Japanese from the coastal area between Buna and Gona was to be a joint Australian-American endeavor, scheduled to begin on December 18. The Urbana Force would ram its way through creeks and swamps to the Buna Government Station east of Buna; the Warren Force would take Cape Endaiadere, then link up with the Urbana Force.

The Warren Force led off, supported by two fresh Australian infantry battalions and seven American M3 tanks brought up from Port Moresby via the coastal supply route and landed by barge in the American zone. The tanks smashed through line after line of enemy bunkers and pillboxes. By nightfall the Australian-American force had forged its way along the coastal strip to within 500 yards of Cape Endaiadere. Within the next few days the men edged their way to the Buna Government Station.

At the same time, back in the swamps around Buna, the Urbana Force skirted the heavily fortified Triangle area, crossed a creek that was supposedly unfordable and gained a foothold in the overgrown gardens outside the Buna Government Station.

Two days before Christmas Eve, Eichelberger reported to MacArthur, "I think we are going places." He was right. By January 3, the entire Buna area was in Allied hands.

In the Sanananda sector, the Australians pushed hard and the Japanese fought back vigorously, buoyed by the promise of reinforcements. Days passed, and no men appeared: Imperial General Headquarters had decided to pull out of Papua because of the staggering losses to their invading forces and the insuperable supply problems posed by Allied control of the air. Reinforcements would be sent, instead, to Japan's bases in Lae and Salamaua in Northeast New Guinea.

Not knowing they were to be evacuated, the Japanese

An Australian soldier wounded in the fighting near Buna is gently guided to safety by a Papuan who found him—partially blind and left for dead—in a thicket. The Papuan led him through jungles and over rivers for two days and nights before reaching an Allied camp.

hung on tenaciously but with growing doubt. "Enemy shelling and bombing every day," Private First Class Kiyoshi Wada, a medical orderly, scribbled in his diary on January 10. "It is about time that we received some divine aid. Starvation is a terrible thing. It seems all the grass and roots have already been eaten." His wasted body was among those cast into a common grave a few days later, when Australian troops cleared the Sanananda area of its last remaining Japanese defenders. By January 22, 1943, resistance at Sanananda had crumbled, and the Papuan campaign was over.

But the Japanese still had not abandoned their goal of taking Port Moresby. Thwarted now in their efforts to get there by the overland route from Buna and Gona, they decided to launch a new drive from their bases at Lae and Salamaua. On the 7th of January, about 3,000 troops under Major General Tooru Okabe arrived at Lae, in spite of heavy bombing by Allied B-17s that deprived them of half of their supplies. Okabe's men then began making their way inland via a mountain track to the village of Mubo. From there, they headed for the little town of Wau in the heart of the Bulolo Valley.

Thirty miles over the mountains from Salamaua and 150 air miles from Port Moresby, Wau was strategically valuable as a link between the south and east coasts of the island of New Guinea. Wau's main value derived from its airfield. Located 3,300 feet above sea level in a valley encircled by the jungle-shrouded mountains of the Kuper Range, the 3,600-foot runway presented a challenge to the most experienced pilots even when the capricious mountain weather permitted its use. It had a grade of 10 per cent, or more than 300 feet, so that landings had to be made uphill and takeoffs downhill (because of the surrounding mountains, the wind direction was of less importance to pilots than the slope of the runway).

Immediately following the Japanese occupation of Lae and Salamaua in March 1942, two companies of Australian commandos had been dispatched to Wau to prevent the airfield from falling into enemy hands. The two companies, together with a small band of militia—the New Guinea Volunteer Rifles, a local guerrilla corps—were all that stood between the Japanese and the airport.

Obviously the force was not strong enough to withstand a mass attack. The Allied plan was to airlift the 17th Australian Brigade from Milne Bay via Port Moresby to the tilted airfield at Wau. But a barrier of heavy cloud cover intermittently closed off the Bulolo Valley and when the weather turned really foul on January 26, planes were unable to get through the turbulence over the mountains.

Meanwhile, the Japanese advanced toward Wau over a forgotten trail, laboriously hacking their way through riotously overgrown *kunai* grass and creeping vines. In the pre-dawn hours of the 28th, they attacked an Australian position at Wandumi, four miles from Wau. Though greatly outnumbered, the Australians, under Captain W. H. Sherlock, managed to drive the Japanese back.

Four inches of rain fell during the night, and more fell the following morning. The Japanese advance now simply flowed around Sherlock's men until some units were within 400 yards of the airstrip. Enemy fire was already falling on the outer defenses of the airfield when the rain suddenly stopped, the cloud banks rolled back and sunlight blazed down upon the muddy field. Then, in a race with time, the drone of engines echoed over the mountains and General Kenney's transport planes began to stream in. Plane after plane landed in rapid succession, and as gunfire laced the field the men of the 17th Brigade tumbled out of the aircraft, raced directly to prepared bunker positions and commenced firing.

Fifty-seven landings were made during the day, and more followed for several days thereafter. Although Okabe personally directed an aggressive attack on the airstrip in the early hours of the 30th, the battle had already been decided with the arrival of the planes. Beaten and disorganized, the Japanese retreated toward Salamaua and Lae.

Six months after the beginning of their overland drive to Port Moresby, almost a full year after securing their foothold on the northeast coast, the Japanese in New Guinea were back where they started.

A PAINFUL PATH TO VICTORY

High in the Owen Stanley Range, a lone Australian soldier crosses a clearing on the Kokoda Track—the only passable land route over the Papuan peninsula.

JUNGLE COMBAT WITH A FANATIC FOE

Australian soldiers hoist their flag after recapturing the village of Kokoda in November 1942. Japanese forces had held the settlement for three months.

In the summer of 1942, the jungle-clad region of southeast New Guinea known as Papua suddenly became one of the most important pieces of territory in the southwest Pacific. For six months, what historian Samuel Eliot Morison would later describe as "certainly the nastiest" fighting of the War surged back and forth over this narrow strip as Australians and Americans struggled to repel Japanese forces attempting to take the Allied base at Port Moresby.

Much of the worst fighting occurred around the Kokoda Track, a narrow, precipitous path over the 13,000-foot Owen Stanley Range that was drenched almost daily by rainfalls of as much as one inch in five minutes, and was so steep and slippery in many places that troops crawled single file and clung to vines to keep from sliding down mountainsides. "The few level areas," said Australian Colonel Frank Kingsley Norris, were "pools and puddles of putrid black mud." It was, said Norris, a "track through a fetid forest grotesque with moss and glowing phosphorescent fungi."

Yet the Japanese moved along the track to within striking distance of Port Moresby in September 1942, before the terrain—and stiffening resistance—stemmed their advance.

As Australian troops, assisted by Papuan carriers, drove the weakened, starving Japanese back to the Buna-Gona coast in November, they passed human skeletons picked clean by jungle ants and found evidence that some desperate survivors had cannibalized the dead. Meanwhile, American units had landed at crude airstrips near Buna to join the combat. In two months of savage struggle at Buna, the Allies lost 3,095 killed and 5,451 wounded—an even bloodier fight than the better-known Guadalcanal campaign.

The horror of Buna struck home with the picture at right by LIFE photographer George Strock. His grim shot of three lifeless GIs was withheld from publication by the censors for seven months, then was released with President Roosevelt's consent. Explaining its decision to print the shocking picture, LIFE said: "The American people ought to be able to see their own boys as they fall in battle; to come directly and without words into the presence of their own dead."

Crawling with maggots, the corpses of three American soldiers killed by fire from a hidden machine-gun nest lie sprawled in the wet sand of Buna Beach.

Gaunt Australian foot soldiers, exhausted after spending 13 days on patrol in the bush, dig into cans of food at a jungle outpost at Itiki in October 1942.

Teetering across a makeshift footbridge, Australian soldiers head for the far bank of the Kumusi River.

DAYS OF AGONY ON THE KOKODA TRACK

The Kokoda Track exacted a heavy toll in life and limb from the Australian soldiers who pursued the Japanese up and down its muddy slopes. Although many of the men were battle-hardened veterans of fighting in North Africa, most agreed that the desert war had been a holiday in comparison with the Papuan campaign. They fought hard and well. "Although the Australians are our enemies," said one Japanese officer on the Kokoda Track, "their bravery must be admired."

The Aussies lived for weeks in clothes saturated and rotting from torrential rains and jungle damp. Broad-brimmed felt hats were caked with mud, helmets red with rust, boots pocked with holes. Many men threw away their groundsheets, blankets and tent halves to lighten their 40- to 60-pound packs, and slept uncovered on beds of muck. Soles of feet, swollen to a pulp from ceaseless walking, peeled off in lay-

ers as socks were removed. Skin riddled by insect bites was scratched raw in sleep.

To compound their miseries, the men were starving. Aerial drops of food fell off target and burst on impact because parachutes were in short supply and seldom used. If the food was found—often only 10 per cent was recovered—it was almost always eaten immediately so it would not spoil. A single can of bully beef was sometimes stretched to feed a couple dozen men. Many soldiers lost up to 20 pounds on the Kokoda Track.

In spite of their hunger, the Australians kept on with their dogged advance, even when it meant crossing flimsy wood and wire bridges under enemy fire. Japanese suicide squads, equipped with hooks on their boots for climbing trees, perched on branches and there, hidden by the foliage, pinned down Australian patrols for days on end. Other Japanese would lie motionless among dead comrades, allow Allied patrols to pass by, then shoot them in the back. The Aussies finally took to bayoneting every enemy corpse as a precaution.

CARRYING THE WAR OVER THE PEAKS

Aiding the Allies during the fighting on the Kokoda Track were more than 10,000 Papuans, who lugged backbreaking loads —weapons, ammunition, foodstuffs, medical supplies and wounded men—across the Owen Stanleys. Barefoot and often naked except for loincloths, the carriers sweltered by day under more than 40 pounds of gear and shivered in the mountain chill at night, two men to a blanket.

Recruited from villages, the porters were given food and medical care, paid nominal sums by the Allies and treated with kindness. Though many broke under the strain and deserted, Australian authorities saw a curious pattern: stretcher bearers—having the hardest job of all—rarely did. The Papuans accepted the wounded as a personal responsibility. Usually eight men to a stretcher, they delivered their human cargo to medical stations almost unfailingly.

Although the local inhabitants were primarily employed as carriers, some assisted Australian engineers in building roads and airstrips, and in hacking steps in mountainsides to make climbing easier.

One steep pathway, the "Golden Stairs," rose hundreds of feet up Imita Ridge in the foothills of the Owen Stanleys. The steps were 10 to 18 inches in height and were made of small logs held in place by wooden stakes. Behind the logs were puddles of mud and water that made hundreds of advancing troops take bruising tumbles. "Gradually men dropped out utterly exhausted," wrote an Australian officer of the climb up the Golden Stairs. "You'd come to a group of men and say 'Come on! We must go on.' But it was physically impossible to move. Many were lying down and had been sick."

Seated in rows, Papuan carriers listen attentively to their instructions at Kokoda in October of 1942.

Four Papuans use a stretcher to transport a wounded Australian to a medical tent on the Kokoda Track.

Using walking sticks for balance, muscular porters tote 70 pounds of cargo. The carriers' shoulders often were raw and bloody at the end of a day's journey.

Young Papuans paddle an outrigger dugout up a river to deliver cases of vital supplies to Australian soldiers who were fighting along the Kokoda Track.

The Golden Stairs up Imita Ridge offer a perilous challenge to two Australian soldiers and their carrier. Engineers cut more than 2,000 steps in the mountain.

Men and horses transport equipment, including a 25-pounder gun, down a zigzagging stretch of the Kokoda Track near Ower's Corner in October 1942.

Crouching behind a log barrier, American troops at Buna man a .30-caliber machine gun; its bullets were all but useless against the deeply entrenched enemy.

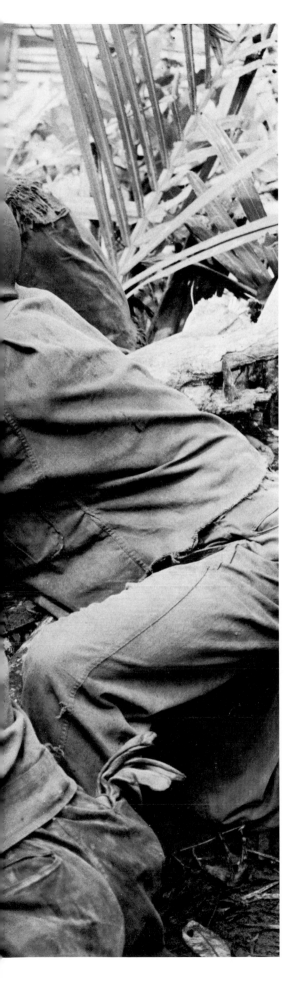

An Australian fires a Bren gun at a sniper concealed in a tree during the battle for Buna-Gona.

A dead Japanese soldier lies outside his smashed pillbox as an Australian checks for survivors.

THE CAMPAIGN'S DEADLY CLIMAX

After their harrowing advance over the Kokoda Track, the Australians joined American forces on the Buna-Gona coast to confront the Japanese in one of the bloodiest battles of the War. For two months the Japanese, manning bunkers built of foot-thick coconut logs reinforced by oil drums filled with sand, held off the Allies. Losing 100 men a day from starvation alone, they stacked dead comrades outside bunkers as an additional buffer, and piled other corpses inside to stand on while they fired. Bogged down in neck-deep swamps, the Allies were killed off by malaria, dengue fever, dysentery and scrub typhus.

But the Allied infantry, backed up by tanks, cleaned out the bunkers one by one. By January 22, 1943, most of the surviving Japanese had been evacuated from the Buna-Gona sector by barge, and the Allied command proclaimed that it had won "a striking victory" in Papua. When the fighting was over, General Douglas MacArthur pledged: "No more Bunas."

In the final assault on Buna, an Australian-manned M3 light tank blasts a Japanese pillbox (smoking at left), as infantrymen fan out alongside the tank to fire at fleeing enemy soldiers. Tanks were decisive in routing the Japanese from their meticulously constructed coconut-log fortifications.

Cocky Australian troops, certain of victory, emerge from swampland during the final days of fighting in the Gona sector. This photograph was taken less than 100 yards from heavily armed Japanese positions.

3

Early in 1943, with the Japanese clearly facing defeat on Guadalcanal and in Papua, planners in both Washington and Tokyo began to rethink their strategy. Up to then Allied leaders had held that no major offensive against Japan could be launched before Germany was crushed. But the success of the Guadalcanal and Papua operations, originally conceived only as emergency moves to defend Australia and its supply routes, opened up new opportunities to press the war in the Pacific. Steps could now be taken to capture or neutralize Rabaul, the big Japanese base on the island of New Britain, and thus make Australia fully secure. But the time was also ripe to look beyond Rabaul and map out a long-range strategy that would defeat Japan conclusively.

Opinions differed sharply as to the best way to achieve that ultimate objective. General MacArthur argued that the quickest route to victory lay through the Philippines. This view surprised no one; the general's desire to redeem the celebrated pledge he had made on leaving the Philippines in March of 1942—"I shall return"—had become, as one observer put it, "an obsession." But MacArthur's argument also made strategic sense. His recapture of the Philippines, using New Guinea as the jump-off point from the south, would cripple the Japanese by cutting off their access to the oil riches of the nearby Dutch East Indies.

The Navy's strategists saw a better way to bring Japan to its knees—by a drive across the central Pacific that would make full use of their new fast carriers. Japan, they argued, was most vulnerable on its eastern flank, and would be made more so by the seizure of the island bases the Japanese held in the central Pacific. In American hands these bases would not only impede the free movement of the Japanese Navy, but would also serve as a springboard from which, in time, air attacks could be launched on Japan's home islands. There was, moreover, the possibility of a landing on Japan's nearest offshore stronghold, Formosa; that would bypass the Philippines entirely. Even if the Philippines had to be taken, the argument went, they could best be approached from the central Pacific.

In May of 1943 the Joint Chiefs of Staff resolved the MacArthur-Navy dispute by approving a "dual drive" in which MacArthur's forces were to advance northwest from New Guinea and Admiral Nimitz' forces were to move west across the central Pacific. The decision to use both routes,

UP THE SOLOMONS LADDER

one military historian later noted, was intended "to prevent the Japanese from knowing where and when the next blow would fall." But in one vital respect MacArthur and Nimitz were also left hanging. The Joint Chiefs' carefully worded order specified only that the dual drive was to be directed "toward" the Philippines. The decision as to whether they were to be taken or bypassed was deferred.

Tokyo's revised strategy was summed up at an uneasy audience with Emperor Hirohito, which his ministers had sought in order to inform him of the decision to evacuate Guadalcanal. On hearing the news, His Imperial Majesty asked an embarrassing question: what did his warlords plan to do next? "Stop the enemy's westward movement," he was told. In this oblique way a fundamental change of strategy was signaled: the Japanese thrust eastward in the Pacific was over. Henceforth the emphasis would shift to strengthening areas now held. Rabaul was to be reinforced. To the southeast, in the part of the Solomons still under Japan's control, the Imperial Navy would rush to build a string of airfields from which to hit at Guadalcanal. To the southwest, in New Guinea, the Japanese Army would beef up its defenses with 100,000 fresh troops, funneled in from Rabaul.

The Army's plan soon met with disaster. Shortly after midnight on March 1, 1943, eight Japanese troop transports and eight escorting destroyers slipped out of Rabaul's Simpson Harbor and made their way through the Bismarck Sea toward the Huon Peninsula, the northeast tip of New Guinea. Their chief destination was Lae; since seizing it the year before, the Japanese had built it into a sizable forward air base. Packed tight in the transports were 6,900 soldiers of the Eighteenth Army's 51st Division. Units, equipment and supplies had been prudently divided among the transports so that the loss of a ship or two to enemy action would not strip the division of any one element.

In the afternoon, a plane from MacArthur's air arm, the Fifth Air Force, spotted the convoy. Then, for two days Australian Beaufighters strafed the ships, and American B-17s and B-24s bombed them from on high, while new P-38 Lightnings—the first Allied fighter that could slug it out with a Zero on a one-to-one basis—kept the Japanese fighter escort at bay. The bombers sank one of the transports and damaged two others, but this was just a curtain raiser.

On the third day, the rest of the convoy was still steaming through the Vitiaz Strait, between New Guinea and New Britain. Then General Kenney, the commander of the Fifth Air Force, sprang a surprise: "skip bombing," a new technique for bombing ships at sea. First a dozen Beaufighters strafed the convoy at deck height to silence antiaircraft guns. Behind the Beaufighters came a dozen B-25 light bombers and a dozen A-20 attack bombers. Skimming in far below the Japanese fighters, they dropped 500-pound bombs that bounced across the water to strike the hull of the enemy ship, causing as much damage as if the vessel had been struck by a torpedo. The bombs' five-second delay fuses gave the planes time to pull away to avoid the impact of the explosions.

When the Battle of the Bismarck Sea was over, all eight Japanese transports and four of the destroyers had been sunk; the other four destroyers got away. At least 61 Japanese planes were downed; Kenney's group lost four. Thousands of Japanese soldiers drowned or burned to death in the oil-slicked waters of the Vitiaz Strait. Many more were killed when American PT boats and fighter planes moved in to rake their lifeboats. Every bit of the carefully loaded equipment and supplies went to the bottom. Approximately 2,400 soldiers, including Lieut. General Hatazo Adachi, commander of the Eighteenth Army, were plucked from the sea and taken back to Rabaul by the remaining destroyers. Only 950 men of the division reached New Guinea.

The Japanese never again dared to send a convoy or a regular troop transport to the Huon Peninsula. From then on their reinforcements for New Guinea had to be fed in, a little at a time, from submarines, barges and small coastal vessels operating by night.

Undeterred by the Army's disaster, the Japanese Navy proceeded with its own dramatic attempt to forestall the Allies' westward movement. Its supreme commander, Admiral Yamamoto, added some 200 carrier planes to the shore-based aircraft at Rabaul and at Bougainville, in the western Solomons; in all, the air armada numbered nearly 400 planes. On April 7, in the biggest Japanese raid since Pearl Harbor, 67 Val dive bombers escorted by 110 "Zekes" (the Americans' new code name for the Zero) hit Guadalcanal and Tulagi, sinking a destroyer, a tanker and a New Zealand corvette. Over the next few days Yamamoto point-

A PUNCTUAL MEETING WITH DEATH

Only a week before his death, Yamamoto addresses Japanese pilots at Rabaul.

On April 14, 1943, U.S. intelligence experts intercepted a message revealing that Admiral Isoroku Yamamoto, Commander in Chief of Japan's Navy, would be flying to Bougainville four days later. Bougainville lay within range of U.S. P-38 fighters at Henderson Field on Guadalcanal, and Allied planners seized the chance to get rid of one of their most formidable foes.

Admiral Chester W. Nimitz, Commander in Chief of the Pacific Fleet, authorized a plan to shoot down Yamamoto's plane. Because of the Japanese admiral's importance, however, approval had to be obtained from Secretary of the Navy Frank Knox and President Roosevelt.

Yamamoto was invariably punctual, and American planners were confident that his plane would appear over Bougainville on schedule—9:35 a.m., April 18. At that moment, 16 P-38s from Henderson spotted two Japanese "Betty" bombers—one carrying the admiral—and six Zero escorts.

As the bombers broke formation to escape, two P-38s dived to the chase. Lieutenant Thomas Lanphier, in one of the fighters, bore down on Yamamoto's plane, shot off the right wing and sent the Betty plummeting to the ground. The other plane was also disabled, and plunged into the sea. Japanese searchers later found Yamamoto's charred body in the jungle.

A shirtless and sun-tanned Lieutenant Thomas Lanphier relishes his success after downing Admiral Yamamoto's plane.

ed his powerful air fleet at Papua and bombed Port Moresby and Milne Bay, the Allied base at Papua's southeast tip. But forewarnings had dispersed an Allied supply fleet in time. Yamamoto's pilots made such exaggerated claims of ships sunk and planes downed that the admiral did not think it necessary to follow through on the operation. It was to be his last venture. Within a week, Yamamoto was dead, shot down by an American pilot (left).

By now the Allies were cranking up for the task of knocking out Rabaul. The problems were formidable. Rabaul's magnificent natural harbor could shelter a host of Japanese warships; moreover, the Japanese had built five airfields, fortified the surrounding mountains and brought in great numbers of troops and quantities of supplies. Long-range bombers from Guadalcanal and Papua had been raiding Rabaul for several months, but with only limited effect; the bombers lacked fighter support because the Allies had no fields within fighter range of Rabaul. So the Allies' first job was to capture or build forward airstrips from which fighters could reach Rabaul, both to protect the bombers and to provide air cover for later troop landings.

General MacArthur had nominal control of the campaign, since it lay within his Southwest Pacific Area Command. But the eastern half of the operation was in the hands of the dynamic chief of the adjoining South Pacific command, Admiral Halsey. Despite his growing reputation as a "fire-breathing swashbuckler," as one admirer described him, Halsey surprised his Navy colleagues by instantly hitting it off with the autocratic MacArthur. The two had never met before Halsey flew to Australia from his headquarters in Nouméa, New Caledonia, to confer with the general at his headquarters in Brisbane. "Five minutes after I reported," Halsey recalled, "I felt as if we were lifelong friends."

It turned out that their fathers had met in the Philippines more than 40 years earlier. But beyond that link Halsey was impressed with MacArthur's erect carriage, "a diction I have never heard surpassed," and the stately way the general paced his office between "his large, bare desk and the portrait of George Washington that faced it." The two men were to have a number of arguments, the admiral wrote, "but they always ended pleasantly."

The complex campaign hammered out by MacArthur and

Halsey called for a series of attacks focused on Rabaul as the ultimate goal and coordinated to keep the Japanese off balance. MacArthur's troops were to capture Lae and other remaining Japanese-held points in northeast New Guinea, then jump across the Vitiaz and Dampier straits to New Britain itself; beachheads acquired at the island's western end would make it all the easier for MacArthur's air arm to strike at Rabaul, at the eastern end. Halsey's forces, meanwhile, were to move toward Rabaul from the opposite direction, the Solomons chain, seizing a number of islands that lay between Rabaul and American-held Guadalcanal.

Three islands, above all, figured in Halsey's plans: New Georgia and Kolombangara in the central Solomons, and Bougainville, at the western end of the chain. Halsey liked to picture the Solomons as a ladder, with each newly won island as another handhold upward. Wresting New Georgia and Kolombangara from the Japanese entrenched there would provide two such handholds. By seizing part of Bougainville, the main Japanese headquarters in the Solomons, Halsey would be poised on the topmost rung of the ladder: Rabaul lay less than 250 miles away.

The Americans' campaign was to begin with simultaneous landings by MacArthur's and Halsey's forces along the entire arc of islands southwest, south and southeast of Rabaul. Appropriately, the operation was code-named Cartwheel, and D-day was set for June 30, 1943.

That day, some 300 miles southwest of Rabaul, a component of MacArthur's forces, the 162nd Infantry Regiment of the 41st Division, moved by sea up the east coast of New Guinea to Nassau Bay, 60 miles below the Japanese base at Lae. Rain, winds and a 12-foot surf combined to swamp many of the landing craft, but all the men got ashore before dawn. Japanese troops nearby heard the sound of grounded LCMs (Landing Craft, Mechanized) trying to work themselves free. Mistaking the noise for tanks coming ashore, they fled into the jungle. By the time they decided to attack, the beachhead had been reinforced and the Americans were moving inland to link up with Australian troops coming down from the surrounding mountains. Despite Japanese attempts to dislodge them, the Australians had stoutly held on to the area around the mountain town of Wau, about 25 miles from the coast; laboring against massive natural obstacles, they had built roads out of some of the primitive mountain tracks that led coastward. By mid-July the joint Allied push was to come within 30 miles of Lae.

The landing at Nassau Bay was one of two moves MacArthur made on June 30. The second took place off the eastern tip of New Guinea about 325 miles south of Rabaul, and the targets, though tiny, were strategically vital. Some 5,000 soldiers of Lieut. General Walter Krueger's U.S. Sixth Army, dubbed the Alamo Force, landed unopposed on the islands of Woodlark and Kiriwina. Airfield construction was quickly begun, and in two weeks planes were flying from both islands. Lightning fighters could now operate over Rabaul for the first time.

Admiral Halsey set his part of *Cartwheel* turning on June 30 with an invasion of the island of New Georgia and its near neighbors in the central Solomons, southeast of Rabaul. To strengthen his hand, Halsey had previously sent in some 10,000 troops of the 43rd Division and the 3rd Marine Raider Battalion to occupy and build up a group of small undefended islands, the Russells, that lay between Guadalcanal and the New Georgia group. By the time *Cartwheel* began, the Russells contained two airstrips, a radar station, a PT-boat base and storage facilities for large quantities of

fuel and other supplies; meanwhile, three more airfields had been built on Guadalcanal to supplement Henderson Field. Strong and close-by support for the New Georgia operation was thus assured. Yet despite these precautions, the fight for New Georgia turned out to be the toughest in the entire campaign.

To *Cartwheel*'s planners, New Georgia had been just another miasmic, jungle-covered island until December 1942, when the Japanese began building an airstrip at its southwest tip, Munda Point, only about 30 minutes' flying time to Guadalcanal. Japanese camouflage experts had concealed the site by stringing heavy cables between the tops of tall coconut palms and hanging fronds from the cables.

Neither aerial cameras nor sharp-eyed pilots could spot the strip until it was almost completed. But the Allies knew it was there, thanks to one of the busiest coastwatchers in the Australians' entire network. Captain Donald G. Kennedy had set up his transmitting station at Segi Point, on the southeast tip of New Georgia 45 miles from the Japanese airstrip at Munda. The location was ideal for his purposes. No trails led to Segi from other parts of the island, and any

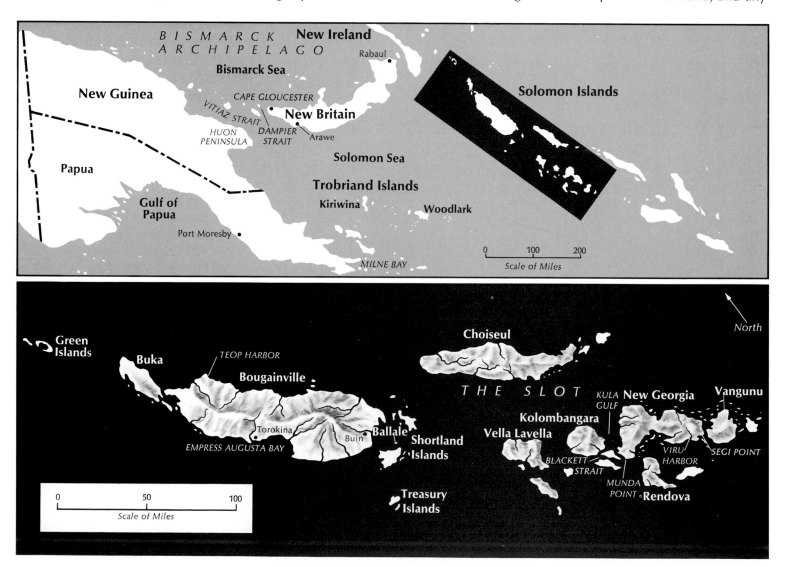

attempt to approach by beach could be detected. The waters around Segi were uncharted and reef filled. Though the Japanese had scouted the area before the War, using craft disguised as fishing vessels, only New Georgia's natives knew the channels through the reefs to the deep, sheltered anchorage inshore. Kennedy, who had served as the prewar district officer, could count on their help and loyalty.

To Kennedy's post, information on the movements of Japanese planes, ships and troops came in by runners from scores of villages and from coastwatchers operating on other islands. Kennedy's scouts guided Allied reconnaissance patrols, sometimes slipping them by canoe, at night, right past the coastal guns at Munda and smaller bases the Japanese had set up. Kennedy and his Melanesian cohorts also operated a rescue service for downed American pilots; for each flier brought safely to Segi, Kennedy rewarded the natives with a bag of rice and a case of canned meat. The same bounty was paid for Japanese fliers, who were overpowered, trussed up with vines, delivered to Kennedy's stockade, then taken by seaplane or destroyer to Guadalcanal for questioning. All told, 22 American and 20 Japanese pilots were to pass through Kennedy's hands.

Though all coastwatchers had been instructed to avoid combat and flee if discovered, Segi was too strategically valuable to be abandoned, and Kennedy turned to guerrilla warfare to protect its secret. Whenever a Japanese supply barge moored at night in his area, he and his men would emerge from the jungle along the shore and pounce on the enemy. They would kill the crew, sink the vessel and make off with food, guns and ammunition.

Kennedy's tactics included ground fighting as well. His guerrillas came from a long line of head-hunters and were well versed in the art of jungle ambush. Once Kennedy had trained them to use firearms, no Japanese patrol was safe. One group of scouts paddled silently to an island where some Japanese were bivouacked, crept among the sleeping soldiers and picked up their weapons. The Japanese awoke to find themselves staring into the muzzles of their own rifles—and soon were staring out of Kennedy's stockade.

After a time, the Japanese became extremely annoyed at coastwatcher Kennedy's escapades. Major General Noboru Sasaki, commander of the New Georgia garrison, ordered an expedition overland to wipe out whoever it was at Segi.

On June 17—less than two weeks before D-day for Halsey's forces—Kennedy's scouts reported that enemy reinforcements had arrived at Viru Harbor, a Japanese outpost 12 miles to the west, and that half of a Japanese battalion was moving toward Segi. Realizing that he would be unable to hold against such a force, Kennedy radioed for help.

The threat to Segi involved more than Kennedy's safety. Segi was one of four landing sites Halsey had scheduled in the New Georgia group, and he planned to build an airstrip there. Since he lacked the shipping to support four full-scale combat assaults, relatively small forces were to go ashore initially at Segi and at three other places where there were few Japanese. If the Japanese bearing down on Kennedy occupied Segi beforehand, more troops might be required to take the area and the complicated *Cartwheel* timetable might be upset. On the other hand, if the Americans could land at Segi ahead of schedule, the area would be denied to the Japanese, Kennedy would be saved and a head start could be made on building the airstrip—but this might also alert the Japanese.

Admiral Turner, who had been commander of the amphibious force at Guadalcanal, was now exercising the same responsibility under Halsey. Turner weighed the alternatives and risks and made his decision fast. On the night of June 20, two destroyer-transports sneaked into the Segi channel. Some of Kennedy's scouts went aboard as pilots, while the coastwatcher himself lit bonfires on the beach as beacons. At dawn two companies from the 4th Marine Raider Battalion, led by Lieut. Colonel Michael S. Currin, went ashore at Kennedy's camp. Halsey's part of Operation *Cartwheel* had begun nine days ahead of schedule. Next day, two more destroyer-transports brought in a naval survey party to start on the airstrip, as well as two infantry companies to free the Raiders for a new action.

The Japanese who had set out for Segi unaccountably stopped short at a village six miles away. Viru Harbor, from which they had started, was another of Halsey's targets; he wanted to establish a base there for his patrol boats. High cliffs surrounded the harbor mouth, there were no beaches, and now that the Japanese had reinforced their small garrison, frontal assault looked risky. So Currin's Marines were to attack Viru from the land side at the same time that a

A FLOTILLA OF ISLAND-HOPPING LANDING CRAFT

The island nature of so much of the Pacific war gave rise to a whole new array of landing craft and ships. Some of the most common types are shown here, with actual size relationships indicated in the box.

The troop-carrying vessels ranged from small landing craft like the LCP or the LVT, which could crawl right up on the beach, to the 200-man LCI. The LCVP was big enough to carry a jeep as well as men, while the LCM and the LCT conveyed bull-dozers, medium tanks and heavy trucks ashore. All of these were dwarfed by the oceangoing vessels, the LST and the LSD. One of the most effective work horses, the LST carried everything from troops and tanks to cargo and landing craft. The biggest of all the vessels was the LSD, which had space enough for troops and smaller landing craft—up to an LCT in size—and could double as a repair ship.

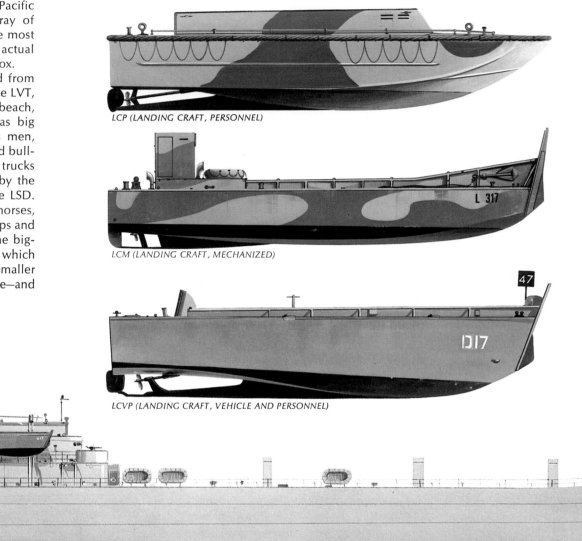

LCP (LANDING CRAFT, PERSONNEL)

LCM (LANDING CRAFT, MECHANIZED)

LCVP (LANDING CRAFT, VEHICLE AND PERSONNEL)

LST (LANDING SHIP, TANK)

LSD (LANDING SHIP, DOCK)

LCT (LANDING CRAFT, TANK)

LVT (LANDING VEHICLE, TRACKED)

LCI (LANDING CRAFT, INFANTRY)

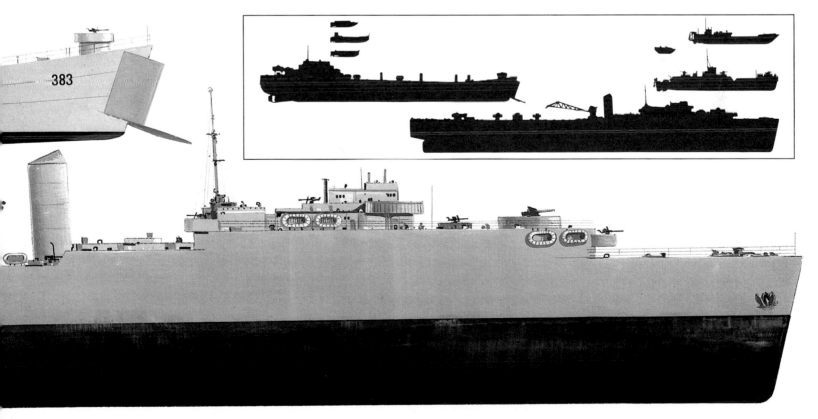

seaborne force arrived on D-day. Though reconnaissance patrols had easily covered the ground between Segi and Viru, Currin's Marines were to learn the simple, painful but vital fact that a heavily armed combat unit takes far longer than a reconnaissance patrol to move through the jungle.

On the night of June 27, Currin's two companies, guided by Kennedy's scouts, silently paddled west from Segi in small rubber boats, freezing all motion whenever the moon shone through the clouds. Shortly after midnight they landed at a deserted village about a third of the way to Viru, and at daybreak set out through the jungle, eating their breakfast—chocolate bars—as they went.

The trek to Viru, Sergeant Anthony P. Coulis recalled, was "nightmarish." That day the men kept on the move for 11 hours, "and every foot was a struggle." Skirmishes with enemy patrols slowed the march, but the big problem was the jungle and the night rain: "Crouching under our ponchos, we ate scraps of cheese from our C rations. A few minutes later I was asleep. . . . I was dead tired, and I didn't give a damn if my throat was slit as I lay sleeping."

The second day was even tougher; it took 12 hours to traverse a stretch of jungle and a mangrove swamp. Three times the Marines forded the same meandering river, gripping hands to pull one another through the muddy, chin-deep water. To march around the loops of the river would have taken longer, for on supposedly solid ground the men leading the column churned the trail into such ooze that those in the rear found it hard to keep their footing.

Because of a change in his original orders, Currin had started out from Segi a day earlier than planned. But his men were still a long way from Viru when, on D-day morning, three American destroyers arrived at the harbor mouth carrying the two Army companies that were scheduled to land. Lookouts aboard ship scanned the shore in vain for the white parachute flare that was to have signaled that the Marines had the situation in hand. Unable to raise Currin by radio, the flotilla commander edged his ships cautiously toward shore. Then a few salvos from a coastal gun made it clear that the Japanese were still in control. The ships retreated and took the soldiers back to Segi.

Throughout D-day, Currin's Raiders continued to slog on toward Viru. "I heard men curse the jungle," Coulis remembered. "We cursed in hoarse, hysterical whispers." Profanity seemed little enough to hurl against "the snake-like roots that reached out to trip us; the damnable mud that sucked us down; the million and one vines and creepers which clawed at a man and threw him off balance." That night, the Marines "flopped in the goo and slept like dead men." The next day those "dead men" had to attack the enemy.

The fight for Viru proved an exercise in total confusion. Since headquarters knew that Currin had not yet reached there, dive bombers were sent to work over the Japanese positions. As they arrived, some U.S. supply ships entered the harbor; the skippers assumed Viru had been taken on schedule. But they managed to move the gasoline-laden LCTs (Landing Craft, Tank) out of the way while the dive bombers went to work. Then the Japanese, believing that they faced a combined sea-air attack, fled into the jungle, where they ran into Currin's advancing Raiders. A few minutes after the Marines clamped their bayonets to their rifles and fell upon the final Japanese position with wild yells, the LCTs reentered the harbor and began unloading.

Unfortunately for the Americans, there was no time for any other commander to learn from Currin's experience with the New Georgia jungle. Cartwheel was now in full swing, and bigger units than Currin's were soon to pay dearly for their ignorance of the terrors the island held.

The prime objective on New Georgia was Munda, site of the Japanese airfield. But to avoid battle until a strong beachhead could be established, the troops that landed on D-day went ashore not on New Georgia itself but on a smaller island, Rendova, about six miles across from Munda. From Rendova, and from a few islets in between, artillery could shell Munda and support the attack on its airfield. Rendova would also be a staging area for the attacking troops.

Rendova was defended by only 120 Japanese, who resisted for just a few hours. The chief problem came from the sky. Japanese air raids killed at least 30 Americans and wounded more than 200 others during the first three days on the island. Those who escaped injury had to contend with heavy rains that turned the soil into mud. Men sank in up to their knees, and machinery bogged down.

Much of the equipment belonged to the Navy's Construction Battalion, the remarkable aggregation of skilled construction workers—called CBs, or Seabees, for short—who had volunteered their know-how and muscle to turn jungle and coral into airstrips and supply bases. The speed with which they could work was to become legendary all across the Pacific, but even the rugged Seabees had trouble with the rain and mud at Rendova.

"The men ceased to look like men," Seabee Commander H. Roy Whittaker recalled. "They looked like slimy frogs working in some prehistoric ooze." For four days they labored through air raids and under sniper fire to build a road from the landing site to another beach where 155mm "Long Tom" guns were to be set up. By the fourth day the road was ready, and that afternoon the guns opened up against Munda, six miles across the water. Whittaker's Seabees "stopped work and cheered almost insanely."

A direct assault on Munda by sea was out of the question; coral reefs and shore defenses protected the approaches. The nearest accessible beaches were at Laiana, two miles east of Munda. But Laiana was thought to be fortified; also, it lay within range of Japanese coastal guns. So Major General John Hester, commander of the Army's 43rd Division, put his troops ashore at Zanana, an undefended beach three miles east of Laiana, out of reach of the enemy guns. Covered by artillery on Rendova and the smaller islets, and protected from Japanese air attack by a constant fighter umbrella, the 43rd was expected to push through the jungle and capture Munda in less than two weeks.

But Hester, like Currin and his Marine Raiders, underestimated New Georgia's jungle. The island lacked the open grassy hills that had given infantry and pilots common reference points on Guadalcanal. The terrain between Zanana and Munda was totally patternless, a thick matting of jungle vegetation, dank, fetid and seemingly endless.

Into this green morass came the 169th and 172nd regiments of the 43rd Division. Advance elements established a small perimeter at Zanana on the 3rd of July. For the next three days landing craft sped in from Rendova bringing the bulk of Hester's forces to the beachhead. The infantrymen were well armed. They wore the new leopard-spot jungle camouflage uniform and carried the new M-1 rifle; they had such special jungle gear as waterproofed miniature flashlights, and hammocks with built-in mosquito nets and rainproof canopies. There were engineer battalions to cut roads for them through the jungle, divisional artillery to support

their attack and eight 13-ton M5 tanks, manned by Marines.

Psychologically, however, the men of the 43rd, a National Guard division from New England, were wholly unprepared for New Georgia. All were new to combat. They had gone through a few weeks of jungle training on Guadalcanal and the Russells; but the amenities the Americans had by now installed on those islands made them seem positively wholesome compared to the central Solomons. Moreover, the Marines had landed on Guadalcanal on a relatively broad coastal plain; they had not needed to deal with the jungle there until later. At Zanana, the officers and men of the 43rd found a world that suddenly closed around them, a terrifying hell where a man might walk within three feet of an enemy and never see him.

Less than two miles separated the landing beach from the Barike River, the jump-off point for a scheduled July 7 attack on Munda. But supply trucks quickly churned the mud into a slime like Rendova's, vehicles sank to axle depth, and ammunition and supplies had to be hand carried. The troops had so much trouble just getting to the Barike that Hester postponed the attack for two days.

The Americans had expected to reach the river without interference from the Japanese and, indeed, General Sasaki, the Japanese commander on New Georgia, was content to wait for the attackers to hurl themselves at his Munda fortifications. But he sent out harassing patrols. One platoon crossed the Barike, built a log barricade across a trail about 1,000 yards inland, set up machine guns on both sides of it and hacked away the undergrowth to provide open fields of fire. On July 5 an American reconnaissance patrol was stopped by the block and withdrew.

Next day the 169th Infantry Regiment's 3rd Battalion, already on the march toward the Barike, was ordered to wipe out the Japanese position. When they bivouacked for the night somewhere east of it, the battalion commander neglected to establish a perimeter defense, he allowed his men to dig foxholes more than six feet apart—thus leaving room for infiltration—and he did not have them string either barbed wire or a simple trip wire with tin cans attached that would rattle when someone brushed by.

After dark a few Japanese slipped up to the battalion's position and went into what was to become a nightly routine—moving about noisily, sometimes firing, yelling taunts and obscenities in English. Some approached calling out company code names and shouting "come out and fight." Hysteria gripped many of the men of the 169th. As the Army's official history put it: "The imaginations of the tired and inexperienced American soldiers began to work. . . . In their minds, the phosphorescence of rotten logs became Japanese signals. The smell of the jungle became poison gas. . . . Men of the 169th are reported to have told each other that Japanese nocturnal raiders wore long black robes, and that some came with hooks and ropes to drag Americans from their foxholes."

In the morning the 3rd Battalion, though shaken, moved on. At about 11 a.m. it ran into machine-gun fire from the Japanese trail block. For five hours the battalion flung itself at the enemy position. The heavy-weapons company tried to use its 81mm mortars, but banyan trees blocked trajectories, and cutting aerial pathways for the shells took several hours. Hand grenades proved all but useless; the men could not get close enough to throw them accurately. Late in the afternoon the battalion pulled back and dug in for another sleepless night, and another onslaught by enemy patrols.

The delay at the trail block had left a dangerous gap in General Hester's lines. Another of his regiments, the 172nd, had reached the Barike to the south of the 169th. But there was little contact between the regiments and nothing like an outpost line, and more Japanese patrols had slipped through the gap. On the morning of July 8, the weary 3rd Battalion, aided by a company from the 172nd Regiment, again attacked the enemy trail block. In the afternoon, mortars were brought to bear and the block was overrun. One Japanese platoon on the narrow trail had barred the advance of a whole division for three days.

That night, as the 169th and 172nd regiments deployed along the river, Japanese prowlers returned. This time, according to Army historians, the result among the Americans was "a great deal of confusion, shooting and stabbing. Some men knifed each other. Men threw grenades blindly in the dark. Some of the grenades hit trees, bounced back, and exploded among the Americans. . . . In the morning no trace remained of Japanese dead or wounded. But there were American casualties: some had been stabbed to death, some wounded by knives. Many suffered grenade fragment wounds, and 50 per cent of these were caused by fragments from American grenades." Large numbers of soldiers broke down entirely and had to be evacuated with what was officially listed as "war neuroses."

The division's attack on Munda was set for the same morning. It was preceded by one of the heaviest artillery barrages thus far in the Pacific war. In one hour, Marine and Army artillery pieces on Rendova and at Zanana fired 5,800 high-explosive shells at Munda. Four destroyers stood in close to shore and poured in another 2,300 rounds; then came 88 bombers dropping 70 tons of bombs.

Then it was the infantry's turn—and the paralyzing effects of the previous night's horror showed immediately. As the official history summed it up, "H Hour, 0630, came and went, but not a great deal happened." Compounding matters, the Barike was flooded, and soldiers laden with packs and ammunition had to wade across chest-deep. On the far bank the troops were deployed in an orthodox skirmish line, but their leaders soon lost control; the foliage was so thick that the men could not even see the others on either side of them. So they reverted to moving single file, thus allowing one or two Japanese riflemen to halt an entire column. By 10 o'clock the 172nd Regiment had advanced only 100 yards beyond the river. The hapless 169th had not yet crossed it, and supply lines were far behind.

General Sasaki, in his command bunker at Munda, wondered at the slowness of the American advance and reported his surprise to Rabaul. To the Americans, the lack of progress brought quick shake-ups. General Hester dismissed the lieutenant colonel in charge of the 3rd Battalion, 169th, as well as the colonel commanding the regiment itself. Then he temporarily called off the advance and ordered the 172nd Regiment to strike south to the beach at Laiana—where hindsight strategists insisted he should have landed in the first place—so that he could establish a new supply beachhead closer to Munda.

The exhausted 172nd spent three days covering the 1,500 yards of jungle and swamp to Laiana. Behind them the 169th, trying to reorganize under a new commander while simultaneously engaged in battle, had to be supplied chiefly by parachute drop. As the two regiments floundered in the jungle, their morale hit bottom. Every day between 50 and

A SKINNY LIEUTENANT'S CLOSE CALL

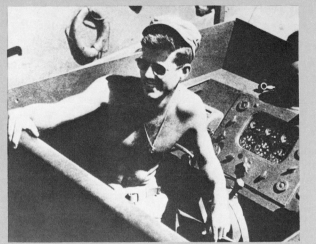

Kennedy sits at the wheel of the PT 109, before its last foray.

While patrolling in Blackett Strait off the Solomon Islands with 14 other American torpedo boats on August 2, 1943, the *PT 109* was rammed by the Japanese destroyer *Amagiri*. As the destroyer sliced through his vessel, the skipper, a skinny lieutenant named John Fitzgerald Kennedy, was slammed against the cockpit wall. "This is how it feels to be killed," he thought.

The fuel tanks ignited, and the flaming boat sank. Of the 13 crew members, two died and one was badly burned. The survivors decided to swim to safety. Kennedy clenched the ties of the burned man's life jacket between his teeth and towed him. When a crew member from Massachusetts whose leg had been injured said he could not make it, Kennedy growled at him: "For a guy from Boston, you're certainly putting up a great exhibition out here." The man struggled on.

After four hours the 11 men crawled ashore on Plum Pudding Island. Fortunately, Lieutenant Arthur Reginald Evans, an Australian coastwatcher on nearby Kolombangara Island, had observed a blaze in the strait the night the boat was hit. He reported it by radio to coastwatchers on nearby islands and was told the *PT 109* was missing. Two of his scouts later found the marooned men, and a rendezvous was arranged with another torpedo boat.

When the *PT 157* showed up and rescued the men after the six-day ordeal, Kennedy was offered food. "Thanks," he wryly responded. "I've just had a coconut."

100 soldiers cracked up. They plodded back to the aid stations with a leaden, mechanical gait. The doctors who took charge of them described the pattern they presented: face expressionless, knees sagging, body bent forward, fingers trembling. About 20 per cent of them cried, wrung their hands, mumbled incoherently and jumped at the least sound; they wore a look "of utter fright . . . of trying to escape impending disaster." Another 30 per cent had become truly unhinged, with "bizarre somatic disturbances."

All told, 2,500 Americans on New Georgia were diagnosed as victims of war neuroses. Of these, 700 came from the 169th—about one man of every four in the regiment. An Army report gave poor leadership as the basic cause, noting that men who did not know what was expected of them, or who were not given clear orders, were the most likely to break under the combined pressures of combat fatigue, nocturnal harassment and noise—not just the noises of war but the unfamiliar sounds of a jungle night.

From his Nouméa headquarters, Admiral Halsey moved to put the New Georgia campaign back on track. At the first signs of delay he had dispatched elements of another division, the 37th, to reinforce the drive on Munda. Now, with the July 9 offensive stalled, he ordered Major General Oscar W. Griswold, XIV Corps commander and Hester's superior, to fly to the island to see what should be done. Griswold pulled no punches. The 43rd Division, he radioed Halsey, "will never take Munda" and was in fact "about to fold up." He urged that the rest of the 37th Division, plus another division, the 25th, be committed to the battle at once "if this operation is to be successful."

Halsey agreed—and put Griswold in charge of the Munda campaign. Halsey later gave his reasons for the command changes. "The ground forces' real weakness," he wrote, "was not in the lower echelons. This became evident as day succeeded day, yet our advance was measured in yards instead of miles. We controlled the air and the sea; we outnumbered the enemy 4 or 5 to 1; we bombed his positions every day and supported our troops with ships' fire on request. Rugged as jungle fighting is, by now we should have been within reach of our objective. . . . When I look back . . . the smoke of charred reputations still makes me cough."

Halsey had still another cause for discomfort—from his own beloved Navy. Since the start of the New Georgia offensive, thousands of fresh Japanese troops had been slipping ashore, brought in at night on barges convoyed by destroyers. The barges—metal-hulled, diesel-powered and carrying as many as 120 troops—were some 40 feet long and had a speed of about eight knots. On a one-to-one basis, they were fair game for the Americans' larger, faster PT boats. Four PT squadrons, based at Rendova and at a point on New Georgia's north shore, prowled the waters nightly, their guns ready to blast the barges in what one historian called "their tender hindquarters."

But taking on the destroyers convoying the barges was another matter. Attempts by U.S. cruisers and destroyers to break up the convoys failed. Aboard the enemy warships was the formidable oxygen-fueled "Long Lance" torpedo, which could carry a half-ton war head more than 20 miles and leave no telltale track on the surface; the maximum range of American torpedoes was less than eight miles. When a Long Lance sank the destroyer *Strong* on July 4, the torpedo was fired from so far away that the Americans on the ship literally did not know what had hit her.

The next night a light-cruiser task force under Rear Admiral Walden L. Ainsworth tried to intercept a Japanese convoy of 10 destroyers, seven of them loaded with troops. Before Ainsworth's ships could come within firing range, three Long Lances hit the cruiser *Helena,* sending her to the bottom with 169 of her crew. Ainsworth's guns sank one Japanese destroyer in the engagement—known as the battle of Kula Gulf—but the other destroyers delivered their troops and supplies.

A week later Ainsworth tried another intercept. Once again, in a battle off the island of Kolombangara just west of New Georgia, Japanese torpedoes more than made up for the Americans' bigger guns and radar. The Long Lances sank the destroyer *Gwin* and put the cruisers *Honolulu, St. Louis* and *Leander,* a New Zealand ship, out of action. The Japanese lost one light cruiser and again managed to unload troops. In time, the Americans learned to detach their destroyers from the cruisers and send them on quick torpedo runs of their own. But by then the fresh Japanese soldiers on New Georgia numbered several regiments.

General Griswold had scarcely begun reorganizing his troops when General Sasaki attempted a three-pronged counterattack. American artillery stopped two of the forces before they started. But the third—a newly arrived regiment led by Colonel Satoshi Tomonari—trekked through the jungle to the north of the Americans, and at nightfall on July 17 swept down out of the jungle at Zanana and surrounded the headquarters of the 43rd Division.

Osmar White, the Australian war correspondent, was on hand. At the first exchange of fire he jumped into a foxhole. Then, he wrote, "a new sound came out of the cold white moonlight—the sound of Japanese voices, shrill and high toned. . . . One Japanese . . . began squalling ludicrously: 'Aid, aid, Doc, give aid to me. I am wounded.' A few nights before, the troops might have fired on him, and the muzzle flashes would have betrayed their position. Not now."

Soon shells began exploding near White's foxhole. "I thought: Well, this finishes it. . . . Suddenly I realized that the shells were not Japanese at all; they were American! . . . The guns were putting down a box barrage on three sides of the command post to prevent the Japanese from bringing mortars close enough to bombard accurately."

In cutting the telephone wires that led from the command post, Tomonari's men had overlooked one line. Captain James Ruhlen, a division artillery-liaison officer, was using it to call in fire from the big American guns on the offshore islets. Through the night Ruhlen maintained a ring of flying steel around the beleaguered post. "It was a gunner's masterpiece," wrote White. "One trivial error of calculation and the guns would have done the job the Japs so far had failed to do—blown the whole camp area to glory. . . . For six hours the guns dropped a curtain of high explosive about us. Never once was a burst farther than 200 yards from the perimeter and only twice was one closer than 20 yards." Tomonari did not get through.

A Japanese battalion stood between the command post and the Zanana beach supply area, a few hundred yards away. Marine Lieutenant John R. Wismer, in charge of a Marine special-weapons platoon guarding the beach, knew that if the Japanese overran his position the bulk of the Army's supplies on New Georgia would be lost. But his defense guns pointed seaward and could not be moved quickly. Leaving half of his platoon to man them, he took the other half, along with an Army antitank platoon and some service troops, and set up a defense line of riflemen on a knoll above the trail to the command post. A hurried search of a salvage dump had turned up enough parts from damaged .30-caliber machine guns to make two serviceable weapons. Wismer placed these in the center of his line, sighting down the trail, and Corporal Maier Rothschild and Private John Wantuck volunteered to man them.

Soon, Wismer remembered, "approximately 100 Japanese came into the draw and started to set up mortars. . . . Upon opening fire, we drove back the Japanese into the jungle. They regrouped and made a banzai charge. The forward positions were overrun and individually we made our way back to the beach, where we prepared to defend against the next charge. To our surprise, it did not materialize."

In the morning Wismer learned why. Wantuck and Rothschild, cut off, had stayed with their spare-part machine guns. More than 100 Japanese bodies littered the slope below their position. Wantuck lay dead beside his empty gun, encircled by Japanese he had killed with knife and grenade. Rothschild lay wounded, also surrounded by dead enemies. General Sasaki's bold flank attack had ended before dawn, thwarted by a virtuoso display of American artillery and the doggedness of two Marines.

Henceforth, Sasaki could wage only defensive warfare, but he waged it superbly. Months before, he had trans-

Shirt off and tattoo showing, Admiral William "Bull" Halsey, commander in chief in the South Pacific, holds an informal interview with members of the press and Marine officers while on an inspection tour of the newly established Bougainville beachhead. The tattoo, dating back to his Naval Academy days, was a sign of what Halsey called his "sea-dogginess."

formed the jungle around Munda into an invisible fortress. His pillboxes were dug five feet deep in the coral under the mud. They were about 12 feet square, and roofed by crisscrossed layers of coconut logs; chunks of weathered coral stacked around the sides gave each pillbox a natural-looking sloping profile. Camouflaged with earth, grass and leaves, the pillboxes looked like hummocks in the jungle.

Hundreds of these strong points studded the approaches to Munda. Rifles, machine guns and light mortars could not damage them, bomber pilots could not see them, and they presented too small a target for artillery, since only a direct hit was effective. The armor-piercing 37mm shells of tanks could blast apart a pillbox, but Japanese antitank experts, sent from Rabaul, had taught Sasaki's men how to knock out an American tank by inching past its blind spots and disabling it with magnetic mines or Molotov cocktails.

General Griswold set July 25 as the date for cracking the Japanese defense line. The American front was now only 3,000 yards from the Munda airstrip. Against three Japanese battalions, Griswold had 12 battalions on line and more troops coming; he had tanks and flamethrowers and new supply roads from Laiana. To kick off his offensive, seven destroyers and 254 planes pounded Munda.

But the Japanese had learned that American shelling was rarely directed close to U.S. lines. When the bombardment began, they simply crept forward into no man's land and waited there in relative safety until it was over. Some used another ploy. They fired heavy mortars at nearby American positions whenever the enemy artillery opened up; this usually convinced the Americans that their own artillery was falling short, and they would call off the barrage. As a result, the offensive got off to a slow start.

For a week Griswold's troops painfully edged forward, one enemy pillbox at a time. When the 2nd Battalion, 145th Infantry, and the 2nd Battalion, 161st Infantry, finally took Bartley Ridge, one of the strongest Japanese positions on the whole line, they counted 46 pillboxes and 32 lesser dugouts in an area not much bigger than two football fields.

North of Bartley Ridge, the 148th Regiment made a wide sweep through the jungle, outflanked the entire Japanese line, approached within 1,000 yards of the airstrip—then was cut off by Tomonari's regiment, which Sasaki had kept hidden in the jungle for that purpose. As the 148th fought its way back to the American lines, a wounded private crawled through the brush toward a machine-gun nest that was pinning down his platoon. Fire from the machine gun wounded him a second time and damaged his rifle, but he kept going and threw a grenade. At that instant he was killed by a fresh burst of fire—but his grenade wiped out the Japanese gun crew and enabled his platoon to escape. The soldier was posthumously awarded the Medal of Honor, and America was stirred by a new patriotic song, "The Ballad of Private Rodger Young."

Experience was seasoning the Americans. Marine tankmen became expert at determining the direction of an enemy position by the sound of the bullets bouncing off the tanks' armor plate. Infantry officers devised a technique for knocking out pillboxes. A combat patrol would force the pillbox to reveal its position; artillery and flamethrowers would clear the jungle around it; 81mm mortars, firing heavy shells with delayed fuses, would crack open the pillbox roof and drive the occupants into the open; then, from several directions, the infantrymen would blast away with machine guns and automatic rifles.

The individual soldier also learned some lessons of jungle warfare. At night, on Bartley Ridge, one man in a foxhole was hit by a grenade fragment, but the Japanese were all around and he made no sound; not until morning did his buddies in the same hole discover his condition and rush him to an aid station. Another man bled to death in silence rather than endanger his squad by calling for help.

At last the incessant pounding of Munda became too much for the defenders. Their aboveground installations were all destroyed, their casualties were mounting, and they too began suffering from combat nerves. Sasaki was ordered to pull most of his remaining troops out of Munda.

On August 1 an American patrol reached the edge of the airstrip. On August 5 the last Japanese were blasted from their bunkers next to the field. Griswold radioed Halsey: "Our ground forces today wrested Munda from the Japs and present it to you . . . as the sole owner." A week later the field was ready for Allied planes.

The battle for New Georgia, planned as a quick operation by one division, had used up elements of four. Some 10,000 Japanese, standing off nearly 40,000 Americans, had set back the Allied timetable by a month. Half a year after the fall of Guadalcanal the Allies were only about 200 miles closer to Rabaul and still had only two fighter bases—Kiriwina and Woodlark—within range of that goal. And a few miles north of New Georgia lay Kolombangara, another jungled island with another Japanese airstrip and at least another 10,000 Japanese troops, many shifted from New Georgia. "The undue length of the Munda operation and our heavy casualties made me wary of another slugging match," Halsey wrote later, "but I didn't know how to avoid it. I could see no victory without Rabaul, and no Rabaul without Kolombangara."

Then Halsey's staff officers came up with an idea he found irresistible: they suggested bypassing Kolombangara. To its northwest lay Vella Lavella, an island with flat areas suitable for airstrips. With its capture, Halsey's ships and planes would be able to harass the Japanese supply route from Rabaul to Kolombangara, thus blockading and starving out the Japanese on Kolombangara. On August 15, American troops landed on Vella Lavella, which was occupied by only a few hundred Japanese. In September a new airfield was in operation—and the Japanese began to pull their garrison out of Kolombangara. Again, as at Guadalcanal, the Tokyo Express came down The Slot for a nightly evacuation routine. U.S. destroyers and PT boats, supported by Navy Corsair fighters, put a deadly crimp in the proceedings, sinking as many as 20 troop-laden barges a night. Kolombangara was finished as a threat. The leapfrog technique had worked, and it was to remain basic Allied strategy.

After Vella Lavella it was MacArthur's turn. Through July and August the Australian and American troops who had joined forces near Nassau Bay on New Guinea's eastern coast had been advancing toward Lae, the main Japanese base to the north. Lae had an airfield, an anchorage and a strategic location; MacArthur needed it to capture the Huon Peninsula, which in turn had to be taken before his forces could jump across the Vitiaz and Dampier straits to New Britain. But the drive on Lae from the south was a feint to lure its defenders from the base while two other approaches were made from the east and west. On September 4 the 9th Australian Division, under Major-General G. F. Wootten, landed on marshy beaches 20 miles east of Lae.

Next day the U.S. 503rd Airborne Regiment parachuted down on an airfield at Nadzab, 20 miles west of Lae.

The airfield, built by the Australians before the War but unused in recent months, was quickly put into commission. The next day the C-47s started ferrying in General Vasey's 7th Australian Division. Vasey had bet Wootten 20 cases of whiskey that his division would reach Lae before Wootten's 9th did. The two divisions began a race for the town. Wootten's troops, to the east of Lae, had to contend with streams that had been flooded by heavy rainstorms; they had to cross the swollen Buso River under Japanese rear-guard fire. Vasey's 7th Division moved in so quickly from Nadzab that American planes were still bombing Lae when the advance elements arrived. Vasey won his bet. His troops found the town "indescribably filthy and thoroughly wrecked." The Japanese, outnumbered, hard hit by disease and short of supplies, had been ordered by Rabaul to evacuate; some 9,000 of them, helped by bad weather that hampered extensive Allied air operations, escaped to the mountains in the north.

With the Japanese in disarray, MacArthur moved to capture the Huon Peninsula. Vasey's division raced back to Nadzab and past it up the Markham River valley, to cut off the peninsula from the northwest. The 22nd Infantry Battalion of Wootten's 9th Division moved eastward along the coast toward a Japanese stronghold at Finschhafen, on the tip of the peninsula, while the 20th Infantry Brigade was put ashore just north of Finschhafen.

The Japanese, determined to hold the peninsula and the shores of the vital Vitiaz Strait, put up a last-ditch defense, including a seaborne counterlanding on the Australians' beachhead. Though Finschhafen fell to the Australians on October 2, three of their brigades spent two months clearing the Japanese from the surrounding mountains.

In November it was Halsey's turn again. Bougainville, the last big Solomons island on the road to Rabaul, was now within his reach. Halsey's aim—"to change the name of Rabaul to Rubble," as he zestfully put it—would be all the more swiftly achieved if American planes were to fly from Bougainville and from carriers that controlled its waters.

But taking Bougainville would not be easy. The island is 125 miles long, with narrow beaches bordered by vast swamps, and with a tangled, mountainous interior dominat-

A LEGENDARY FIGHTER SQUADRON

Boyington trades stickers signifying the downing of 20 Zeros for 20 caps from the Cardinals.

The brashest, most widely publicized pilots of the Pacific theater belonged to the appropriately named "Black Sheep Squadron." Rowdy, profane, hard-drinking and fun-loving, the Black Sheep credited themselves with so many Japanese planes that they became a legend in their own time. The pace was set by the 30-year-old squadron commander, Major Gregory "Pappy" Boyington, a former Flying Tiger. Boozing, brawling Boyington claimed 28 planes—more than any other Marine pilot.

Buoyed by their success, Boyington and his cohorts made a startling offer in October 1943. Having run out of baseball caps—their traditional headgear—they promised to shoot down a Japanese Zero for every cap sent to them by a major league baseball team. In December, when the St. Louis Cardinals forwarded 20 caps, the daredevils had more than kept the bargain—with 48 planes shot down, 14 of them attributed to Boyington himself.

On January 3, 1944, the Black Sheep lost their high scorer. During a fighter sweep over Rabaul, Boyington parachuted from his flaming Corsair into St. George Channel, just after bagging his 28th plane. He was picked up by an enemy submarine and spent the rest of the War in a prison camp.

With baseball caps and bats, the 20 original members of Pappy Boyington's famous Black Sheep Squadron pose on top of the wings of a Corsair fighter.

ed by two active volcanoes. Adding to these hazards were the powerful installations of the Japanese. They had made good use of the 21 months since their take-over. At Buin, on the island's southern tip, they had built four airfields and a seaplane base. At Buka and Bonis, on the northern tip, were two more airfields. Some 40,000 men of the Japanese Seventeenth Army defended the ground. They were well seasoned; they included the notorious 6th Division, which had sacked and raped Nanking, China, in December of 1937.

Halsey preceded his assault with several moves designed to confuse the Japanese as to his real target. Army, Navy and Marine planes of Airsols—the Americans' air force in the Solomons—made low-level photoreconnaissance and bombing flights over the Shortland Islands, a few miles southwest of Bougainville, and caused a hurried Japanese movement of troops and artillery across from Bougainville. On the night of October 27, the 8th New Zealand Brigade Group, veterans of the North African campaign, seized the Treasury Islands, southwest of the Shortlands. At midnight the 725 Americans of the 2nd Marine Parachute Battalion went ashore on the large island of Choiseul, southeast of Bougainville, and destroyed some Japanese facilities there. The Marines knew that this was to be a raid of limited duration; the Japanese thought otherwise. They estimated the number of invaders at 20,000 and concluded that Choiseul was to be the scene of the big American push.

In the predawn hours of November 1—D-day for the Bougainville landing—Halsey's naval forces went into action. Under Rear Admiral Aaron Stanton "Tip" Merrill, four light cruisers and eight destroyers moved close inshore to the island's northern end and pounded the Buka and Bonis airfields. By sunrise, the ships had raced down the length of Bougainville and shelled the Shortlands as well as Ballale, a small island where the Japanese had built a fifth airfield. The two bombardments in seven hours cost Merrill five wounded men and minor damage to one destroyer. Meanwhile, planes from the carriers *Saratoga* and *Princeton*—steaming in from the lower Solomons—completed the havoc Merrill's ships had wrought at Buka and Bonis.

Halsey's selection of a landing site on Bougainville surprised the Japanese beyond all else. In a variation on the leapfrog technique, he chose to hurdle Buin, the formidable complex of installations at the island's south, and send his troops ashore at Cape Torokina on Empress Augusta Bay, about halfway up Bougainville's west coast. With the bulk of the Japanese garrison guarding Buin and Buka-Bonis, Torokina's defenders numbered only a few hundred. But this advantage for the attackers was offset by a surf that played hob with landing craft, and by Torokina's lack of an airstrip; Halsey's men would have to build one from scratch. The Japanese could not understand why the Americans would prefer to carve an airfield out of swamp and jungle rather than expend lives capturing one that was ready made.

For the assault on Torokina, Halsey was using the fresh 3rd Marine Division and the Army's 37th Division, which had fought on New Georgia. On D-day-plus-1 some of the men and supplies were yet to be landed when the Japanese tried to recover their initial fumble. Rabaul dispatched three heavy cruisers, a light cruiser and six destroyers to Torokina—only to have them intercepted about 45 miles from the beachhead by Admiral Merrill's four light cruisers and eight destroyers. In a savage three-hour exchange of torpedoes and gunfire—known thereafter as the Battle of Empress Augusta Bay—Merrill's force succeeded in driving off the enemy, now minus a light cruiser and destroyer, with four of his own destroyers damaged but no ship lost.

Within days after the landing at Torokina, Rabaul itself had a new taste of the expanding air power of the Americans. On the 5th of November, 97 planes off the carriers *Saratoga* and *Princeton* roared in on Rabaul's harbor and badly damaged seven Japanese warships, at a cost of 10 American planes. An attack by General Kenney's Fifth Air Force followed; 27 B-24 bombers and 58 P-38 fighters unloaded 81 tons of bombs on the wharf area. On the 11th of November "as an ironic memorial to Armstice Day," Halsey later explained—Rabaul was hit once again. This time MacArthur's pilots and pilots from the *Saratoga* and *Princeton* were joined by pilots from the carriers *Essex, Bunker Hill* and *Independence*. Japanese losses that day were one destroyer sunk, three destroyers and two cruisers damaged, and more than 100 planes downed; the Americans lost 11 planes. On the morning following the second raid, reconnaissance showed Rabaul's Simpson Harbor entirely cleared of ships: the Japanese were pulling them back to Truk, their principal base in the central Pacific, 800 miles to the north.

But no such way out was in store for their troops on Bougainville. The Seventeenth Army's commander was the same General Hyakutake who had incurred the final Japanese defeat on Guadalcanal, and he was determined not to repeat that "mortification," as he called it. But the general made a fateful error in judgment. Convinced that the Torokina landing was a mere sideshow preparatory to a main American thrust somewhere else on the island, Hyakutake bided his time—thus allowing the American invaders to entrench themselves on the shores of Empress Augusta Bay.

As they began setting up supply depots, draining swamps, clearing land and cutting roads through the jungle, the chief dangers they faced from the foe were intermittent attacks by planes from Rabaul and sporadic shelling by artillery in the hills beyond the beachhead. One such point, dubbed Hellzapoppin Ridge by the Americans, proved a particular threat; from its heights the enemy gunners had a sweeping view of the American enclave. More than a week was required to dislodge them. Time and again the attacking Marines were driven off Hellzapoppin's steep slopes, and

An American LST disgorges a tank at Cape Gloucester, New Britain, during the Allied invasion of the Japanese base. On the jungle-clad cape, tanks frequently became bogged down in swamps, and soldiers had to wait for them to be freed. The armored vehicles were invaluable in routing the Japanese from pillboxes and other stubbornly held fortifications.

air strikes failed to hit its narrow crest. Finally, a closely coordinated assault succeeded. On Christmas Day of 1943, Hellzapoppin was taken by the 21st Marine Regiment, aided by 100-pound bombs dropped by Marine Avengers.

That ended the fighting—for a while. Hyakutake at last realized that Torokina merited his full concern and that it would not fall either to air attacks from Rabaul or to the comparatively few troops he could trickle in by sea east and west of the beachhead. His sole alternative was to withdraw thousands of his men from the big Japanese defenses at Bougainville's northern and southern ends, and send them through the labyrinthine interior to attack Torokina from the land side. The move took weeks—much of the heavy artillery had to be dragged by hand—and it was not until March that the battle was joined.

The Americans had taken full advantage of the interim. A horseshoe-shaped perimeter defense line, by now 22,500 yards long, was studded with automatic weapons, mortars, antitank guns and artillery. Fields of fire had been cleared. The swamp approaches had been mined, and the Numa-Numa and East-West trails—the main roads into the perimeter—had been blocked. Foxholes and trenches had been dug. Two Army divisions, the 37th and the Americal, which had replaced the 3rd Marines, stood ready.

The Japanese, on their part, were motivated as never before. A captured document attested to the ferocity of their spirit. It was a rallying cry by the 6th Division's commander, Lieut. General Masatane Kanda, to his Nanking veterans, saying: "There can be no rest until our bastard foes are battered, and bowed in shame—till their bright red blood adds yet more luster to the badge of the 6th Division."

The battle of the perimeter raged for 17 days, often tree to tree and hand to hand. In the end the Japanese were outgunned and outmanned. By the end of April 1944, Bougainville was secured. The cost was high for both sides: more than 7,000 Japanese dead, more than 1,000 Americans.

But long before then—by mid-December of 1943—U.S. fighters from not one but three new airfields at Torokina were flying over Rabaul. They could thus provide partial cover for MacArthur's next move. On December 15, the U.S. 112th Cavalry Regiment crossed the Vitiaz and Dampier straits from New Guinea and landed on the southwest coast of New Britain at Arawe—270 miles from Rabaul at the island's northeast tip. Though the landing met little opposition, for the next three days Japanese planes from Rabaul flew 250 sorties against the beachhead. But coastwatchers gave warning of the attacks and American fighters, flying from Nadzab and Lae as well as from Torokina, met and bested the attackers in the air.

On December 26, MacArthur dispatched the 1st Marine Division, the veterans of Guadalcanal, to capture the only piece of New Britain real estate he really needed: Cape Gloucester, on the island's western tip, overlooking the waterway through which his troops heading for the Philippines would have to pass. Again the Japanese at Rabaul sent aloft all the planes they could muster, 70 or 80 at a time, and again the U.S. P-38s shot them down by the dozens. By the end of 1943, Japanese air activity over Cape Gloucester had virtually ceased. But on the ground the Marines still faced 10,000 enemy troops and had to fight in monsoon rain that sometimes added up to 16 inches a day. Three weeks of battle in terrain much like New Georgia's were required before the Cape Gloucester area was cleared of Japanese.

By now the Allied leaders had decided that Rabaul itself need not be taken. That once-great base, focus of so much American and Australian effort, was no longer regarded as a threat. Allied bombers and fighters ranged over it regularly, in increasing numbers and from several directions. To counter the blows, Admiral Mineichi Koga, Admiral Yamamoto's successor as commander in chief of the Imperial Combined Fleet, had decided to pull his planes and pilots off his carriers and land-base them at Rabaul. But they were systematically chewed up by their adversaries. Koga's decision was to have a longer-range effect as well. Japanese carrier planes, flown by inexperienced and ill-trained new pilots, were never again an important factor in the War.

Some 135,000 Japanese were still dug in at Rabaul. But with hundreds of miles of jungle between them and Cape Gloucester, they could have presented a greater problem than the one the Americans had faced on New Georgia. No one in the Allied camp welcomed the prospect of a repeat of that experience. Besides, Nimitz' central Pacific drive had begun, and MacArthur's attention was turned back to New Guinea, his war machine probing along its north coast for a jump-off point for the Philippines. Rabaul had been reduced to impotence, and could be safely bypassed.

KENNEY'S FLYING DEVILS

Low-flying U.S. Fifth Air Force B-25s plaster the Japanese airstrip at Dagua, New Guinea, in 1944 with "parafrags," 23-pound parachute fragmentation bombs.

AN INNOVATOR AND HIS "GANG OF GANGSTERS"

General Douglas MacArthur decorates Fifth Air Force commander George C. Kenney. After the capture of Nadzab, Kenney decorated MacArthur.

Throughout the War, Allied operations in the bitterly contested southwest Pacific were supported by the U.S. Fifth Air Force, which struck with such fury and imagination that the Japanese often could do little more than scurry for cover and complain of "fiendish warfare." Whether engaging in aerial combat, bombing ships or strafing airfields, the Fifth kept coming up with new techniques that caught the Japanese off guard and gave the Allies a crucial advantage.

The driving force behind the Fifth was its unorthodox commander, Major General George C. Kenney. A veteran of World War I who had shot down two German planes and been shot down himself, Kenney encouraged his pilots to be innovative and forget about the rule book. He taught them to fight in packs, and under his guidance they became such skilled hunters that Tokyo radio called Kenney "The Beast" and his men "a gang of gangsters."

The Fifth Air Force's bag of tricks was large and varied. When enemy antiaircraft interfered with its missions, pilots dropped white phosphorus to blind Japanese gunners on the ground. To distract the Japanese from air bases being built on New Guinea, a dummy airfield was set up, and Kenney noted with satisfaction "the great amusement of the natives" as the Japanese attacked his ghost field.

Kenney was one of the first to use a technique called "skip bombing," which enabled his men to fly in at extremely low altitudes, bounce their bombs across the water at enemy ships and get away before their targets erupted in smoke and flame. He engineered massive paratroop drops, and even airlifted two-and-a-half-ton trucks—by sawing them in half to fit aboard C-47s, then welding and bolting them together afterward. One of Kenney's most ingenious devices was the parafrag, a small fragmentation bomb with a parachute attached to slow its descent so that bombers could fly in at treetop height, drop their bombs and still have time to escape the explosions. By bombing Japanese airstrips with parafrags, the Fifth could demolish scores of enemy aircraft at a clip. By late 1944, the Fifth had blown up more than 1,000 enemy planes.

Three members of the Fifth Air Force stand proudly outside their officers' club on New Guinea in 1943: their squadron bagged 17 fighters in two days.

The top-scoring American ace of all time, Major Richard Bong, glances out of the cockpit of his P-38 before takeoff from a New Guinea airfield in 1943.

Daredevil pilot Major Thomas B. McGuire Jr. smiles confidently before a 1945 mission. Three days later, McGuire disappeared over the Philippine Islands.

ACES HIGH IN A DEADLY GAME

The Fifth Air Force produced some of the greatest fighter pilots in aviation history—men who would not hesitate to attack even when the odds were as much as 6 to 1 against them or when their planes had been riddled by enemy fire. They were a cocky crew; operating on the same radio frequency as the Japanese, they traded insults with them in the air.

The Fifth's aces included many different kinds of pilots: acrobats, daredevils, sharpshooters. The best shot, Lieut. Colonel Jerry Johnson, once sent three Japanese fighters into the sea in 45 seconds with just three bursts from his .50-caliber machine guns. Another of the Fifth's great gunners, Captain William A. Shomo, shot down six Japanese fighters and a bomber in his first aerial combat—a record never surpassed. When asked by Kenny why he had let two more fighters get away, Shomo tersely replied, "I ran out of bullets."

The Fifth's most celebrated ace was Major Richard "Bing" Bong. He came to Kenney's attention in San Francisco in 1942, when an irate housewife complained that Bong had buzzed so low in his P-38 that he had blown her clothes off the line. Bong became the top American ace of all time, with 40 enemy planes to his credit. A poor gunner, he won his victories by swooping in and firing at dangerously close range, then pulling up at the last minute to avoid colliding with his targets.

Bong's reputation was rivaled only by that of Major Thomas B. McGuire Jr., who made 38 kills. He won fame for himself over Wewak, New Guinea, by refusing to give in to an equally stubborn Japanese fighter closing head on. They grazed each other in mid-air. When McGuire returned to his base, he had the evidence of his encounter for everyone to see—a paint smudge on his wing, picked up when the two planes brushed. It had to be removed by the ground crew with steel wool.

By late 1943, the Fifth's aces had obtained supremacy of the air. By then the nature of the opposition had changed, and the self-satisfied American pilots used to say of their Japanese adversaries: "The eager pilots are not experienced; and the experienced not eager."

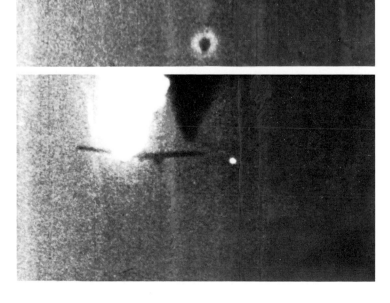

At top, Captain Thomas J. Lynch, who downed 20 enemy planes, leans nonchalantly against the propeller of his P-38. Below, footage from Lynch's gun camera records his destruction of a bomber over Wewak, New Guinea, in 1943.

After landing, one of the 1,400 paratroops
who participated in an airborne assault
by the Fifth on the island of Noemfoor, off the
northwestern coast of New Guinea, in 1944 is
pulled along a muddy airstrip by his parachute.

A battalion of paratroops descends on Nadzab
under the cover of a smoke screen in 1943.
Ninety-six C-47s participated in the daring drop.

THE FIFTH'S SPECTACULAR AIR INVASIONS

Among the Fifth Air Force's many pioneer-
ing achievements were the first large-scale
airborne operations of the Pacific war. The
greatest of these was the paratroop assault
against Nadzab, New Guinea, in 1943, as
part of a crucial drive on nearby Lae. A
total of 302 planes from eight Allied fields
converged on Nadzab on the morning of
September 5. After preliminary bombing
and the laying of a thick smoke screen,
C-47 troop carriers flew in low over the
landing site. Then, in a little more than a
minute, all of the 1,700 paratroops made
their jumps.

Taken by surprise, the Japanese offered
no resistance. High above, in a B-17, General MacArthur was—in Kenney's words—
"jumping up and down like a kid," amazed
and delighted by the ease of the operation.
Using Nadzab as a staging base, the Allies
took Lae in a few days.

A low-flying Fifth Air Force B-25 skips two bombs off the water in a run at Wewak, New Guinea.

BOMBS THAT SKIPPED TO TARGET

One of the Fifth's trickiest assignments was sinking enemy shipping. Traditional high-altitude bombing, while minimizing enemy antiaircraft fire, proved generally ineffective against moving ships. To improve the Fifth's accuracy, Kenney began experimenting with skip bombs.

The theory was simple: if dropped at a low altitude a few hundred yards from an enemy ship, a bomb would hit the water's surface and skip across it like a flat stone until it bounced into the target. Then, if equipped with a fuse set to go off five seconds after impact, the bomb would explode deep inside the ship, where it would do the most damage.

During trial runs the bombs had a tendency either to sink or to bound right over the target. But the Fifth's pilots quickly discovered that by releasing bombs from approximately 200 feet above the water, while flying at 200 mph, they could get them to strike the mark.

The skip-bomb technique proved to be deadly effective. The Fifth helped put a big crimp in Japanese shipping in the southwest Pacific—on one occasion scoring 28 direct hits with only 37 bombs.

Geysers erupt around a barge caught in a skip-bombing attack by the Fifth off Kokas, New Guinea, in 1944. One bomb can be seen sailing through the spray.

EXTRA FIREPOWER FOR LOW-FLYING BOMBERS

Because so many of the Fifth's missions, from paratroop drops to skip bombing, involved low-altitude flying, the planes were particularly vulnerable to antiaircraft fire. In the early days over New Guinea, it was not unusual for a bomber to limp back to base with as many as 200 holes in its sides.

To give his B-25s more firepower and enable them to strafe enemy positions as they came in on their bombing runs, Kenney turned to a "super-experimental gadgeteer and all-around fixer," Major Paul "Pappy" Gunn. Gunn ripped out the bombardier's position in the nose of a plane and had it fitted with eleven .50-caliber machine guns armed with 500 rounds of ammunition apiece. When the additional weight made the bomber nose-heavy, Gunn removed three of the guns and added an extra 200-gallon gas tank behind the wings to correct the balance. And as a final touch, he modified the plane's two standard top turret guns so they could be locked in an automatic forward-firing position. The 10-gun plane became the prototype for a whole line of bomber-strafers used throughout the islands with devastating effectiveness.

Japanese manning 75mm antiaircraft guns take cover in dugouts as a Fifth Air Force B-25 bomber—

its nose fitted out to hold additional .50-caliber guns and painted to resemble a falcon—skirts treetops on a strafing run at Boram, New Guinea, in 1943.

4

As a battleground, the islands of the central Pacific posed problems encountered in no other arena of the War. Their strategic value, so far as the U.S. Navy planners of the campaign were concerned, was beyond question. Wresting them from the Japanese would open an avenue westward either to the Philippines or Formosa. In the longer run, the central Pacific islands would serve as bases from which growing American air and naval power could strike closer and closer to Japan itself. But the very nature of the islands made their capture potentially far more complicated than was generally believed.

In contrast to the mountainous, jungle-clad Solomons to the south, the typical central Pacific island is flat and sparsely vegetated, a low platform of coral rising only a few feet above the surface of the sea. Usually, it is part of a curious formation called an atoll—the result of the build-up of coral atop an extinct and sunken volcano. Variously shaped like a circle, a horseshoe or a triangle, atolls enclose a lagoon that is open to the sea through only one or two narrow channels. Here and there along the rim of the atoll the coral stands high enough above water to form a string of tiny islands where scattered coconut palms and pandanus trees may grow, but not much else. A large atoll may be 20 or more miles long, and a smaller one no more than the size of a sports stadium. But even on a large atoll no island is much more than a couple of miles long.

From the standpoint of an air force or a navy, atolls are tempting objectives. The flat terrain makes good airstrips, and there is an unlimited supply of coral for the construction of runways. The lagoons provide protected ship anchorages, while the vast stretches of ocean between atolls allow for large-scale maneuver.

For ground forces, however, atoll warfare can spell trouble. Landing craft risk being hung up on the treacherous and often hidden coral reefs that rim both the lagoon and ocean sides of an atoll. Once ashore on a strongly defended atoll, attacking troops must fight for every foot. They have no room to maneuver, no forests or thickets or hills to use as cover. They have just the sea or the lagoon at their backs and coral sand and a dug-in enemy in front.

Kwajalein Atoll, in the group known as the Marshalls, was Admiral Nimitz' obvious prime target as he contemplated his drive across the central Pacific in the summer of 1943.

LESSONS IN ATOLL WARFARE

The Japanese had ruled the Marshalls under a League of Nations mandate since the 1920s; they had built 65-mile-long Kwajalein, the world's biggest atoll, into a major air and naval base. But U.S. planners decided that before the Marshalls could be approached, the Gilberts, a cluster of atolls more than 500 miles to the southeast, had to be taken. Long under British control, the Gilberts had been seized by the Japanese soon after Pearl Harbor. Attacking the Marshalls while the Gilberts were still in Japanese hands would expose the Americans to danger from the rear.

The two main Gilbert atolls occupied by the Japanese were Makin and Tarawa. Tarawa was the larger and more heavily fortified, but the Japanese prized both. While serving as outposts on the eastern approaches to the Marshalls, they also posed a threat to Allied communications between the central and southwest Pacific. That the Japanese would not easily yield the Gilberts was a foregone conclusion.

In November of 1943, Nimitz' drive across the central Pacific was ready to be launched. Its top commander, directly responsible to Nimitz, was the officer whose decisive action had proved a key factor in winning the Battle of Midway 17 months earlier: Vice Admiral Raymond A. Spruance. At his disposal Spruance had a formidable assemblage of American land, sea and air power. From the United States, Hawaii and from bases in New Zealand and the South Pacific some 200 American ships made their way by circuitous routes toward the point where the equator crosses the international date line; Makin and Tarawa lie just northwest of that junction. In the armada were three dozen transports carrying the 2nd Marine Division and elements of the 27th Infantry Division—some 35,000 soldiers and Marines in all. Protecting the transports were 17 carriers, 12 battleships, eight heavy and four light cruisers and 66 destroyers. Of the carriers, 10 were new fast carriers—bigger than the flattops that had fought at Midway—and seven were small escort carriers. On the carriers were more than 900 planes, and they were to be backed by Army planes, land-based in the nearby Ellice Islands, which were still British held.

The armada was divided into three task forces: a southern force to take Tarawa Atoll; a northern force for a simultaneous assault on Makin Atoll, more than 100 miles away; and the fast-carrier force to protect the other two forces from Japanese planes based at Kwajalein, as well as from the warships of the Imperial Combined Fleet.

Though it was expected that Tarawa would be the tougher fight, both Admiral Turner, the amphibious force commander, and Marine Major General Holland M. "Howlin' Mad" Smith, commander of the landing forces, chose to go first to Makin with the northern force. They assumed that the battle for Makin would be finished so quickly that the battleship *Pennsylvania*—on which both men sailed—could take them to Tarawa in time to make any critical decisions that might be required there. And indeed Makin should have been a pushover. A probing raid in August of 1942, conducted by Lieut. Colonel Evans Carlson and his Marine Raiders, had met with only feeble resistance. Now, after more than a year, the Japanese had only about 300 trained troops and 400 civilian laborers on the one fortified island of the atoll to pit against 6,500 Americans—the entire 165th Regimental Combat Team of the 27th Division.

But clearing that one little island, Butaritari, took four days. In the course of the landing, much vital equipment was soaked. Waterlogged radios fouled up communications; damp flamethrowers could not be used to clear out Japanese bunkers. Moreover, the Americans were untried in combat; they had been on garrison duty in Hawaii. Frightened and trigger-happy, they wasted time and effort firing at nonexistent snipers in palm trees. Morale plummeted when the regimental commander was killed early in the fight and his body remained in plain view for two days. Artillery was misused. Squads of Japanese riflemen held up entire companies for hours. General Smith, whose short temper had helped earn him his nickname of "Howlin' Mad," thought the advance "infuriatingly slow," and he went ashore to chew out Major General Ralph Smith, commander of the 27th Division.

The wrangling was due in part to a difference between Army and Marine tactics. The soldiers had been instilled with the idea of keeping casualties low by advancing cautiously and making sure no enemy remained to threaten their rear. The Marines were accustomed to moving fast, at almost any cost, because the fleet supporting them was vulnerable to attack every extra hour that it had to wait near a beachhead for an island to be secured.

In this instance, the Marine doctrine proved tragically

correct. On the last day of the fight for Makin, a Japanese submarine torpedoed the escort carrier *Liscome Bay* amidships as she stood by off the atoll. The bombs and ammunition she was carrying exploded, and she sank in 23 minutes. More than 600 men were lost, 10 times the number of American soldiers killed on the atoll. Had the battle gone more quickly, the *Liscome Bay* would have left long since.

The Americans' misfortunes at Makin were vastly compounded at Tarawa. The fight there, waged over an area less than half the size of New York's Central Park, was destined to go down in history as one of the bloodiest battles of World War II. The high cost in American lives was to come as a profound shock not only to the people back home but also to the planners of the invasion; every subsequent move in the drive across the central Pacific was to be made with the mistakes of Tarawa in mind.

Of the atoll's 47 islands, the Americans' chief target was Betio, on the atoll's southwest corner. Though just over two miles long and only half a mile at its widest, Betio is Tarawa's largest island, and on it the Japanese had built a fighter airstrip and their principal installations.

Before the battle, two opposing admirals had made grand predictions. "A million men cannot take Tarawa in a hundred years," contended Rear Admiral Keiji Shibasaki, commander of the 2,600 seasoned troops defending the atoll. Rear Admiral Howard F. Kingman, commander of the ships that were to deliver the preinvasion bombardment of Betio, was no less sweeping in his optimism. "Gentlemen," he promised the 2nd Marine Division, "we will not neutralize Betio. We will not destroy it. We will obliterate it!"

Both admirals proved to be poor prophets—but both initially had cause for confidence. Some 1,000 Japanese construction workers and 1,200 Korean laborers had turned Betio's 291 acres into the most heavily fortified bastion of its size in the world. Fourteen coastal defense guns, four of them quick-firing 8-inchers bought from Britain before the War, guarded the shoreline. At least 40 more artillery pieces were sited at key points to hang a devastating curtain of fire over every avenue of approach and every beach. A coconut-log sea wall four feet high lined the lagoon side, and more than 100 machine guns were emplaced to fire over the lip of the wall at approaching men or boats.

Moreover, each of Shibasaki's pillboxes was a fortress in

itself. His laborers had dug deep holes in the coral, lined them with steel and concrete, overlaid them with coral and coconut logs, and rounded them into small hillocks that cast no clear shadows in aerial photographs; hits by shells and bombs would glance off and do little damage. Shibasaki's command posts and ammunition dumps were just as secure in a series of bombproof bunkers, some of them two stories high, with walls eight feet thick and steel-and-concrete roofs. Not even a direct hit by heavy naval guns was certain to crack open these structures. Adding to the

Hip-deep in water, men of the U.S. 27th Infantry Division wade ashore at Butaritari Island on Makin Atoll as black smoke from enemy oil dumps hit by naval gunfire clouds the sky. Although they outnumbered the Japanese troops by more than 20 to 1 and were supported by tanks, the poorly trained Americans, in combat for the first time, took four days to capture lightly defended Makin and suffered 218 casualties.

sense of safety they gave the defenders was an intricate network of trenches; by racing through these tunnels, even while under a bombardment, the crack riflemen of the Special Naval Landing Forces could quickly shift to any threatened sector of the defense line.

Finally, Shibasaki could take comfort from the reef that fringed Betio—a shelf of coral that was wider than the island itself. On the ocean side the reef had been mined and the shallows between it and the shore studded with concrete pyramids and barbed-wire entanglements so arranged that approaching boats and wading men would be funneled directly toward the muzzles of the Japanese guns. Though similar traps on Betio's lagoon side had not been completed, the reef there was even wider and higher than the one facing the open sea.

Yet in spite of these redoubtable obstacles, natural and man-made, Admiral Kingman, like Admiral Shibasaki, had reason to believe that his side would prevail. Kingman's prediction that Betio would be obliterated was based on his knowledge of what lay in store for the island even before

the men of the 2nd Marine Division went ashore. Betio was to undergo a concentration of aerial and naval bombardment unsurpassed in the history of modern warfare. Flying from airfields in the Ellice Islands, B-24 Liberator bombers had been plastering the island for days, and were scheduled to keep on doing so right up to H-hour. Dive bombers and fighters from the carriers *Essex, Bunker Hill* and *Independence* were set to give the island a low-level working-over for half an hour at dawn on D-day. Before and after the carrier strike, the battleships *Tennessee, Maryland* and *Colorado,* as well as five cruisers and nine destroyers, were to hurl 3,000 tons of shells at Betio, or about 10 tons of high explosive per acre. Nothing could survive this massive onslaught—at least so the Navy gunners believed.

What most concerned the attackers was the landing operation itself. A third General Smith—Major General Julian C. Smith, commander of the 2nd Marine Division—planned to send his men in on Betio's lagoon side in order to avoid Shibasaki's obstacle course on the ocean side. Most of the men were to go ashore from LCVPs (Landing Craft, Vehicle and Personnel), more popularly known as Higgins boats after their flamboyant builder, Andrew Jackson Higgins of New Orleans. The Higgins boats were shallow-draft, but Smith was not certain that there would be enough water over the lagoon's reef for even these craft to cross, and he had asked for more LVTs (Landing Vehicle, Tracked). These were amphibian tractors called "amtracs" for short—or "alligators," after their original use by civilians for work in swamps—and they were actually lightly armored personnel carriers that could hold about 20 fully armed men. They had

propellers to move them at about four knots through water, caterpillar tracks to carry them forward on land at 20 mph, and power enough to roll over barbed-wire barriers and other minor obstacles. They could approach a reef from deep water, then start their tracks going, and move across the reef and up onto a beach and dry land.

Smith had to argue a good deal before he could persuade Admiral Turner, the amphibious force commander, that more amtracs were needed. Turner felt that the troops could just as effectively be landed on Betio's lagoon side by Higgins boats. The admiral's information was based in part on hydrographic charts made during an American Navy expedition in 1841 and in part on more current data provided by a handful of Britons, Australians and New Zealanders who had lived on Tarawa Atoll or sailed its waters.

These informants agreed that the lagoon itself was easily navigable and that the surf on the inner beach posed no problems for landing craft. However, on the crucial question—the depth of water that would cover the fringing reef the craft would have to cross—they disagreed. Judging by the tide at that hour of day and time of year, most of them estimated that five feet of water would cover the reef; but they were prudent enough to warn that they might be overestimating the depth by as much as a foot. Thus, a fully loaded Higgins boat, which draws about three and a half feet, might scrape the reef and be grounded. The planners of Tarawa chose to accept the estimate of five feet—a decision that was to have disastrous consequences.

Still, Admiral Turner was sufficiently won over by General Smith's plea for more amtracs to have 50 of them rushed

Aboard a Navy transport prior to the assault on Tarawa, a Marine intelligence officer (center) uses a relief model to point out Betio Island's topographical features and defenses to a group of platoon leaders scheduled to go ashore.

The U.S. offensive in the central Pacific (top map, right) started with an invasion of Tarawa and Makin atolls in the Japanese-held Gilbert Islands. U.S. amphibious forces entered Tarawa's lagoon through a break in the reef (bottom map, inset), and struck at Betio. On November 20, 1943, U.S. Marines came ashore on Red Beaches 1, 2 and 3. The next day, Marine reinforcements landed at Green Beach. Betio was secured on the fourth day of battle.

from the U.S. to join the convoy on the night before D-day. But that made a total of only 125 of the odd-looking vehicles, barely enough to transport the rifle companies of the first three assault battalions. Follow-up troops, ammunition and supplies would have to approach in Higgins boats. Colonel David M. Shoup, the assault force's commander, had misgivings about the plan and, en route to Tarawa, voiced them to Robert Sherrod, a TIME-LIFE war correspondent. Shoup foresaw that the first waves of his men would

get in all right on the amtracs, but that if the Higgins boats failed "we'll either have to wade in with machine guns maybe shooting at us, or the amtracs will have to run a shuttle service between the beach and the end of the shelf."

Early on D-day morning, November 20, even before the boatloads of Marines reached the fringing reef, the complicated assault timetable began to unravel. Debarking of the troops from the transports was delayed when the ships found themselves positioned in the path of the projected

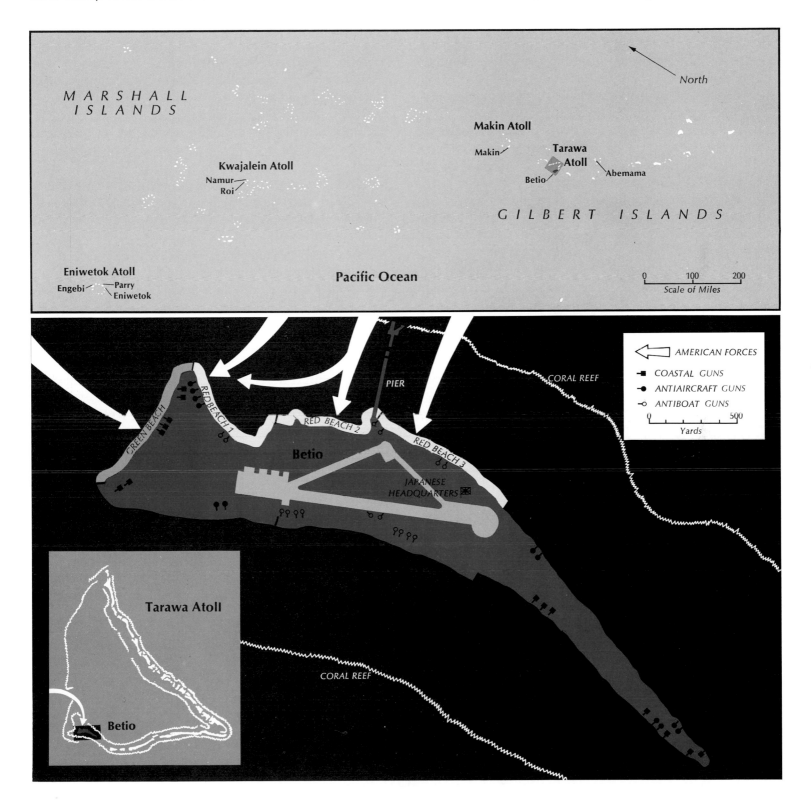

bombardment as well as in range of Japanese guns on shore. They were forced to move, with partially loaded Higgins boats and amtracs scurrying along behind. The battleships, after bombarding Betio for 35 minutes, ceased fire to make way for the air strike by carrier planes. But because of an inexplicable failure to coordinate, the carriers and battleships were operating on different schedules, and the planes did not show up until half an hour later. In this interval the Japanese started shelling the transports, compelling them to move again and further scrambling the organization of the landing waves. The delayed air strike was allotted only seven minutes instead of half an hour, and the scheduled big raid by B-24s from the Ellice Islands never materialized.

Tarawa's lagoon is about 17 miles long and nine miles wide, with one entrance about three miles north of Betio. Choppy seas and an unexpected current at the lagoon entrance made rough going for the incoming craft. Many of the men were seasick and all were drenched, but they could see the effect of the planes and the naval guns and they felt confident. Standing on the gunwale of a Higgins boat, correspondent Sherrod made a quick survey: "I tried to count the number of salvos—not shells, salvos—the battleships, cruisers and destroyers were pouring on the island. A Marine who had a waterproof watch offered to count off the seconds up to one minute. Long before the minute had ended I had counted over one hundred, but then a dozen more ships opened up and I abandoned the project. . . . There were fires up and down the length of the island. . . . The feeling was good." Watching the roaring flames and the smoke, a Marine private said: "It's a wonder the whole goddam island doesn't fall apart and sink."

H-hour had been set for 8:30 a.m. The bombardment and the strafing were supposed to continue until just before the Marines hit the beach, so as to keep Japanese heads down until the last possible moment. But the morning's delays and the fast current in the lagoon put the leading amtracs far behind schedule. The flagship of the supporting force, the *Maryland*, radioed frantic messages to her sister ships and to planes to keep up the pressure. But because of the smoking fires, the beach could not be seen clearly and it was feared that the landing craft might be hit instead. The bombardment ended and the strafing planes zoomed up

and away 18 minutes before the first wave of Marines touched shore. In that tense interim the huddled men in the wallowing amtracs were virtually without cover except from the destroyers *Dashiell* and *Ringgold,* which had also entered the lagoon. Their gunners, able to see the amtracs up ahead, kept shelling Betio until the first wave beached.

But that suppressed the Japanese only on one sector of the landing area. Those of Shibasaki's troops who were posted on the island's ocean side rushed to the rifle pits on the lagoon side. Though the bombardment had knocked out the communication lines of the Japanese, their weapons were virtually undamaged and every man knew his assignment: to destroy the invaders at the water's edge.

The Japanese began firing while the three lines of amtracs were 3,000 yards from shore. At 2,000 yards Japanese long-range machine guns opened up. At 800 yards the drivers of the amtracs started their treads going and the vehicles waddled up onto the reef fringing the island's lagoon side— only to meet a barrage from every gun in range.

Marine Private Newman Baird, an Indian of the Oneida tribe, was a machine gunner on an amtrac in the first wave. "They were knocking boats out left and right," he recalled. "A tractor'd get hit, stop, and burst into flames, with men jumping out like torches. . . . Our boat was stopped, and they were laying lead to us from a pillbox like holy hell. . . . I grabbed my carbine and an ammunition box and stepped over a couple of fellas laying there and put my hand on the side so's to roll over into the water. . . . Only about a dozen out of the twenty-five went over the side with me." Of these, Baird and perhaps three others made it to shore.

Many amtracs blew up when Japanese guns hit their fuel tanks. Others foundered in shell holes. Others, their drivers dead at the controls, ran wildly off course, spilling shaken, wounded and dead passengers. Some amtracs managed to reach shore but not at the assigned beaches, with ruinous consequences for the Americans' original plan. Amtracs that got to shore and tried to climb the log wall Shibasaki's workmen had built jammed against it. Of the original 125 amtracs, well over half were put out of action by Japanese gunfire; others simply broke down, and by the time the battle was over, only about 20 would be in working order.

One of the first-wave amtracs that made it all the way to shore was dubbed "The Old Lady." Among the Marines aboard was Corporal John Joseph Spillane, a baseball player whose throwing arm and fielding ability had already attracted the attention of two major-league teams. As The Old Lady rumbled up to the sea wall, the Japanese began lobbing hand grenades into her. Spillane picked the first one off the deck like a hot grounder and threw it back. He caught the second in mid-air and tossed it overboard. His fellow Marines watched, horrified but fascinated, as Spillane fielded the third, the fourth and the fifth grenade and pegged them back to the Japanese. Screams were heard and a machine gun on the sea wall stopped firing. Then came a sixth grenade. The Japanese Marine who had thrown it had delayed a few seconds, and it exploded in Spillane's right hand. The 20 riflemen whose lives he had saved vaulted over the sides of The Old Lady and dashed to the sea wall. Spillane could not go with them. His pitching hand was in shreds; a surgeon on a transport later amputated it.

The Higgins boats following the amtracs in got stuck on the lagoon reef—confirming the fears of the assault-force commander, Colonel Shoup. Many of the boats ran aground at the edge of the coral and were quickly blasted by Japanese guns. A few managed to transfer their passengers to battered amtracs that were on their way back to deep water and in exchange picked up wounded men the amtracs were evacuating. A desperate shuttle service began. But not enough amtracs were running and most of the Marines in the later waves had to wade in under fire.

Correspondent Sherrod and about 15 Marines transferred from their Higgins boat to an amtrac, but the driver warned he could carry them only part of the way to shore before he would have to go back for more incoming troops. He let them out in neck deep water; then they started wading, bullets whizzing all around them. Finally they reached the end of a long pier that dominated the lagoon side of Betio, extending from the shore to deep water across 500 yards of reef. Sherrod and the Marines lay panting on the coral rocks of the pier foundation, hidden from the enemy by coconut-log stanchions. Almost an hour was to pass before they were able to make the last 400 yards to shore, by crawling in most of the way under the protection of the pier.

At that moment, the safest spot for the Americans on Betio was the area east of the pier—named Red Beach 3 in the attack plan. Thanks to the destroyers *Dashiell* and *Ringgold,* which had concentrated their last-minute fire on this area, Major Henry Crowe's 2nd Battalion, 8th Marines, had landed virtually unscathed. Two of Crowe's amtracs had even punched through a gap in the sea wall and established a precarious toe hold at the edge of the airstrip's taxiway, about 50 yards inland. But the rest of Crowe's men were pinned down on a strip of beach at the water's edge, under heavy fire from a complex of Japanese pillboxes nearby. Admiral Shibasaki's headquarters, the biggest concrete blockhouse on the island, stood just in front of Crowe's left flank.

On Red Beach 3, at least, an intact battalion was functioning under the control of its commanding officer. But elsewhere the precisely organized landing plan—under which three reinforced battalions were to have moved in abreast, each assigned to a particular section of beach—had completely come apart, turned into a monstrous jumble of blasted amtracs, bodies awash in the lagoon and small groups of leaderless men, out of touch with other units, crouching on slivers of shoreline under direct enemy fire. As one man later recalled: "It was like being in the middle of a pool table without any pockets."

To the west of the pier, on Red Beach 2, the 2nd Battalion, 2nd Marines, had lost its commander. Wading in, Lieut. Colonel Herbert Amey had raised his pistol over his head, yelled "Come on, these bastards can't stop us," and was heading toward shore when a burst of machine-gun fire struck him in the chest and stomach, killing him instantly. The next ranking officer in his group was Lieut. Colonel Walter I. Jordan, an observer from the 4th Marine Division. Though Jordan had assumed charge, he did not know the men of the battalion and some resented taking his orders. His new command was completely snarled, his radios waterlogged and silent, and he had no idea where the rest of the men of the battalion were or how many had survived.

Jordan got some help when a corporal named Osbaldo Paredes slid into the command post—a bomb crater under the sea wall—and volunteered to run messages. Jordan gratefully put him to work and soon Paredes was back with dire news. One company had landed near the pier but was under such fire that it could do nothing but dig in. In another company, five of the six officers were dead. So many sergeants and junior officers were wounded and out of action that those still unhurt found themselves in charge of total strangers. Most of the battalion was cut up into isolated groups of three or four men huddling at the base of the sea wall while Japanese guns fired over their heads at newer arrivals. All along the beach casualties were mounting: little had been done to silence the enemy machine guns. Jordan sent Paredes to find a working radio and send a message to Colonel Shoup: "We need help. Situation bad."

Shoup was getting even grimmer messages from Red Beach 1, the westernmost landing area. There the lagoon shore curved sharply inward, forming a deep cove; amtracs and wading men entering it faced fire not only frontally but also from their flanks, especially from a complex of Japanese gun positions at the border between Red 1 and Red 2. The sea wall offered no protection from this sweeping cross fire, and soon there were so many dead and wounded Marines on the beach that the battalion's six Sherman tanks could not get ashore without running over them. The drivers moved off to try another sector of the beach, and four of the tanks promptly fell into holes in the reef. Of the 700 men of the 3rd Battalion, 2nd Marines, who had left the transports to land on Red 1, nearly half had been killed or wounded; only about 100 were ashore, fighting to stay alive. The rest, including the battalion commander, Major John F. Schoettel, were hung up in boats at the reef's edge.

Schoettel had watched the slaughter of his first waves in mounting horror. Unable to contact his assault companies, he believed they were totally wiped out. Most of his amtracs lay wrecked on the reef; few were returning to shuttle him and his remaining men across the reef to shore. In agony over the fate of his men, Schoettel decided to hold the rest of his force at the reef instead of leading it into the murderous cross fire in the cove. He radioed Shoup: "Unable to land. Issue in doubt." A few minutes later he added, "Boats held up on reef of right flank Red 1. Troops receiving heavy fire in water." Shoup curtly replied: "Land Beach Red 2 and work west." Then came a message from Schoettel that stunned all who heard it: "We have nothing left to land."

But the situation on Red 1 was not as hopeless as Schoettel thought. One of his company commanders, Major Michael Ryan, had observed a few first-wave Marines going ashore at the extreme right end of Red 2, near Betio's northwest corner. Ryan directed his company that way, jumped from his Higgins boat and led the long wade to shore. More than a third of the company suffered casualties on the way in, but Ryan rallied the survivors of the earlier wave and took command of the battalion's remnants. He had no artillery, no mortars, no functioning radios with which to report his position or call for air or naval support. But soon the remaining two of the six tanks that had earlier been unable to land at Red 1 rolled ashore, and a little later Ryan was unexpectedly reinforced by 100 men of a reserve battalion; they had been heading for Red 2 but had been driven off course by the Japanese guns at the strong point between Red 1 and Red 2. Ryan set up the tanks and his ragtag force for a sweep down Green Beach, facing the open sea on Betio's western shore. If he could clear the Japanese off Green Beach, he reasoned, fresh troops could land without having to face the terrible fire in the lagoon.

Meanwhile, Colonel Shoup was on his way in to Red 2 with his staff. When shellfire hit their amtrac, Shoup managed to reach the pilings of the long pier where, standing in the water, he set up his temporary command post and watched the reserve battalions arrive.

Only a handful of amtracs remained to shuttle them in across the lagoon reef. In fact, there were no amtracs at all in sight when Major Robert Ruud's 3rd Battalion, 8th Marines, reached the reef opposite Red Beach 3 in Higgins boats. As the ramps of the boats came down, Marines on shore heard a sound "like a steel girder hitting concrete," and one of the boats disappeared. "It had been there," said one eyewitness, "and then suddenly it was not. In its place, for a split second, there was a blur in the air, and there was nothing." Then came another grinding crash, and a second boat vanished. The Japanese had the exact range. Beyond the reef; the coxswain of a third boat panicked. "This is as far as I go," he yelled, and let down his ramp—and a boatload of heavily laden men drowned in 15 feet of water.

The remainder of Ruud's battalion began wading in. Few lived to tell of it, but there were many witnesses. Shoup radioed Major Crowe: "Ruud is landing to your rear and catching hell." Crowe and his men could see for themselves. So could a sailor on the *Dashiell* in the lagoon, watching through binoculars. Later he recalled: "It was like a war movie. Those poor guys plodding in chest-high water

ABEMAMA: AN ODDBALL INVASION

Friendly islanders on Abemama help Seabees—who arrived after the invasion—construct a causeway of logs and oil cans.

When American troops invaded Makin and Tarawa, a third Japanese-held atoll in the Gilberts chain, Abemama, was also targeted. Little more than a speck in the ocean, Abemama was not expected to provide serious resistance. The landing force numbered only 78 Marines, and their offshore support consisted of only one vessel, the submarine *Nautilus,* which had also served as their transport.

They very nearly did not make it to Abemama. The night before D-day, November 19, 1943, the U.S. destroyer *Ringgold,* en route to Tarawa, spotted the *Nautilus,* mistook her for a "skunk" (Navy parlance for an "unidentified surface radar contact"), scored a direct hit on her with a 5-inch shell and went on, sure she had sunk. In fact, the shell had not exploded, and the *Nautilus* was able to take a quick dive.

Once ashore on Abemama the Americans were welcomed by two islanders who said there were only 25 Japanese on the atoll, dug in around the radio station. The Marines called in fire from the *Nautilus* and then attacked; but when the Japanese fought back fiercely, the Marines decided to wait them out. Four days later one of the Abemamans returned to tell the Americans that "the Saps are all dead" (Gilbert Islanders pronounce "j" as "s"). The Japanese captain in charge, rallying his 15 survivors for a new onslaught, had shot off the top of his own head while waving his pistol around; his men, deciding there was no more they could do, had killed themselves.

and getting shot down. I tried not to look, but I couldn't turn away. The horror of it hypnotized me. If I get to be a hundred years old I'll always remember." Overhead, in the battleship *Maryland*'s scout plane, Lieut. Commander Robert MacPherson watched too. He wrote in his log: "The water seemed never clear of tiny men, their rifles held over their heads, slowly wading beachward. . . . They kept falling, falling, falling . . . singly, in groups, and in rows."

Some of the waders made it to relative safety under the pier. Others trudged on toward shore through water tinged pink and whipped by bullets. Many died quickly. Some died slowly, wounded and struggling to keep their heads above water as the blood drained out of them and their packs pressed them down. Some stepped into holes and drowned. Some died trying to help wounded buddies. Heads and limbs of the newly slain bobbed gently in the swell; the dead from the first assault waves floated stiffly, like logs. Of Ruud's first wave, only 30 per cent reached Betio unhurt. His second and third waves fared little better. The battalion was finished as a fighting unit; the fragments were fed into Crowe's lines on Red Beach 3.

In the chaos, the life of every Marine depended quite simply on his willingness to risk it. Unless the Japanese guns could be silenced, the entire American force would be annihilated at the water's edge, as Shibasaki had ordered. And there was no easy way to knock out the Japanese pillboxes and gun emplacements. It was not a matter of digging in while artillery, tanks, naval fire or airplanes did the job; no artillery and few tanks had been landed, and the ships' guns and the planes' bombs were still inflicting but little damage on Shibasaki's maze of constructions.

Only at close range, with flamethrowers, or with hand grenades or demolition charges tossed into narrow firing slits, could the pillboxes be destroyed. That meant suppressing the instinct for self-preservation. It meant standing up, climbing over the sea wall and charging into a hail of bullets. Fewer men did this than did not—despite the traditions and training of the Marine Corps. Many had to be inspired by the exploits of men like Corporal Spillane, or bullied—in some cases literally kicked—into reluctant action by those officers and noncoms who were not themselves paralyzed by fear. With the chain of command in shambles, the outcome of the battle hung on the ability of the surviving leaders to take command of whatever men were available and to galvanize them into a fighting team. And there were leaders who could do this.

One of the most inspiring officers in the battle for Betio was First Lieutenant William Deane Hawkins. "Hawk," as everyone called him, commanded the 2nd Scout-Sniper Platoon, a select group of daredevil commandos whose skills and bravery made them the elite of the Marines. Burned in a childhood accident, and apparently haunted by the scars, Hawkins had spent his young life seeking out tough challenges. After Pearl Harbor he enlisted in the Marines and told a friend, "Mac, I'll see you someday, but not on this earth." He won a battlefield commission at Guadalcanal, and on the transport en route to Tarawa he told correspondent Sherrod: "I think the 34 men in my platoon can lick any 200-man company in the world."

Hawkins and his platoon had reached Betio a few minutes ahead of the first wave, their mission to clear the long pier of Japanese machine gunners. With a flamethrower and grenades, they did the job in a few minutes. Then Hawk led his men over the sea wall and stayed in the forefront of the battle most of D-day, shooting up Japanese positions and returning to the beach only to get more ammunition. "He's a madman," said one admiring fellow officer who saw Hawkins on one of his ammunition-gathering forays, standing erect on an amtrac, "riding around with a million bullets a minute whistling by his ears, just shooting Japs." Someone yelled at Hawk to get down. "Aw, those bastards can't shoot," he said. "They can't hit anything." A little later he was wounded, but he kept on fighting into the night.

Colonel Shoup—destined in later years to become the Commandant of the Marine Corps—was another natural leader of men. He was also witty and erudite. Few Marines were aware that he wrote poetry; most knew him as a tough, bullnecked, red-faced officer who chewed on cigars and bellowed orders with all the creative profanity of a top sergeant. Still under the pier at noon, Shoup saw a Higgins boat coming by along a narrow channel that had been discovered next to the pilings. He and his command group climbed aboard and Shoup ordered the coxswain shoreward. But they met with such fire that the colonel decided to transfer to an amtrac that was just then backing off the

shore with a load of wounded men. Shoup, seeing that most of the men were dead, grimly ordered the amtrac's crew to help him toss the bodies overboard. Then he waded back to the Higgins boat where his staff and a few other men were cringing to avoid the rain of fire overhead.

"All right, who's coming with me?" Shoup shouted. The only man to stand up was Lieut. Colonel Carlson of the Marine Raiders, who was at Tarawa as an observer. Shoup began barking orders, calling his staff officers by name, shaming them one by one into the waiting amtrac.

A few minutes later, on the beach, Shoup was knocked to his knees when some mortar fragments hit him in the legs. He rose and hobbled on. As he did so, he noticed a pair of Marine boots sticking out from a pile of coral rubble; when the boots twitched, he rapped on the soles and kept shouting until a dusty corporal wriggled out. Shoup identified himself and roared: Have you got a mother back home?" The corporal said he did. "Well, do you think she'd be proud of you, curled up in a hole like that, no damn use to anybody?" The corporal shook his head. "Where's your squad?" asked the colonel. The corporal glared and said that his squad had been wiped out. "Well," said the colonel, "why don't you get yourself another squad?" The corporal didn't know how. "I'll tell you how," said Shoup, pointing to a string of men crouching under the sea wall. "Pick out a man, then another and another. Just say, 'Follow me.' When you've got a squad, report to me." Soon the corporal did just that. By then Shoup had set up a command post about 15 yards inland. It was just three feet away from a Japanese blockhouse, but the troops inside its coconut-log walls could not get at him and he could not get at them.

By noon on D-day, five reinforced battalions had been committed to Betio, but they were clearly not enough. Aboard the *Maryland,* General Julian Smith, the 2nd Marine Division commander, radioed General Holland Smith at Makin Atoll. "The issue is in doubt," he reported, and he asked for the reserves to be sent in. It worried Holland Smith to get such a request so early in a battle. Still, despite the slow progress on Makin that had him fuming, he concluded that the men of the Army's 27th Division could do the job there alone; at his order the 6th Marines' combat team, which had been standing by in transports at Makin, was dispatched to Tarawa. With these added troops coming, Julian Smith felt that he could commit his own last reserve, Major Lawrence Hays's 1st Battalion, 8th Marines.

Poor communications had bedeviled the operation all morning; now they became unbelievably snarled. The radios on shore were wet and malfunctioning, and the radios on the *Maryland* seemed to stop working every time the battleship's guns fired. Moreover, her transmitters, receivers and antennas were too close together, causing mutual interference. Julian Smith sent a message to Shoup asking whether a night landing of the reinforcements was possible and whether they could come in on Green Beach, at the western end of the island. Shoup never got the message. Then Smith ordered Major Hays, whose 1st Battalion was already in boats inside the lagoon, to land to the east of the beachhead and strike west. Hays never got that message.

Had the radios functioned properly, a great many American lives would have been saved and the battle might have ended much sooner. Unknown to any of the top commanders, Major Ryan and his pickup force at the western end of Betio, moving along Green Beach toward the ocean side, had penetrated more deeply into the island than any other unit. The Japanese guns on Green Beach faced out to sea, and though Ryan had only the 75mm guns of two tanks for heavy fire-support, he managed to overrun most of the turrets and pillboxes by a flanking attack. But without flamethrowers or explosives, he could not eliminate all the Japanese in those positions, and after his main force had passed them, some of them popped out of the bunkers to waylay Ryan's ammunition carriers. Unable to inform Shoup that part of Green Beach was cleared to receive reinforcements, and in danger of being cut off himself, Ryan abandoned his gains and pulled his makeshift battalion back to a safe perimeter. In the evening, a runner Shoup sent to get a situation report somehow contrived to sneak around the Japanese strong point at the edge of the cove and find Ryan, but the messenger never made it back to Shoup.

On Major Crowe's beachhead near the long pier, four more tanks managed to get ashore. Taking on the Japanese pillboxes one by one, they helped Crowe's battalion in their yard-by-yard advance inland to the edge of the airstrip. But after a few hours only one of the tanks was still operating. This was Lieutenant Louis Largey's "Colorado," which was to become a Tarawa legend. The Colorado was hit by a Japanese antitank gun, showered with grenades and Molotov cocktails and blasted by a land mine in its path. Though it was fire-blackened and battered, and its crew was bruised and weary, machine and men kept ripping up the smaller Japanese emplacements.

But Admiral Shibasaki's huge concrete headquarters and the steel-reinforced pillboxes that ringed it were impervious to tank fire. Carrier planes and naval gunfire hit at them most of the day without doing much damage. Major Crowe sent demolition teams to try to blow up the blockhouse and a platoon to try to encircle it, but the demolition men were thrown back and the platoon was nearly wiped out. Shibasaki had tanks too, and one of them came chugging and clanking toward Crowe's men. Two of the Americans' 37mm antitank guns had been dragged onto the beach after the boat that had brought them in was sunk, but there seemed no way to get them over the sea wall into firing position. "Lift 'em over," came the cry. The Marines nearby grabbed hold and the 900-pound weapons fairly soared over the wall. They fired, and the Japanese tank retreated.

All through the night of D-day, the men of Hays's battalion waited in Higgins boats offshore for landing orders that did not come. They could smell death; the strong, sweetish odor of decaying flesh wafted across 1,000 yards of lagoon water and sickened and frightened them. The Marines on shore were also waiting, well aware of the Japanese tactic of counterattacking at night. They had no way of knowing that Shibasaki's telephone system had been blown apart, that his headquarters blockhouse was out of touch with all of his forces (although he still had radio contact with Tokyo), and that he could not coordinate or even order an attack.

But some of Shibasaki's officers needed no instructions. The Americans had managed to bring in small quantities of supplies along the pier, and in the moonlight the pier's coral surface gleamed; anyone on it became a perfectly silhouetted target for Japanese gunners. Suddenly it became clear that part of the fire directed against the men on the pier was coming from machine guns that had been left in disabled American boats and amtracs in the lagoon. In the darkness, the Japanese had swum out to the boats and were manning the machine guns. Some of the watching Marines had reason to remember a line from a mimeographed sheet of tips they had received en route to Tarawa concerning the fighting tactics of the Japanese. "Don't be a Boy Scout," it read. "Kill or be killed is their creed."

When the men of Major Hays's battalion finally started wading ashore to Red Beach 2 at dawn—20 hours after they had boarded the landing craft—bullets and shells flew at them from every direction: from wrecked American amtracs and tanks, from the strong point at the edge of the cove at Red 1, from machine guns and cannon beyond the beachhead, and from a bombed-out Japanese freighter grounded on the reef, where another Japanese suicide squad had set up several machine guns during the night. The tide had receded and Hays's men could not even crouch low in the water to hide. Though Dauntless dive bombers and Hellcat fighters screamed down to bomb and strafe the Japanese freighter, most of them missed. A few newly arrived 75mm pack howitzers were rushed up the beach to fire on the strong point at the cove, but that helped only a little. Desperately, Colonel Shoup ordered all of his units to attack to take the heat off the men sloshing across the reef and to clear an area where they could land. But 350 of the 800 men in Hays's rifle companies were killed or wounded before they could reach shore.

Lieutenant Hawkins and his scout-snipers got the toughest assignment of the morning: to knock out a cluster of enemy machine guns that were protecting the strong point at the cove. While his men laid down covering fire, Hawk dashed from gun to gun. He stood up in full view to shoot point-blank into the firing slits of the pillboxes; then he tossed in grenades to finish off the occupants. A mortar shell killed three of his men and wounded him again, this time more seriously, but he reorganized his platoon and single-mindedly returned to the attack. "I came here to kill Japs, not to be evacuated," he snapped at a corpsman who tried to hold him back. Three more pillboxes were blown up. Then, as one of his sergeants later described it: "We were attacking a sort of fort at the base of a sandy knoll. Hawk started tossing grenades from close up. He had got rid of maybe half a dozen when a heavy machine gun opened up and an explosive shell hit him in the shoulder. The blood just gushed out of him." Hawk died. The Betio airstrip was

later named Hawkins Field—the first time a nonaviator was so recognized—and the daring lieutenant was awarded a posthumous Medal of Honor. Thanks to him, the 450 survivors of Hays's battalion were able to take over the right flank of Red Beach 2.

Except for a few short cat naps during the night, Shoup had been on his feet for 30 hours and his leg wounds hurt. Gloom pervaded his command post. Since early morning he had been on the radio asking the flagship to send more ammunition, water, rations and medical supplies. His medics had so little to work with, and so many wounded to work on, that during the night some of them had waded out to the lagoon reef to strip dead bodies of the little first-aid kits that all Marines carried hooked to their belts. At one point during the morning, Shoup's superiors on the *Maryland* asked if he had enough troops to do the job. His answer was a blunt no. "We're in a mighty tight spot," he said. Orders went out from the flagship to send in the 6th Marines' combat team as soon as it arrived from Makin.

But sometime around noon on D-day-plus-1, the Marines on Betio noticed that the erratic Tarawa tide was flooding in—and with it, the tide of battle began to turn. Though the rising water threatened to drown wounded Marines lying on the beach, it also allowed Higgins boats to come across the reef to pick them up and to bring in greater quantities of supplies. Meanwhile, the infusion of more than 400 fighting men from Major Hays's battalion enabled the two battalions already on Red Beach 2 to punch their way across the airstrip and seize a section of the island's south shore. And from every sector Shoup began receiving reports that Japanese soldiers were committing suicide in their bunkers.

Meanwhile, a Navy liaison officer with a working radio reached Major Ryan on Red 1. With his tanks in support and the liaison officer calling in naval shellfire, Ryan and his men swiftly retraced the advance they had made along Green Beach the day before, then continued on to Betio's southwest corner. Green Beach was clear—and this time, thanks to the radio, Shoup knew about it. The 6th Marines, arriving from Makin on the afternoon of D-day-plus-1, were ordered to land one battalion on Green Beach. At dusk, Major William Jones's 1st Battalion, 6th Marines, paddled over the reef and ashore in rubber boats, to be greeted with joy by Ryan's ragged force. For the first time a battalion had landed on Betio not only intact, but with all its weapons. Shoup concluded his evening situation report with this laconic summary: "Casualties: many. Percentage dead: unknown. Combat efficiency: we are winning."

In his big bombproof blockhouse, Admiral Shibasaki was also composing a situation report. He had not really believed his own boast that his forces could hold out on Betio indefinitely. What he had counted on was an assurance by the High Command in Tokyo that if the Americans attacked Tarawa he would get every sort of help—troops, planes, ships, submarines. From the headquarters of Admiral Koga, Commander in Chief of the Imperial Combined Fleet, had come word that "a hornets' nest for the Yankees" had been prepared.

But in the weeks preceding Tarawa a number of moves by the Americans elsewhere in the Pacific had shattered Tokyo's plans. With the invasion of Bougainville in the Solomons on November 1, Japanese troops had been rushed there rather than to Tarawa. The American air strikes at Rabaul on November 5 and November 11, made in support of the Bougainville operation, had destroyed scores of Japanese planes intended for Betio and put a number of Japanese warships out of action.

In effect, Shibasaki had been abandoned by his helpless superiors. Hundreds of wounded, hungry and panicky men jammed his headquarters; the stench was unbearable. He was out of touch with the rest of his garrison. The Americans were crawling ever closer and bringing up artillery and fresh tanks. But Shibasaki's radio to Tokyo was still operating, and over it he sent a last message: "Our weapons have been destroyed. From now on everyone is attempting a final charge. May Japan exist for ten thousand years!"

On the morning of D-day-plus-2, Major Crowe's mortars on Red Beach 3, aided by the tank Colorado, finally cracked apart the pillboxes protecting Shibasaki's headquarters. This cleared the way for First Lieutenant Alexander Bonnyman's assault engineers, who had been trying to get at Shibasaki's stronghold for two days. Japanese guns still prevented Bonnyman and his men from going around the two-story bombproof structure to reach the entrance, but now they could walk right up to the other side. Covered by Marine rifle fire, Bonnyman and five of his engineers clambered up the rounded, sandy side of the structure. Bonnyman had made it to the top—the highest point on Betio—when the Japanese came swarming up the other face to drive him off. The lieutenant stood there, blazing away with carbine, then flamethrower, for about 30 awful seconds until the Japanese retreated in disorder. But as they did so Bonnyman himself fell, fatally wounded.

By his exploit—later recognized by a Medal of Honor—Bonnyman held the roof long enough to allow his men to race up and drop grenades down the bunker's air vents. Scores of Japanese rushed from the entrance and were cut down by rifle fire and canister shot. A Marine bulldozer heaped sand against the portal and the firing slits, entombing the Japanese still inside. Gasoline was poured into the vents, followed by TNT charges, muffled explosions and screams. Then silence. When the Marines were able to go in, they found nearly 200 blackened corpses. Shibasaki's

At the height of the fighting on tiny Betio, Marine assault leader Colonel David M. Shoup (holding map case) receives a battle report from one of his officers. Informed that Japanese still occupied the coconut-log bunker on the left, Shoup decided to order its apertures plugged rather than relocate his command post.

was thought to be among them, but it was never identified.

As D-day-plus-2 wore on, the freshly arrived troops of the 1st Battalion, 6th Marines, swept from Green Beach along the southern shore to link up with the Marines who had crossed the airfield the day before. The 3rd Battalion, 6th Marines, landed on Green Beach to back them up. By nightfall the airfield and the entire western end of Betio were in American hands, except for the now-isolated strong point at the edge of the cove, at Red Beach 1.

Hundreds of Japanese were still dug in on the narrow eastern end of Betio. That evening, when General Julian Smith came ashore to take direct tactical control of his 2nd Marine Division, he cautiously predicted that it would take five more days to root out all the resisters. But the Japanese simplified the task. That night they launched a series of savage counterattacks against the Marine line athwart the island. Their final, heaviest charge erupted against a company of Major Jones's battalion, the troops who had landed unopposed on Green Beach the previous evening. In the face of artillery and naval shelling, screaming Japanese broke into the company's lines, and the fight turned into a hand-to-hand melee. First Lieutenant Norman Thomas radioed Jones: "We are killing them as fast as they come at us but we can't hold much longer; we need reinforcements." "We haven't got them to send you," Jones replied; "you've got to hold." The men did. More than 300 Japanese bodies were counted around the company's position at dawn.

A few hours later a Navy Hellcat landed at Hawkins Field and at 1:10 p.m. on D-day-plus-3 Betio was declared secured. Except for a few strays who kept turning up for days afterward, most of the Japanese had been killed or had committed suicide by placing the muzzles of their rifles in their mouths and pulling the trigger with their toes; the last of the defenders had fled across the reef to the neighboring islands of the atoll, where they were chased down in short order. Only 17 Japanese—and 129 Korean laborers—surrendered at Tarawa Atoll. The rest of Shibasaki's men—some 4,700 troops and construction workers—died; Imperial General Headquarters in Tokyo acclaimed the soldiers as "the flowers of the Pacific."

The American loss was smaller in numbers but greater in impact upon a country that had not yet begun to realize the cost of war. In a 76-hour fight for a chunk of coral, 1,027 Marines and 29 Navy officers and men—most of them medics—were killed, died of wounds or were missing and presumed dead; 2,292 men were wounded but recovered. Back home, Americans were shocked by news pictures of dead Marines on Betio's beaches, and angry editorials demanded a Congressional inquiry into "the Tarawa fiasco." Admiral Nimitz himself was flooded with accusing mail from bereaved parents. "You killed my son on Tarawa," one mother wrote.

But the lessons learned in the battle were quickly put to use and were to save many lives. More amtracs were built, strengthened with better armor—some equipped with turrets and 37mm guns or 75mm howitzers—and rushed to the Pacific. LCIs (Landing Craft, Infantry) were converted into supporting gunboats that could come in close on a beach. Aerial intelligence techniques were refined to provide accurate data about water depths and tide levels. Underwater demolition teams were trained to destroy natural and man-made impediments before any landing took place.

The most important lesson learned was that fortifications as strong as Betio's could not be knocked out simply by blanketing the island with bombs and shells. As one Marine officer put it after the battle, the Navy had assumed that land targets were like ships: they would sink when hit by enough shells and never be heard from again. Though much damage was done to Betio by the massed "area" bombing and bombardment, many of its blockhouses and pillboxes remained intact. What was needed to destroy these was precision bombing and accurately aimed gunfire, with time out to let the smoke clear and to judge the success of the hits. Moreover, the Navy's shells, fired on a flat trajectory, had failed to penetrate the heavier blockhouses and pillboxes. Duplicates of Shibasaki's defenses were hurriedly constructed in Hawaii, and after practicing against them the Navy found that airplane rockets and armor-piercing naval shells, fired at a high angle, were the most destructive.

From the Betio airstrip, as well as from newly built fields on Makin and a third atoll, Abemama, scouting and bombing missions to the Marshall Islands began as soon as the battle was over. Under Rear Admiral Marc A. Mitscher, newly designated as commander of the Fast Carrier Task Forces, carrier strikes at Japanese ships and planes in the region virtually wiped out the possibility of interference with the American invasion. On February 1, 1944, less than three months after Tarawa, Admiral Nimitz' fleet, rearmed, reequipped and prepared with new tactics, attacked Kwajalein Atoll in the central Marshalls. At the northern tip of the atoll the newly formed and untested 4th Marine Division took the causeway-connected islands of Roi and Namur, the main Japanese air base in the Marshalls. At the atoll's southern tip, the Army's 7th Division—all its troops landing from amtracs—took Kwajalein Island, site of an almost completed bomber strip. Some 300 miles to the southeast of Kwajalein Atoll, undefended Majuro Atoll was occupied in a few hours; its lagoon, 26 miles long and six miles wide, quickly became an advance base for Mitscher's fast carriers.

On February 4 the campaign in the central Marshalls was over. It had taken a few days longer than Tarawa, but at a lower cost in lives—334 Americans died compared to 1,056 at Tarawa. Many steps had been taken to reduce the risks. The firepower delivered before the invasion was more effective. The amtracs were sheathed in extra armor, and there were enough of them to prevent the need for assault troops to be transferred at the reef line. Newly designated headquarters ships, employing improved radio communications and unburdened by fire-support duties, monitored the action. On other vessels, unit commanders were posted to guard against failures to coordinate.

With the relative ease of the Kwajalein campaign, Nimitz decided not to have the fleet return to Hawaii to regroup. Instead he sent it on to invade Eniwetok Atoll, 380 miles from Kwajalein in the western Marshalls. Charts captured at Kwajalein had provided valuable information about Eniwetok's defenses and about water depths in its lagoon. To cover the landings, scheduled for February 17, nine of Mitscher's fast carriers hit at Truk, the powerful Japanese air and naval base 770 miles to the west of Eniwetok in the Caroline Islands. In two days and one night of raids, Mitscher's planes destroyed some 200 Japanese planes on the ground and sank 41 ships; the total tonnage sunk—more than 200,000 tons—was to remain a record for a single action throughout the War. Truk, which the Japanese had been secretly building up for years, was such a vital linchpin in their entire Pacific strategy that after the raids were over Admiral Koga ordered his remaining planes from Rabaul to

protect it, thereby abandoning the Japanese forces in and around New Guinea to the mercy of MacArthur's air arm.

Despite the removal of the threat from Truk, the Eniwetok operation might have turned into a disaster had it not been for the chance discovery of certain Japanese documents. Engebi Island, the Americans' first target in the atoll, fell within a few hours; softened up by prior bombardment, the small garrison there was too dazed to put up much resistance. On Engebi the Americans found papers that revealed the existence of sizable garrisons of tough, veteran troops on two other islands of the atoll slated for invasion—Eniwetok and Parry. Since the ships passing these islands on their way to Engebi had noticed no sign of life on them, Marine Brigadier General Thomas E. Watson had assumed that there were few Japanese there; he planned to send in only small forces to capture the two islands simultaneously. In fact the garrisons there had been ordered to lie low when the American fleet came by. As a result of the discovery of the documents Watson changed his plan, and Eniwetok and Parry were taken one at a time.

On Eniwetok Island some 800 Japanese were in underground bunkers with connecting tunnels and trenches, or in holes concealed by palm fronds; others were hidden in the underbrush that covered much of the island. The attackers—soldiers of the 106th Infantry, 27th Division, and Marines of the 22nd Regiment—had to scrutinize every yard of their advance. At one point an Army squad tossed grenades down a hole, then heard voices singing a Christian hymn: out came a local village chief and six companions, none hurt. After cigarettes and expressions of good will had been exchanged, the battle with the Japanese resumed. Eniwetok Island fell in two and a half days and yielded still another important document, showing the defensive plans for Parry Island, just across the channel. Three days of bombardment and one day of sharp ground fighting won Parry and completed the conquest of Eniwetok Atoll.

Within a few weeks U.S. Navy parties occupied about 30 other small Marshall atolls and islands, bypassing four atolls still in Japanese hands but isolated and useless. In the entire Marshalls campaign, 594 Americans were killed, about half the losses sustained on Betio alone. The lessons of Tarawa had been well learned—but the fight for the central Pacific was far from over.

THE TARAWA KILLING GROUND

Dynamite charges blast a Japanese blockhouse as U.S. Marines, clad in camouflage suits, prepare to advance across Tarawa's battle-scarred Betio Island.

AN IMPREGNABLE ISLAND FORTRESS

A concrete bunker (top) and two powerful 8-inch guns, which the Japanese bought from the British before the War, attest to Betio's strength.

Before the U.S. Marines landed on Betio Island in the Tarawa Atoll, intelligence experts studying an aerial photograph had spotted a row of latrines along the shoreline of the tiny island. By counting up privies and calculating how many of the enemy would probably be assigned to each, they estimated Betio's defenders to number about 4,800. The estimate proved to be almost on the nose—the actual figure was 4,836—but Japanese manpower figures gave no clue to the toughness of the island's fortifications.

The Japanese had concluded that the American drive across the central Pacific would concentrate on islands with airfields, and they had left nothing to chance in preparing their defenses for Betio, with its prized 4,000-foot airstrip. Offshore, a double curtain of barbed wire barred the way to the beaches. Mines and reinforced concrete pillars were planted underwater to deter landing craft. The shore bristled with pillboxes and emplacements, housing weapons that ranged from 13mm to 8-inch guns. On the lagoon side of the island, not more than 20 feet from the water at low tide, a four-foot sea wall of heavy coconut logs rose from the beach. Next came more pillboxes, blockhouses, and riflemen hidden in pits and trenches.

The Japanese had had 15 months to work on Betio's defenses, and they had gone to extraordinary lengths to make their positions invulnerable. Blockhouses and pillboxes were dug into the ground, encased in concrete, reinforced with steel rods and green, splinter-proof coconut logs and then covered with up to 10 feet of crushed coral or sand. The interiors of many of these blockhouses were divided by partitions of more green coconut logs, which helped shield the defenders from any exploding shells or hand grenades that might be tossed through the firing slits.

The Marines in turn were testing a new amphibious doctrine: a fortified island, no matter how heavily defended, could be taken by an all-out frontal assault. After 76 hours of the Pacific war's most concentrated violence, the Marines had an answer: a fortified island could be taken, but only if the assaulter was willing to pay a staggering price.

Betio Island—less than half a square mile in area—lies ravaged after the battle. Underwater bomb craters became pitfalls for the Marines wading ashore.

Following other landing craft, a Higgins boat jammed with troops splashes toward the smoke-obscured island. To storm its defenses, the Marines had to commit more than 12,000 men.

The first wave of amphibious tractors heads toward shore. Dubbed "little boats with wheels" by the Japanese, the amtracs ferried Marines from the Higgins boats to the beach.

Their boat having been sunk, three Marines slowly work their way along the edge of Betio's pier. The Japanese destroyed or damaged 72 of the 125 amtracs used in the invasion.

CHURNING TOWARD A RUDE RECEPTION

After U.S. Navy warships pounded Betio for two and a half hours and carrier-based planes dropped 400 tons of bombs on it, the men of the 2nd Marine Division wondered how the enemy could survive such a bombardment—indeed, some joked that all they would have to do upon landing would be to use their entrenching tools to bury the dead.

But the reality was otherwise. The Navy's firepower had had little effect inside the island's network of fortifications. Japanese artillery opened up on the Marines while the landing craft were still moving toward shore. So accurately presighted were the weapons that some shells exploded on the ramps of the craft even as these were being lowered. And this was only a taste of the fury to come.

Beside an amtrac that has run ashore, Marines crouching behind Betio's sea wall return enemy fire.

Protected by sandbags, a Marine hurls a grenade as an exhausted buddy (right) takes a breather.

A CRUSHING REJOINDER FROM THE MARINES

Though the Marines used everything they had on the Japanese pillboxes and blockhouses, they soon realized that the only way to knock out the enemy's fortifications on the island was to kill all of the men inside. But how to get at them? Flamethrowers and demolition teams were called into action.

Reporting on how these specialists did their work, TIME-LIFE correspondent Robert Sherrod wrote: "A Marine jumped over the sea wall and began throwing blocks of fused TNT into a coconut log pillbox about 15 feet back of the sea wall. . . . Two more Marines scaled the sea wall, one of them carrying a twin-cylindered tank strapped to his shoulders, the other holding the nozzle of the flamethrower. As another charge of TNT boomed inside the pillbox . . . a khaki-clad figure ran out the side entrance. The flamethrower, waiting for him, caught him in its withering stream of intense fire. . . ."

Despite the success of this "corkscrew and blowtorch" method, as it was called, the Marine advance was agonizingly slow. There were easily 500 pillboxes crammed onto the little island, and enemy fire was so heavy at times that it took up to seven hours just to crawl 100 yards.

As the battle nears its climax, Marines storm a well-camouflaged blockhouse and drop grenades and dynamite charges through air vents to rout the defenders.

Piled on stretchers loaded on a rubber boat, wounded Marines are towed through the water by their buddies to Higgins boats—a distance of more than 500

Braving a hailstorm of bullets, two Navy corpsmen help a wounded Marine back to an aid station.

THE HIGH COST OF VICTORY

The U.S. victors at Tarawa paid a terrible price. Of the 12,000 attackers, 1,056 died and 2,292 were wounded. Casualties were so heavy that Navy medics retrieved and treated them on an assembly-line basis. One doctor, operating by flashlight in a captured pillbox, patched up 125 Marines in the space of 36 hours.

Once the wounded Americans had been cared for, they were evacuated. But getting them off the island was a major problem. Marines had to pile the patients aboard rubber boats, wade through water under fire, and then transfer the men to waiting Higgins boats.

Some of the Japanese wounded, seeking to avoid the disgrace of being taken alive, pleaded with their comrades to kill them. Many others shot or stabbed themselves or blew themselves up. When at least one soldier tried slashing his wrists with a sea shell, but the edge was too dull. When the fighting was finally over, he and 16 other prisoners were the only Japanese still alive on Betio.

128

In the wake of battle, Admiral Chester W. Nimitz (center, carrying jacket), Commander in Chief, Pacific Ocean Areas, inspects destroyed Japanese fortifications. Leading the tour of the battlefield is Major General Julian C. Smith (right), commander of the 2nd Marine Division.

The wreckage of the bitter fighting is strewn over the landscape as Marines (left) gingerly advance toward a massive blockhouse, which was destroyed by medium tanks firing high-explosive shells into its narrow gun ports. Dead Japanese soldiers lie sprawled everywhere. The sheet metal scattered in the foreground was used to buttress the enemy pillboxes.

5

General MacArthur's mood at the start of 1944 was less than happy. Over the past 16 months, Australian and American troops of his southwest Pacific command had driven the Japanese out of Papua and much of Northeast New Guinea and regained a firm Allied foothold on neighboring New Britain. But in all they had advanced only about 280 miles closer to MacArthur's cherished goal. By the end of 1943, he was later to recall, "I was still about 1,600 miles from the Philippines and 2,100 miles from Manila."

The general made no bones about his dissatisfaction, and unlike other commanders he did not feel he had to limit himself to military channels. An added outlet of expression was available to him in exchanges of letters with his fervent admirers back home. Many of them had begun to think of him as the Republican candidate for the White House in 1944, the one charismatic figure who could deny President Roosevelt an unheard-of fourth term. Though MacArthur was careful to skirt that subject in response to delicate queries, he sometimes seized the moment to dwell on what he regarded as his plight in the southwest Pacific—and on what he believed was to blame for it.

"Probably no commander in American history has been so poorly supported," he wrote one influential magazine publisher in October of 1943. "At times it has looked as though it was intended that I should be defeated. . . . My isolation, indeed, is complete. This area is not only the forgotten one but is the one of lost opportunities. Time and again, had I had the support, the opportunity was present for a decisive stroke. I do not know who is responsible but it is a story of national shame."

The statistics refuted MacArthur's sweeping indictment. In the first two years, Washington had allotted more troops and combat ships to the war with Japan than to the war with Germany, and almost as many planes. The real cause of the general's annoyance was a trend he foresaw in the making. With the invasion of Europe now in the planning stage, an increasing percentage of the United States' men and matériel was being earmarked for the European and Mediterranean theaters. Even worse, from MacArthur's standpoint, was the fact that of the most recent allocations for the Pacific theater, a smaller share was going to support his advance toward the Philippines from the southwest Pacific than to Admiral Nimitz' advance across the central Pacific.

MACARTHUR'S ROAD BACK

In linking the Nimitz and MacArthur operations as a "dual drive," planners in Washington had inadvertently touched off a competitive spirit that made the normal interservice rivalries seem pale. Part of the problem lay in the sharply divergent ways in which people reacted to MacArthur's lordly personality.

With few exceptions, his staff thought he could do no wrong. They treated him with a deference that bordered on idolatry, and they shared his belief that his projected return to the Philippines was in the nature of a sacred mission. Among Navy officers, on the other hand, MacArthur was viewed as a pompous windbag and an incurable ham, always playing to the galleries. They hooted when, in late 1943, he took note of press rumors that his part in the War was to be reduced by issuing a statement asserting that "however subordinate may be my role, I hope to play it manfully." They felt certain that MacArthur's massive ego would never allow him to yield his claim to supreme charge of the war against Japan—or to give the Navy proper credit for its vital contribution to that effort.

Dislike of the general reached to the top of the Navy's hierarchy. The hard-bitten Chief of Naval Operations, Admiral Ernest J. King, voiced such hostility to MacArthur in the privacy of Joint Chiefs of Staff meetings in Washington that he eventually drove presiding General George C. Marshall to an uncharacteristic act. The usually mild-mannered Marshall smashed his fist down on the table, declared "I will not have any meetings carried on with this hatred," and cut King off in mid-tirade.

Apart from their personal rancor, Navy officers found fault with the thinking at MacArthur's headquarters. They felt that his operations planners were locked into an "Army mentality" unsuited to dealing with an arena of war that was mostly an expanse of ocean. Captain Raymond D. Tarbuck, who served as Naval liaison with MacArthur, later remembered his surprise at "how little the Army officers at GHQ knew about water." The Navy concept of a body of water as a pathway was foreign to them; they treated "even the smallest stream as an obstacle." Even their maps, Tarbuck claimed, stopped at the water's edge. Coral reefs and other hazards that seagoing men had to take into account did not figure in their calculations. Predictably, the Navy took a dim view of MacArthur's repeated attempts to enlist some of its prized carriers to support his operations.

MacArthur's opinion of Navy thinking was no more flattering. Frontal assaults on heavily defended islands, the strategy chosen by the Navy's planners for the drive across the central Pacific, struck him as an utter waste of men and time. The American losses at Tarawa provoked a blistering MacArthur memorandum to Washington. Directed over the heads of the Joint Chiefs of Staff to Secretary of War Henry L. Stimson, the MacArthur memo denounced the Navy's frontal attacks as "tragic and unnecessary massacres of American lives," and clearly implied that the cause of the tragedy was "the Navy's pride of position and ignorance."

MacArthur's own idea of "how to end the war as soon and as cheaply as possible," as he put it, was summed up at a meeting of his staff concerning his projected operations against certain Japanese bases. As he later reconstructed the conversation, it opened with one of his officers saying: "General, I know your peculiar genius for slaughtering large masses of the enemy at little cost in the lives of your own men, but I just don't see how we can take these strong points with our limited forces." In reply, MacArthur recalled, "I thoroughly agreed with him, but said I did not intend to take them—I intended to envelop them, incapacitate them, apply the 'hit 'em where they ain't, let 'em die on the vine' philosophy."

There was, in fact, no difference between this strategy and the strategy of leapfrogging and starving out the enemy that Admiral Halsey had introduced and successfully employed in his drive up the Solomons in the closing months of 1943. Halsey was one of the rare Navy men for whom MacArthur had any kind words—he called him "a battle commander of the highest order"—but the general did not feel that any accolades were due the Navy for the leapfrogging idea. Though it was hailed as "something new in warfare," MacArthur noted, it was really an old notion—"the classic strategy of envelopment."

The term he preferred for bypassing enemy strongholds was throwing "loops of envelopment" around them. But whatever the semantic shadings, the strategy was to work as successfully for MacArthur as it had worked for Halsey. During the first eight months of 1944, his forces were to streak 1,100 miles along the north coast of New Guinea, then cross the sea to come within 300 miles of the Philippines.

In the War's early months the shock of the fall of the Philippines, the Dutch East Indies, Burma and Malaya had temporarily diverted Allied attention from Japan's quieter moves into the southwest Pacific. Besides taking Rabaul on New Britain, much of the Solomons chain and a stretch of the east coast of New Guinea, the Japanese had occupied a number of sites along New Guinea's north coast, as well as a number of islands in and around the Bismarck Archipelago. Seizing these places from Australian or British or Dutch control had proved easy enough, and promised the Japanese two vital advantages. In addition to bringing them closer to cutting Australia's lifeline, it gave them a valuable edge in case the fortunes of war shifted—a far-flung perimeter of outposts to guard against Allied attack on the Philippines and the Indies from the Pacific side.

By the start of 1944, the perimeter had sizable dents in it. The Solomons were in American hands. Admiral Halsey's success there, along with MacArthur's landings on New Britain, had all but isolated Rabaul. With the Japanese defeats in Papua and on the Huon Peninsula, the east coast of New Guinea was back under Allied control. All these developments enhanced the prospects of MacArthur's drive on the Philippines. But ultimately its success hinged on his

Men of Australia's 18th Brigade inch toward the top of Shaggy Ridge, in New Guinea's Finisterre Mountains. In spite of the danger of being shot by the Japanese who held the crest, one Australian quickly concluded that "the climbing is worse than the firing."

disposing of key Japanese outposts along his projected route. The route lay westward along New Guinea's north coast, then northward through a number of islands between New Guinea and the southern end of the Philippines. In line with MacArthur's philosophy of waging war at the least possible cost in lives, he intended to bypass as many of the enemy's bases as he could, seizing every opportunity that arose as his operations proceeded.

The primary problem confronting the general was New Guinea's rugged north coast. Not only was it now the strongest sector of Japan's southwest Pacific perimeter—as a result of the dwindling power of Rabaul—but it was also the longest. The coastline extended some 1,200 miles, and the Japanese had sited their bases so as to bracket every segment of it. Their major installations ranged from Madang, 200 miles from the island's northeast tip, to Manokwari on the northwest tip.

About midway between Madang and Manokwari lay Hollandia, which before the War had served as the capital of Dutch-owned western New Guinea. The Japanese had turned the port into their chief transshipment center for troops and supplies coming into the southwest Pacific; to protect the facilities, they had built three airfields and fortified the hills around the city. Hollandia was MacArthur's main objective on the New Guinea coast, the point beyond which he expected to veer northward across the sea toward the Philippines.

On the way west to Hollandia, however, he would have to deal with Madang and three other large Japanese bases —at Hansa Bay, Wewak and Aitape. All except Aitape, the nearest to Hollandia, lay within range of MacArthur's Fifth Air Force, and by the end of 1943 had been heavily pounded in softening-up sorties directed by his feisty air chief, General Kenney. But these bases still remained to be finished off as obstacles to MacArthur's advance.

Some other unfinished business also needed attending to. Though the Allies had retaken Lae and Finschhafen on the Huon Peninsula, thousands of soldiers of the Japanese Eighteenth Army had eluded the Allied net by withdrawing westward. Their initial goal was Sio, the nearest Japanese-held port on New Guinea's north coast; their eventual destination was Madang, 140 miles west of Sio and now Eighteenth Army headquarters. Some of the troops were making their way along the coast, others along a roughly parallel course through the mountains just inland. The 9th and 7th Australian divisions, respectively, were in pursuit of the two retreating Japanese forces; unless they were prevented from reaching Madang and joining the 10,000 fresh troops stationed there, MacArthur's subsequent assault on that stronghold would prove much more hazardous.

By late December, 1943, neither the pursued nor the pursuers had achieved their objective. Both were simultaneously involved in fighting a third foe—the New Guinea terrain itself. "Few areas in the world," MacArthur later wrote, "present so formidable an obstacle to military operation." The coastline was one long tangle of mangrove and nipa swamps, studded here and there with sheer cliffs that had to be scaled by rope. Inland, the 13,000-foot Finisterre Mountains evoked memories of the nightmarish struggle across the Owen Stanleys in Papua in 1942. Dizzying heights alternated with plunging gorges, and jungle growth covered all.

An unidentified Australian soldier later gave historians of his country's war effort an account of what it was like to fight in the Finisterres. At stake was control of a 5,000-foot razor-backed peak called Shaggy Ridge; whoever held it would also dominate a nearby pass that led to a road to the coast—an escape hatch for the retreating Japanese. Though many of them were by now in the pass, a blocking force had been left in the Shaggy Ridge area to deny the peak to the pursuing Australians. At its crest there was only a narrow track, wide enough for just one man, with a drop of thousands of feet on either side; athwart the track the Japanese had managed to set up their machine guns and barbed wire.

Successive companies of Australians scaled the cliffs in an attempt to gain the crest. As the anonymous soldier recalled it: "You've got to climb; climb where there are no holds. You're flat, you're upright, you're slipping. Your chest burns with the pain of effort and you fight for gulps of air. You don't care about the bullets much. Up, up, hand over hand. The crest is immediately above you now, and you can see the holes from which comes the Japanese cross fire. You reach the top and, as you tense yourself for the levering over the rim, a burst of fire chews the earth within inches of your hand."

Many of this man's comrades never made it to the top.

Wounded or fatally hit during the ascent, they would roll over and over, their bodies finally coming to a stop at some point so far below that they could no longer be seen by the men watching from above. Those who did reach the crest found the going agonizingly slow. As they edged along the narrow track, hurling grenades to force the Japanese from one strong point to another, their progress was never measurable except in yards. Sometimes the combat was hand to hand; often the "front" consisted of one Australian lying prone on the track, sniping at one Japanese lying prone 20 yards away.

The battle for Shaggy Ridge, which had begun in mid-October of 1943, was still unresolved when on the day after New Year's, 1944, a stunning blow was dealt the Japanese who were retreating along the coast. Many of them had already reached Sio, and were making preparations to move on to what they hoped would be haven at Madang. But on the dark, drizzly morning of January 2, American troops of the 32nd Division's 126th Regimental Combat Team came ashore at Saidor, about 70 miles west of Sio and halfway to Madang. The Japanese at Sio now faced the prospect of being squeezed between the pursuing Australians and the waiting Americans.

Saidor, where the Japanese had a harbor and an airstrip but comparatively few defenders, proved easy to take. The Americans' amphibious landing was covered by guns of the Seventh Fleet, the modest force—widely dubbed "MacArthur's navy"—that America's admirals had consented to turn over to his command after his arrival in Australia in 1942. By nightfall on the 2nd of January, some 8,000 Americans were ashore at Saidor, and to American observers the "loop of envelopment" MacArthur had thrown around Sio looked escape-proof.

Their optimism was premature. The pincers movement that was to finish off the Japanese at Sio failed to materialize. Though the Australians kept closing in from the east, there was no corresponding thrust by the Americans from the west. The Sixth Army's commander, General Krueger, was asked to account for the inaction—or, as he preferred to put it, the delay in "the transition to the offensive." Krueger placed the blame in part on "magnified" estimates by local inhabitants of the threat of Japanese counterattacks, and in part on the weather. "Incessant torrential rains which rendered all tracks and rivers impassable," he reported to MacArthur, "caused great difficulty in the movement of troops and supplies to outlying sectors."

The Australians at Shaggy Ridge were as baffled as their comrades slogging along the coast. With the landing at Saidor, they had expected that some American contingents would be sent inland to help in the fighting in the Finisterres. In the attendant confusion, General Adachi, the Japanese Eighteenth Army's commander, moved to take advantage of the situation.

The term "warrior's warrior," bestowed on many a gen-

Although he was defeated by General MacArthur's forces in New Guinea in 1944, Lieut. General Hatazo Adachi held out in the jungle with the remnants of his army until September 1945, when he learned from a radio broadcast that the War was over. Adachi later committed hara-kiri.

eral by a reverential staff, was in Adachi's case merited. Grandson of a famed samurai (a member of Japan's hereditary warrior class), he had started his military career in the elite Imperial Guard Division, serving for a time as drill instructor to Emperor Hirohito when he was Crown Prince. At the War's outbreak, Adachi was chief of staff of Japan's North China Area Army; when Allied pressure against Rabaul began to mount, he was sent to the southwest Pacific to become head of the newly activated Eighteenth Army.

Adachi was not the brainiest of Japanese generals; nor was he gifted at rhetoric. What his men most admired about him was his fighting spirit. So bent was he on helping achieve Japan's ultimate victory that he never wrote letters home. "I have to give all my wakeful moments to war," he said. His deep sense of responsibility also showed in his concern for his troops; he often had to be talked out of visiting frontline units under fire.

When the Americans took Saidor, flanking the Japanese at Sio, Adachi was at his headquarters in Madang. He promptly decided to go to Sio to supervise, personally, a plan for getting his troops out of the trap. En route, the submarine on which he was traveling was attacked by one of the many American PT boats now patrolling the coast. The sub managed to reach Sio and deposit its star passenger, unruffled; Adachi had faced death before. He had been barely saved from drowning during the Battle of the Bismarck Sea in March of 1943, when Allied planes sank the ship on which he was sailing to New Guinea.

At Sio, Adachi had all available barges packed with troops and sent forth to try to reach Madang by sea. Those men the barges could not accommodate were ordered to move inland, carefully detouring around the Allied-held section of the coast, and make for Madang on foot. Adachi also sent orders to the troops at Shaggy Ridge: they were to give up trying to block the Australians, abandon their defenses and, like their comrades, head for Madang overland.

Adachi had to wait three nights before a second submarine, scheduled to take him off Sio, could succeed in its mission. On the first night the boat carrying him to the sub had already started from shore when PT boats appeared; the sub had to dive. The next night the PT boats were again hovering; the sub moved out to sea. On the third night, with the PT boats back again, the submarine's machine gunners loosed a barrage. The Americans returned the fire, but then hove to more than half a mile away. The sub captain hastily took aboard Adachi, staff officers and 25 bags of equipment and records, and took his craft down. Next morning—January 11, nine days after the American landing at Saidor—Adachi was back in Madang.

The troops he had dispatched overland—some 14,000 men of the 20th and 51st divisions—had rougher going. Those from Sio had to move along the coast for a distance before turning inland, and they were bombed and strafed by American planes. In the interior the Japanese had to hack a route through rain forests high enough up in the mountains to avoid Australian patrols. But their worst enemies were the jungle and the threat of starvation.

Though they had set out with all the food they could carry, it was not enough. Other supplies also dwindled. Sergeant Eiji Iizuka of the 51st Division, who survived the trek, recalled: "We passed many dead and dying soldiers. As we had no fresh uniforms or shoes we would strip the dead and take theirs. Sometimes we took clothes and boots from men who were still alive but who could no longer move, and we said to them, 'You don't need such fine shoes any more.' They would watch us with dull eyes and let us do anything. We even took water canteens from them. That was the worst, to hear a soldier say 'Don't take my canteen away from me, I'm still alive.' "

More than 4,000 of the men were to die en route before the last haggard troops of the 20th and 51st division plodded into Madang on March 1. But any comfort Adachi could take from their reappearance was short-lived. It soon became apparent that even Madang could not be held: MacArthur's forces had landed again, 240 miles due north of Madang across the Bismarck Sea.

MacArthur's new coup, the seizure of the Admiralty Islands, had initially been envisioned as a move to finish sealing off Rabaul, to make sure its isolation was total. The islands stood like sentinels at the northern entrance to the Bismarck Sea, affording a key vantage point from which to thwart the movement of Japanese troops and supplies to Rabaul, and from Rabaul to New Guinea.

But with the start of MacArthur's drive along New Guinea's north coast, the Admiralties offered an immense added advantage—as a base from which American air and sea power could more easily be brought to bear on Madang and other Japanese strongholds farther up the coast. Enclosed within the clustered Admiralties was one of the finest protected anchorages anywhere in the Pacific: Seeadler Harbor, 20 miles long and six miles wide, big enough to hold a huge fleet. The largest island in the group, 50-mile-long Manus, had a Japanese-built airfield and ample space for supply installations. Nearby, the smaller island of Los Negros had a second airfield and flat terrain that would permit the building of more airstrips.

MacArthur's move on the Admiralties, though scheduled for April of 1944, was launched at the end of February. The immediate reason for pushing up the date was a report that Kenney's reconnoitering pilots had seen no signs of enemy activity on the islands. But MacArthur was impatient in any event, determined not to be outstripped by the swiftly moving Admiral Nimitz in the central Pacific. Since early February, Nimitz' forces had swept through the Marshall Islands, securing Kwajalein Atoll by the 7th of February and

Eniwetok Atoll, 330 miles to the northwest, by the 22nd.

On the evening of the 24th, MacArthur decided to strike at the Admiralties on the 29th. With just four days to prepare, the operation was mounted so hastily that the cruiser *Phoenix*, flagship of the task force, had only two hours' notice before departing from Brisbane. When the order came, many of the crew were ashore on liberty; shore patrols frantically made the rounds of Brisbane's bars, with bullhorns blaring a coded recall signal. Some of the sailors had to commandeer harbor craft to catch up with the ship.

En route, another surprise awaited them. On the 27th, when the *Phoenix* put in at Milne Bay in southeast New Guinea to link up with other ships of the naval support force, MacArthur himself came aboard, flown in from Brisbane. As the *Phoenix* continued northward, officers and crew found him far from the aloof autocrat he was said to be. He amiably obliged requests for autographs, asked for the recipe of a corn pudding he was served, and above all impressed the men with the numerous searching questions he asked about the workings of the ship. So far as was

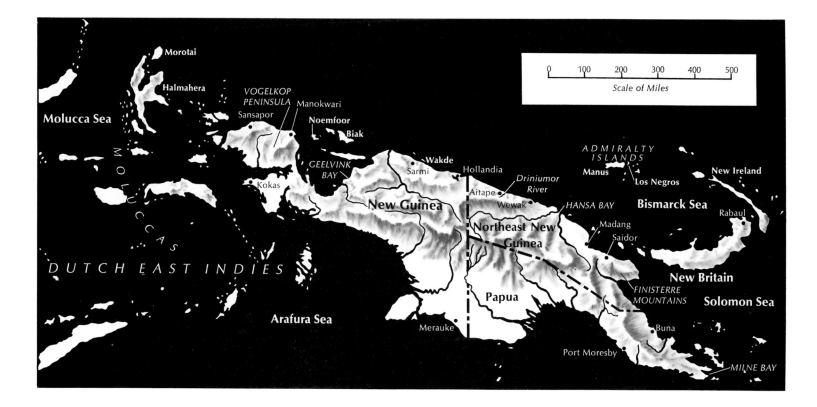

Target of General MacArthur's drive toward the Philippines was a chain of Japanese bases and strongholds on New Guinea's north coast and on its offshore islands. In the first nine months of 1944, Allied forces swept from Saidor to Sansapor on the north coast and took the islands of Manus, Los Negros, Wakde, Biak and Noemfoor. By the 15th of September, 1944, MacArthur, commanding a huge invasion force, had landed on Morotai in the Moluccas and was poised for his return to the Philippines.

known, he had traveled on a naval combat vessel only once before, aboard the PT boat that had brought him out of the Philippines early in 1942.

His presence on the *Phoenix,* however, was intended to serve a purpose more critical than improving his image with the Navy. In spite of the pilots' reports that there were no signs of Japanese activity in the Admiralties, MacArthur had prudently planned the strike as a "reconnaissance in force"—meaning that his troops could be pulled out if the opposition proved heavy or reinforced if it proved light. A quick judgment would have to be made as to whether to stay or withdraw, and MacArthur would make the decision on the spot.

On the afternoon of the 28th, the *Phoenix* was nearing the Admiralties when a disquieting message arrived for the general. Before sunrise on the previous day, a Navy Catalina had set down six scouts some 500 yards off Los Negros, where the American troops were slated to land. The men had paddled ashore in a rubber boat, explored part of the island and brought back a succinct report—the place was "lousy with Japs."

MacArthur had 1,000 troops of the 1st Cavalry Division (dismounted) on the way to Los Negros, with 1,500 more alerted to move in as an auxiliary force. How many Japanese they would be up against could only be conjectured. MacArthur decided to go ahead with the strike.

Except for some firing by Japanese coastal batteries— quickly silenced by the guns of the *Phoenix* and other support ships—the men of the 1st Cavalry met almost no opposition when they landed on the morning of February 29. Colonel Yoshio Ezaki, the Japanese commander in the islands, had expected the invaders to come in through Seeadler Harbor, and had concentrated the bulk of his 4,300 troops accordingly. MacArthur had chosen to avoid the mined waters of Seeadler and instead to send his force ashore at Hyane Harbor, a small bay on the eastern coast of Los Negros, accessible directly from the sea. By the time Ezaki concluded that this was more than a feint to cover a major thrust through Seeadler, it was too late. By 1 p.m., some five hours after the first wave of Americans landed, they had secured a beachhead and the nearby airfield.

That afternoon MacArthur himself came ashore to get a feel of the situation. As he toured the beachhead, he paused for a look at the bodies of two Japanese soldiers, killed less than half an hour before. "That's the way I like to see them," he commented, and moved on. An officer who was showing him around tried to steer him away from a patch of jungle near the beachhead, explaining: "We killed a Jap sniper in there just a few minutes ago." MacArthur replied: "Fine. That's the best thing to do with them," and kept walking in that direction. Clearly he was determined to lay to rest, once and for all, the derisive nickname of "Dugout Doug" bestowed on him by his troops on Bataan in 1942.

After a two-hour visit, a high-spirited MacArthur was ready to render his decision. The "reconnaissance in force" was to stay in the Admiralties and finish off the enemy. He told the troops' commander, Brigadier General William C. Chase: "You have your teeth in him now. Don't let go."

That night, with MacArthur heading back to New Guinea on the *Phoenix,* along with all but two destroyers of the naval support force, the Japanese launched a number of piecemeal attacks on the beachhead. Pulled into a tight perimeter and backed by the guns of the destroyers that had remained offshore, the Americans held.

Two days later their reinforcements arrived—just in time. The following night the Japanese returned in strength, wave after wave charging straight at the Americans' guns; inexplicably, one Japanese unit surged forward singing "Deep in the Heart of Texas." The men of the 1st Cavalry, who had never before been in combat, were also introduced to a Japanese ploy that American troops in the Solomons had learned to their chagrin. Tapping into one of the Americans' telephone lines, the Japanese had an English-speaking officer order an American platoon leader to retreat, even calling him by name. Unsuspecting, the platoon leader complied. The Americans' defenses were breached in several places as a bloody night wore on, but their mortars and artillery prevented the Japanese from following through. At dawn, with Japanese corpses littering the airfield, the attack petered out.

More American troops and more weeks of sharp fighting were required to nail down victory in the Admiralties, at a total cost of 326 American and 3,280 Japanese lives. But the outcome was never seriously in doubt after the first week's fighting. Amid the widespread Allied acclaim that followed,

MacArthur's stock as a master strategist skyrocketed. Even his archcritic in the Navy, Admiral King, pronounced the operation "a brilliant maneuver."

A more oblique tribute came from General Adachi, MacArthur's adversary in New Guinea. At Madang, Adachi ordered his gaunt soldiers to pack up and move on; with the Americans in the Admiralties, Madang could no longer be effectively supplied. Adachi decided to transfer his headquarters and his garrison troops, the 41st Division, 150 miles farther up the north coast to the next Japanese base at Hansa Bay. For his trail-weary 20th and 51st divisions, he decreed another long jungle trek: they were to head for Wewak, the next major Japanese base beyond Hansa Bay, 70 miles still farther west. From there, the 20th Division was eventually to move on another 90 miles west to the next big base at Aitape.

Hansa Bay and Wewak, Adachi thought, were bound to be MacArthur's next targets, and the Japanese commander's moves were intended to throw all his available strength into the defense of those areas. But MacArthur, in the glow of his success in the Admiralties, now had a more ambitious plan. He proposed to bypass Hansa Bay and Wewak and make a 500-mile leap directly to his principal target on the coast, Hollandia. This speed-up in schedule would bring him appreciably closer—in terms of time as well as distance—to realizing his dearest aim, the return to the Philippines. Hollandia's capture would make it possible to seize points farther west along the coast and key islands off the coast. These, in turn, would serve as steppingstones to the southernmost island of the Philippines, Mindanao.

On March 12, the Joint Chiefs of Staff approved MacArthur's plan, including his proposal to invade Mindanao. But MacArthur had hoped for something more from Washington: a mandate to proceed north from Mindanao to the main Philippine island of Luzon—and thus to put the final seal on the islands' recapture. The Joint Chiefs, however, were far from ready to commit themselves to this course. Their directive made plain that Formosa, not the Philippines, was their favored route to final victory over Japan, and that Luzon was to be taken only if necessary as a preliminary to the move on Formosa.

In the same directive, the Joint Chiefs ordered Admiral Nimitz to proceed with his drive across the central Pacific and to add three more island groups—the Marianas, Carolines and Palaus—to the victories already achieved in the Gilberts and Marshalls. But Nimitz, too, was left in suspense as to where he would go afterward—except that the Palaus were to be used to extend American control over the eastern approaches to both the Philippines and Formosa.

There was some good news for MacArthur in two of the orders to Nimitz. The Joint Chiefs instructed the admiral to lend the support of his powerful Pacific Fleet for MacArthur's invasion of Mindanao, and more immediately for the invasion of Hollandia. MacArthur, in turn, was to send heavy bombers from Hollandia to help soften up the Palaus in advance of Nimitz' landing there. For the first time since the beginning of the dual drive, rivalries would have to be set aside and efforts coordinated.

In late March, with the Hollandia operation just weeks away, Nimitz arrived in Brisbane to confer with MacArthur. They knew each other only slightly, and had not met since the War began. Their personalities were poles apart. Nimitz had none of MacArthur's flair for the dramatic or his profound sense of himself as a man of destiny. Self-effacing and low-keyed, the admiral tended to smooth over moments of tension with a folksy or sometimes bawdy joke told in a Texas drawl.

Staff officers who had expected a clash between the two commanders, an airing of past irritations, were in for a surprise. The mood in Brisbane was conciliatory. Nimitz came bearing thoughtfully selected gifts from Hawaii: rare orchids for MacArthur's wife, silk playsuits made of Hawaiian prints for their six-year-old son Arthur. MacArthur warmly embraced Nimitz when his plane set down and that night gave a dinner in his honor.

The next day, at two lengthy sessions, the details of the joint effort at Hollandia were threshed out. Behind the new show of harmony some of the old strains were evident. Nimitz proposed to provide 12 fast carriers of Vice Admiral Marc A. Mitscher's Task Force 58, along with fast battleships, cruisers and destroyers. But he frankly expressed fears for the carriers' safety; the Japanese were estimated to have 200 to 300 planes in the Hollandia area. General Kenney, who was present as MacArthur's expert on such matters, breezily predicted that the enemy's air strength would be "rubbed out" by his pilots days before the invasion. Nimitz, clearly skeptical, stood fast on his insistence that the big carriers would withdraw no later than noon on the second day after the landings. But he gave in on another point, agreeing to leave eight small escort carriers off the beachhead for as long as eight days, to help cover the unloading of supply vessels.

As it happened, less help was required from Nimitz' carriers than had been foreseen—except perhaps by the ever-confident Kenney. By April 22, D-day for Hollandia, he had made good on what most of the conferees in Brisbane had viewed as an idle boast. Raids by his bombers and fighters had effectively destroyed Japan's air power in the invasion area. Though Task Force 58 covered the landings, there was little need for it to linger. The Hollandia operation came off with remarkable ease.

The Japanese had figured that an attack on Hollandia might come eventually—but they had not expected the blow to fall so soon. They had taken only one precautionary measure, and one that was to prove futile. Toward the end of March, General Korechika Anami, whose sprawling domain as commander of the Second Area Army included western New Guinea, ordered General Adachi to move some of his troops to Hollandia to strengthen the garrison there. Adachi, still certain that MacArthur would strike first at Hansa Bay and Wewak, was reluctant to deplete the forces he had concentrated along that part of the coast. But Anami had to be obeyed; Adachi, cut off from his superiors at Rabaul, was now officially under Anami's command.

Nine days before the Americans were to go ashore at Hollandia, Adachi dispatched two of his regiments on an overland march from Wewak, 210 miles away. They would have to struggle through jungle and across swollen and sometimes crocodile-infested rivers, but there was no other way for them to travel. The Allies' control of the sea route was now virtually total. At best, the men could not reach Hollandia before early May. As it happened, they failed to get anywhere near the goal. The two regiments were still bogged down when it became apparent that the attempt to help their Hollandia comrades would be pointless.

Through radio intercepts and code breaking, the Americans were aware of Adachi's misgivings about reducing his

strength at Hansa Bay and Wewak. They did everything they could to reinforce his belief that these bases were to be MacArthur's next targets. Destroyers were sent in to bombard them, reconnaissance planes flew over on ostensible mapping missions and PT boats shot up the nearby coast. To suggest the presence of infiltrators, dummy parachutes were dropped in the area, and empty rubber boats of the kind used by scouting parties were brought in by submarine and liberally strewn on the waters close to shore. To cap matters, there were repeated visits by Kenney's raiders; planes of the Fifth Air Force bombed Hansa Bay and Wewak as often as they pounded their top-priority objectives in and around Hollandia.

The final ruse involved the invasion convoys. The quickest course they could have followed from their assembly points along New Guinea's east coast would have been to go through the Vitiaz Strait, then turn directly westward along the north coast to Hollandia. Instead, once through the strait, they moved north to the Admiralties. Thanks to MacArthur's coup of the previous month, the islands were able to serve as the rendezvous point for the entire invasion armada: transports, warships, supply vessels—217 ships in all—carrying some 50,000 combat troops and 30,000 support personnel, and representing the largest amphibious operation yet undertaken in the southwest Pacific.

From the Admiralties, the armada continued a deceptive course to confound any Japanese reconnaissance plane or submarine that might be lurking in the area. When the ships left the islands on April 21—D-day-minus-1—they headed northwest, seemingly widening the distance from Hollandia; then, in the middle of the night, they swung southwest and made straight for the target.

From first to last, the stratagem worked so well that on April 21 a Japanese intelligence summary put Hollandia at the bottom of a list of possible places where the Americans might land. One officer of the Japanese headquarters staff later recalled: "The morning we found out that the Allies were going to come to Hollandia, they were already in the harbor with their transports and battleships."

What was in the harbor, in fact, was only one of the American Sixth Army's three attack forces: the 41st Division, debarking not far from the town of Hollandia itself, on the shores of Humboldt Bay—the largest anchorage on New

IN THE REMOTE PACIFIC: A MEETING OF TWO WORLDS

Sneaking a peek at today's feature—Wake Island—a local resident sees his first film from outside a thatched theater on Guadalcanal.

Decked out in traditional feathers and shells, a New Guinea tribal chieftain accepts a light for his cigarette from an American newsman.

The war in the southwest Pacific brought together peoples of sharply differing cultures normally thousands of miles apart. Yet islanders and Allied troops were able to communicate with surprising ease. They did so by means of gestures and pidgin, an amalgam of English and tribal tongues that enabled the "nambawan kiap," or "number one officer," to give "straitpela tok," or "straight-fellow talk," to "olman," "all men"—i.e., the local people.

With the language barrier broken, Allied troops and islanders joined in "sing-sings," at which islanders performed their songs and dances—and the GIs theirs.

Exchanges of another kind occurred. The islanders prized cigarettes, soap, combs, decks of cards and medicines—especially iodine, which was not only colorful, but stung when dabbed on cuts.

A New Guinean takes a turn behind a turret gun from a downed plane.

Jitterbugging in front of a crowd of delighted tribesmen and Americans, two Marine privates entertain during a show on the island of New Britain.

Guinea's north coast. Simultaneously, a second force, the 24th Division, was landing 22 miles to the west at another useful big bay, Tanahmerah. The third force—the 41st Division's 163rd Regimental Combat Team—was landing at the Japanese base of Aitape, 120 miles east of Hollandia.

Taking Aitape had a double purpose: to secure two nearby airstrips as backstops to the three airfields at Hollandia and to block the way to Hollandia should General Adachi try a counterattack from the east. The 1,000-man garrison at Aitape was quickly overcome. Only about a fifth of the men were combat troops; the others were pilots—now without planes to fly—and ground crews and service personnel. The airstrips were seized within 24 hours; the entire operation cost 19 American and 525 Japanese lives. The rest of the Japanese, except for a score or so who surrendered, escaped eastward toward Wewak.

The far bigger Hollandia garrison—some 11,000 men, mostly base and support personnel—proved to be almost as little trouble. The Japanese command did not draw up a defense plan until after the invasion fleet appeared. In the heavy bombardment that preceded the landings, troops on the beaches, lacking specific orders from their superiors, simply took to the hills back of the shore. The first wave of Americans to land found boiling teapots and unfinished breakfast bowls of rice in beachside log dugouts, and huge quantities of abandoned supplies everywhere.

But the big prize the invaders sought was well inland, at a large crescent-shaped lake shielded from the sea by the Cyclops Mountains. On a plain along the shores of 15-mile-long Lake Sentani, the Japanese had constructed their three major airfields and a network of roads, supply dumps and barracks. Sentani was about equidistant from Humboldt and Tanahmerah bays. As planned, a pincers movement was quickly launched. By the evening of D-day the Americans from Tanahmerah had advanced six miles up the mountain trails toward their objective, passing pillboxes and other defenses that were now completely deserted. Nearer to Sentani, scattered resistance developed. To help secure control of the lakefront, amtracs were brought up and some of the troops were ferried to their objective.

Four days later, the airfields had been taken and steps had already been initiated to turn the Hollandia area into a gigantic base. The project was assigned to Lieut. General Robert Eichelberger, who had clinched the victory in Papua in 1942 and had directed the assault on Sentani. The sides of mountains would have to be sheared to widen trails into roads; bridges and culverts would have to be thrown across rivers, docks constructed and 135 miles of pipeline laid to feed gasoline to the airfields. Eichelberger was later to write: "Where once I had seen only a few native villages and an expanse of primeval forest, a city of 140,000 men took occupancy."

A total of 152 Americans and about 3,300 Japanese were lost in the Hollandia operation. Another 600 of the defenders were captured or surrendered. Some were rear-echelon Korean laborers, impressed into Japan's service and of dubious loyalty to its cause; still, the number was unprecedented. The rest of the garrison—some 7,000 men—fled into the jungles to the west. The Sixth Army's top commander, General Krueger, summed up the behavior of the foe as "unparalleled in the history of our campaign against the Japanese." As Krueger put it: "Not only did the majority flee without a show of resistance, but those who remained to fight failed to offer any type of resistance we have come to regard as characteristic of the Japanese."

The soldiers who fled headed for Sarmi, a Japanese base 145 miles farther west. Only about 500 of them were to make it; the rest were to succumb to wounds, starvation and sickness. But even as they began moving away from Hollandia, another Japanese force began moving toward it from the east. General Adachi had decided to launch a counterattack against Aitape.

On April 24, a communiqué by MacArthur announcing the Hollandia-Aitape triumph also summed up Adachi's plight. As a result of the "loop of envelopment" that had been thrown around the Japanese Eighteenth Army, it was now "completely isolated." The Americans were to its west and the Australians to its east, gradually mopping up its former strongholds. In the rolling prose characteristic of his communiqués, MacArthur declared that Adachi's garrisons "can be expected to strike desperately to free themselves, and time and combat will be required to accomplish their annihilation." Clearly confident of the outcome, MacArthur concluded on a note of deep personal satisfaction. The Eighteenth Army's situation, he asserted, "reverses Bataan."

Adachi, a realist, would not have quarreled with this assessment of his dilemma. All of his men were weary and malnourished, and many were suffering from tropical diseases. He had only two months of subsistence-level supplies on hand; Japanese submarines bearing food and small arms were finding it increasingly difficult to sneak through the Allied blockade of the coast.

But Adachi's troops, unlike the soldiers in flight from Hollandia, were still a reliable, disciplined force. An assault on Aitape might divert enough American forces to slow MacArthur's westward advance.

For the Japanese, with at least 100 miles of jungle to get through and supplies steadily diminishing, a knowledge of how to live off the land was more essential than ever. Recipes were issued for processing the sago palm, a native staple. ("Crush the trunk of the sago tree to make starch. Mix it with copra, stems of taro, or breadfruit. Serve it as dumplings or soup.") Units held classes on how to make herb medicines, to light fires without matches and weave straw sandals for emergency use.

The lack of shoes was so critical that detailed instructions for their care were distributed. To prevent the leather from decaying in the jungle climate, shoes were to be oiled, or coconut meat was to be used if there was no oil available. Rivers and muddy passages were to be crossed either in bare feet or in *geta*, wooden clogs.

Of Adachi's 55,000 men, he assigned 20,000 of the fittest to the assault on Aitape, 15,000 to logistic support and 20,000 to stay and protect Wewak, the last big Japanese holding east of Aitape. By the end of May, Adachi's advance units were at Aitape's easternmost outposts, some 30 miles from the base, and were clashing with American patrols.

But the main Japanese thrust had to be delayed for a variety of reasons: heavy rains, mud-choked trails, bridges that had been bombed out by Kenney's pilots, PT-boat attacks on Adachi's cargo barges and the attrition of his few remaining trucks. Everything needed for the assault was carried on men's backs, and their pace was further slowed by stops to forage for food.

Adachi was compelled to bide his time, but his determination to press the attack never wavered.

For MacArthur, the month of May was also problem-ridden. Shortly after the securing of Hollandia's airfields, it was discovered that the nature of the soil made them unsuitable for extensive use by heavy bombers, and that much more engineering work than had been anticipated would be required to put the fields into proper condition.

MacArthur had counted on using heavy bombers from Hollandia not only to help soften up the Palaus in advance of Nimitz' invasion—as ordered by the Joint Chiefs of Staff in mid-March—but also to support his own eventual thrust at the Philippines and, more immediately, the drive to complete his control of New Guinea's north coast. There were some 600 more miles of that coast beyond Hollandia, guarded at key points by Japanese Second Army troops who, unlike Adachi's, were well fed and combat-fresh. At the far northwestern end of the coast lay the huge Vogelkop ("bird's head") Peninsula, named by the Dutch for its shape. Japanese supply and troop ships could reach the Vogelkop from the seas to its west and south without risking the Allied-controlled waters of the Bismarck Sea.

Unless the Japanese bases beyond Hollandia and on the Vogelkop were decisively knocked out, they could pose a serious threat from the rear when MacArthur turned north toward the Philippines. In the middle of May he moved to reduce the threat and simultaneously to solve the problem of finding sites for his heavy bombers. On the 17th, a newly formed Tornado Task Force went ashore near the village of Toem, about 125 miles west of Hollandia and some 20 miles east of Sarmi, which the Japanese had built into a major supply and staging area.

The mission was twofold. Part of the force was assigned to seize the Japanese airstrips between Toem and Sarmi on a coastal plain bordering Maffin Bay. The others were to capture Wakde, a tiny island just off Toem. Only about 3,000 yards wide and 1,000 yards long, Wakde contained an excellent Japanese-built airfield that covered almost half the island's surface.

The Tornado Task Force was made up mainly of the 41st Division's 163rd Regimental Combat Team—the same men who had captured Aitape a few weeks earlier, led by the same commander, Brigadier General Jens A. Doe. Those who set out for Maffin Bay soon found they were up against opposition much tougher than Aitape's: Lieut. General Hachiro Tagami's 36th Division, about 10,000 strong and dug in all along the route. It was to take the Americans until early September, with the help of elements sent in from the 31st and 33rd divisions, to secure Maffin Bay, only about eight miles from the starting point near Toem in May. The toll in lives—most of them lost in savage fighting for a heavily defended strong point called Lone Tree Hill—numbered 400 Americans and nearly 4,000 Japanese.

Fighting was also required to capture Wakde Island; the Americans lost 40 men and the Japanese about 800, some of whom were killed in coral caves in which they had holed up. But securing the island took just four days, and American engineers quickly set about extending the airfield the entire width of Wakde, shore to shore. The field was soon to accommodate two heavy-bomber groups, two fighter groups and two reconnaissance squadrons. It was already in operation when, on the 27th of May, MacArthur launched an assault on his next objective, some 200 miles to the northwest: the island of Biak in Geelvink Bay, adjoining the Vogelkop Peninsula.

After 24 hours, MacArthur issued a communiqué heralding Biak's imminent capture and "the practical end of the New Guinea campaign." A second communiqué on June 1 reported enemy resistance "collapsing." A third communiqué on June 3 reported "mopping up" in progress. The facts were wrong and the optimism embarrassingly unfounded. Organized resistance on Biak was not overcome before the third week in July, and sporadic but fierce resistance continued. It was not until August 20 that the Sixth Army's commander, General Krueger, could declare the Biak campaign "officially" at an end.

Looking back after the War, MacArthur was to place part of the blame for the operation's protracted troubles on the island's "peculiar topography." Biak was, indeed, a redoubtable natural fortress. It was virtually all coral, but unlike other coral islands of the Pacific, with their low-lying terrain and visibility unhampered except by scattered palm trees, Biak was hilly and densely covered by tropical rain forest and jungle undergrowth. In many places the coral had formed ridges and terraces, and these were honeycombed by hundreds of huge caves with connecting galleries. Biak's southern shore, on which the 41st Division landed, not only had a hazardous fringing reef but narrow beaches overhung by coral cliffs as high as 250 feet.

The Japanese had 11,000 men on Biak, only about a third of them combat troops. But their commander, Colonel Naoyuki Kuzume, had devised what MacArthur himself was later to describe as a "brilliant defense structure," utilizing the island's formidable natural features. Kuzume did not bother to fortify all of Biak. The island's three airfields—predictably the attackers' objectives—all lay on the southern coast. Kuzume concentrated his defensive positions in the hills overlooking the shore. Inside caves in these hills, howitzers and machine guns were emplaced, supply dumps set up, and equipment and provisions stocked—electric generators, radios, plenty of ammunition and food and, not least, fresh water. Biak had very little of it that was easily available; most streams ran through underground channels, and the coral surface quickly soaked up even the heaviest rainfall. The shortage of fresh water was to plague the Americans from the start.

From their vantage points, the Japanese could pour withering fire on every movement on the beachheads. They could also foil attempts to take the high ground. A preinvasion bombardment by MacArthur's navy and the Fifth Air Force had barely scratched the defenses in the hills. The Japanese would pop out of the caves, fire off a few rounds, then dart back inside. Flamethrowers and artillery did little good because the caves were deep and twisting. Eventually, after hours of flying over the island, American officers discovered the entrances to the various cave networks. At the most critical network, hundreds of barrels of gasoline were poured into crevices and ignited; as a final touch engineers then carefully lowered a charge of 850 pounds of TNT into the cave entrance and blew it up. The fires and explosions killed hundreds of Japanese.

On June 7 the Americans secured one of Biak's airfields, only about 10 miles from the point where they had come ashore 11 days earlier. It took them two more weeks to capture the other two fields. In the interim they had been threatened, without knowing it, by a potentially lethal blow to their entire operation—from beyond Biak.

Three successive Japanese convoys had set out bearing troop reinforcements for Biak. The first was withdrawn after Imperial Combined Fleet headquarters received an erroneous report that a large force of American ships, including a carrier, was in the area. The second was driven off by Allied planes and ships after landing only 100 troops. The third convoy, preparing to set out from the island of Batjan in the Moluccas, 560 miles west of Biak, had special protection: the new super-battleships *Yamato* and *Musashi,* the biggest in the world. Their huge 18.1-inch guns would certainly have caused havoc—and quite possibly defeat—for the Americans on Biak. But as the convoy was about to leave Batjan, word came of Admiral Nimitz' attack on the island of Saipan in the Marianas. Imperial Combined Fleet headquarters ordered the mammoth dreadnoughts to speed north to the Marianas, and the troopships they were convoying never appeared at Biak.

MacArthur had promised Nimitz that heavy bombers flying from Biak would back up the Saipan operation by raids on the Carolines, the next island group Nimitz was to invade. It was now plain to MacArthur that he would be unable to keep his pledge in time to do any good. Irate at the pace of the Biak operation, MacArthur kept pressuring General Krueger, who in turn kept pressuring Major General Horace H. Fuller, commander of the 41st Division. Fuller, who had ably led his troops from Humboldt Bay to Lake Sentani during the Hollandia operation, finally could take no more of what he viewed as needless heckling. He asked to be relieved.

On June 18, Fuller left Biak. Behind him he left a poignant letter to his troops, stating that they were "the finest body of men that it has been my privilege to be associated with in 39 years of service," and ending: "I love you all." The laborious task of bringing the Biak campaign to a successful close fell to General Doe, the division's new leader, under the supervision of General Eichelberger as commander of the United States I Corps. By the time the fight for Biak was over, some 400 Americans had been killed, 2,000 wounded and 7,200 hospitalized because of illness or accident. About 4,700 Japanese had been killed and 220 captured; the rest were left to surrender or face death by suicide, starvation or disease.

On July 2, with only one Biak airfield as yet operational, MacArthur made a move that was to allay his rising anxiety over the air-base problem. The 158th Regimental Combat Team went ashore on the island of Noemfoor, 60 miles west of Biak and about midway to the Vogelkop Peninsula. Noemfoor, like Biak, had three Japanese-built airfields, but they were bigger; one of them had a 5,300-foot surfaced runway and extensive dispersal areas.

Not a shot was fired when the Americans landed, thanks in large part to General Kenney's pilots, flying in from Wakde. In a raid that ended just 10 minutes before the troops went ashore, the planes dropped 300 instantaneously fused 1,000-pound bombs on the Japanese beach defenses. As Kenney reported, the few Japanese who survived "were so stunned by the blast effect of the heavy bombs that they sat by their machine guns staring straight ahead, numb with shock, while our infantry gathered them in."

Back of the beaches, however, other defenders lay in wait. Unsure of how many there were, the Americans took a Japanese prisoner's estimate of 5,000—which later proved to be about double the actual number—and sent out a hurried call for reinforcements. For the next two days C-47s dropped some 1,400 men of the 503rd Parachute Infantry Regiment on Kamiri Drome, the island's main airfield. The drop was not an unqualified success: the C-47s flew in at lower than 400 feet and the paratroops landed on a hard coral surface. The casualty rate was close to 10 per cent, including 59 serious fracture cases.

But by July 6 all of Noemfoor's airfields were secured. One was found to be badly graded and not worth repair. The other two, improved with extended runways and suitable for use by heavy bombers, were operational by the start of the last week in July. MacArthur himself had set the deadline; he intended to use planes from Noemfoor to provide air cover for the invasion of the Vogelkop Peninsula, set for July 30.

By a quirk of fate, the last week of July 1944 marked the general's first absence from the southwest Pacific theater since he assumed its top command in 1942. Up to now he had managed to avoid high-level strategy conferences in Washington and elsewhere, instead choosing to send members of his staff to represent him. But a summons by his Army superior, General Marshall, was in effect an order. Marshall, without explaining why, told MacArthur to be at Pearl Harbor on the 26th of July.

MacArthur correctly surmised that the secrecy portended a visit to Hawaii by the President himself. Newly nominated for a fourth term, Roosevelt had sailed from San Diego on July 21 aboard the cruiser *Baltimore*. His stated purpose was to confer with MacArthur and Nimitz about their next moves in the Pacific; MacArthur saw the trip, rather, as a ploy to demonstrate to the voters back home that Roosevelt, as Commander in Chief of the nation's armed forces, was running the War, strategy and all. En route to the meeting aboard his plane, the *Bataan,* the general angrily paced the aisle and fumed at the "humiliation" of being compelled to leave his command for "a political picture-taking junket."

But the cordiality of the encounter at Pearl was unmarred. MacArthur had served as Army chief of staff in Washington during Roosevelt's first term, and they soon reverted to friendly reminiscing. In more somber talks over two days, Roosevelt listened attentively as MacArthur and Nimitz, using a bamboo pole to illustrate their points on a huge map, presented their cases for the Philippines versus Formosa as the best route to victory.

MacArthur seized the opportunity to expand on a new plan he had in mind.

After taking Mindanao, in the southern Philippines, he proposed to invade Leyte, in the central part of the islands, as a step toward his primary goal, the island of Luzon in the north. Though the Joint Chiefs had not committed themselves on Leyte—let alone Luzon—MacArthur saw a chance to persuade the President of the merit of his idea. When Roosevelt pointed at Mindanao on the big map and asked: "Douglas, where do we go from here?" MacArthur quickly replied: "Leyte, Mr. President, and then Luzon!"

Privately, Nimitz himself had begun to question the wisdom of bypassing Luzon in favor of a strike directly at Formosa. But he felt obliged to present the case for Formosa—still the strong preference of his boss, Admiral King—and he did so in full, objective detail. Then MacArthur turned emotional. He told Roosevelt: "You cannot abandon 17 million loyal Filipino Christians to the Japanese in favor of first liberating Formosa and returning it to China." Almost as an afterthought, the general served his ace. "American public opinion will condemn you, Mr. President," he said, "and it would be justified."

Aboard his plane on the return flight to the southwest

Pacific, MacArthur jubilantly told an aide: "We've sold it!" MacArthur would still need the approval of the Joint Chiefs, but he was convinced that he would now have Roosevelt in his corner.

MacArthur was back in Brisbane on July 30—just in time to savor another triumph. That day a newly designated Typhoon Task Force—7,300 men of the 6th Division—made an unopposed amphibious landing at Sansapor at the far western end of the Vogelkop Peninsula, MacArthur's last objective on New Guinea's north coast. The troops also took the nearby village of Mar, where the construction of an airfield quickly began. The chief Japanese base on the Vogelkop lay 150 miles to the east at Manokwari, site of the Second Army's headquarters. Bypassed by the Sansapor-Mar operation, Manokwari was totally isolated, a counterattack by its 15,000 troops clearly hopeless.

Several days later it occurred to General Marshall, in Washington, to raise the question of what was to be done, ultimately, about the Japanese forces that had been bypassed—not just at Manokwari but all along the New Guinea coast and as far east as the Solomons. "The various processes of attrition will eventually account for their final disposition," MacArthur replied. "The actual time of their destruction is of little or no importance."

Fortunately for MacArthur's standing with the Australians, the comment was to lie buried in top-secret archives until after the War. All through the New Guinea campaign, Australian forces had been engaged in the perilous and costly task of cleaning out the Japanese pockets of resistance that the Americans had swept past. It was to continue to be the Australians' job until the War ended. Their supreme commander, General Sir Thomas Blamey, had been given a signal to that effect in a MacArthur directive in mid-July. Anticipating the end of the New Guinea campaign, MacArthur had informed Blamey that henceforth he was to assume the responsibility for the "continued neutralization" of the Japanese. The mandate extended from the northern Solomons to New Britain to Australian New Guinea, and excepted only the Admiralty Islands.

The dynamic Blamey, who had hoped to take part in the action in the Philippines, dutifully agreed to the assignment and estimated that six of his brigades—the equivalent of two American divisions—could handle it. MacArthur overruled him, insisting on 12 brigades. The nettled Australians managed to find some wry humor in the decision. As their official Army history noted, it appeared that MacArthur's headquarters "did not wish it to be recorded that six American divisions had been relieved by six Australian brigades."

There remained one place on the New Guinea coast where American forces were still deeply enmeshed. In early August of 1944, General Adachi's attack on Aitape was in full swing. The strategically least vital battle of the New Guinea campaign was also to prove the bloodiest.

By now, Adachi himself was in bad shape; he had lost all his teeth and could eat only sago starch. He had also lost any hope that the attack on Aitape would affect the tide of the American advance. In a candid message to his men, he had emphasized the limited scope of his objectives. As he put it: "The presence of the enemy in Aitape affords us a last favorable chance to display effectively the fighting power which the Army still possesses, and to contribute toward the destruction of the enemy's strength."

Since the first clashes between Aitape's advance units and American patrols 20 miles east of Aitape in late May, the Americans at Aitape had taken two measures to prepare for the main Japanese assault. They had set up a new perimeter line closer to Aitape, along the west bank of the Driniumor River, only 10 miles east of the base. They had also beefed up their force. It now consisted of the United States XI Corps—including the 32nd Division, the 124th Regimental Combat Team of the 31st Division and a separate entity, the 112th Cavalry Regimental Combat Team, serving as infantry—under the command of Major General Charles P. Hall.

All together, Hall had at his disposal 15 infantry battalions and two dismounted cavalry squadrons—all of them fresh, well fed and superbly equipped for battle. Three of the infantry battalions and the two cavalry squadrons were on the Driniumor River line itself, with Brigadier General Clarence A. Martin commanding.

Adachi's first big assault took place on the night of July 10. He had massed nearly 17,000 troops within a few miles of the Driniumor and, despite his transportation problems, had managed to equip them with artillery, 13,000 rifles, ammunition and enough rice for about a week. Moreover, his jungle-wise veterans had contrived to assemble under the noses of Martin's troops without being detected. A strong reconnaissance in force, sent out by Martin on the morning of the 10th, failed to find Adachi's troops. The patrols had been taken from the river defense line, thus weakening it at the time of the attack.

Just before midnight, Adachi's artillery opened up, astonishing the Americans; they had no idea he had brought field guns so far west. Five minutes later the leading elements of his 20th and 41st divisions came pouring across the river at the weakest point of the line. A ferocious battle raged all night. By morning the Japanese had broken through to establish a considerable bridgehead on the west bank, isolating the Americans downstream. General Martin pulled his troops back three miles. A sharply worded message reached his superior, General Hall, from Hall's superior, General Krueger. The retreat, Krueger declared, was needless. He ordered a counterattack.

Hampered by poor communications, Adachi took several days to exploit the breakthrough his men had made. By that

time the Americans had been reinforced, and had begun to regain their riverside positions. Soon Adachi's 20th Division and his 237th Infantry Regiment were marooned behind the American lines, while his reserves struggled through the jungle to join up with them and resume the attack.

In late July, Adachi launched his second—and last—assault, in an attempt to outflank the southern end of the Driniumor perimeter. The southern anchor of the line was a riverside village, Afua, in the foothills of the mountains five miles inland. While some of Adachi's forces hurled them-

U.S. soldiers wading ashore in columns churn up the waters off Morotai Island, midway between western New Guinea and the Philippines. MacArthur wanted Morotai so Allied aircraft could operate from there and protect his Philippine landings. The Morotai invaders met no resistance.

selves at Afua, capturing and losing it several times, others fought to hang on to positions they held at the coastal end of the Driniumor and along its central stretches. In a double-pronged maneuver, American forces at the northern end of the line enveloped and entrapped the Japanese.

By the 9th of August the battle was over. Adachi withdrew what remained of his battered Eighteenth Army to 15 miles east of the Driniumor. By his own later estimate, he had lost 10,000 men. The American toll was 440 dead and more than 2,500 wounded.

For weeks, American forces pursued Adachi's retreating survivors as they limped back toward Wewak. The Australians were beginning to close in on Wewak from the east. But none of the Allied commanders wanted to risk more lives in what had become a meaningless campaign. General Adachi held Wewak against the Australians until May of 1945. He then retreated to the hills, still in sporadic radio contact with Japan, still maintaining the empty shell of military organization. Not until World War II ended did he surrender, in a formal ceremony, handing over his sword and the few thousand survivors of his army to the Australian commander in the area.

More anguish lay in store for Adachi. Charged by the Australians with a number of war crimes, including the killing of prisoners, he was sentenced to life imprisonment. In September of 1947 he committed suicide in his quarters in a prison compound at Rabaul. He left an extraordinary letter revealing that his decision to take his life had been made while he was still in command of his troops, observing their dedication.

"My officers and men all followed my orders in silence without grumbling," Adachi wrote, "and when exhausted they succumbed to death just like flowers falling in the wind. . . . At that time I made up my mind not to set foot on my country's soil again, but to remain as a clod of earth in the Southern Seas with the 100,000 officers and men, even if a time should come when I would be able to return to my country in triumph."

At the start of September 1944, the Americans were on the way to ensuring against any Japanese triumph. The campaign for New Guinea and its offshore islands was officially, if not entirely, finished. MacArthur's attention was now focused on the southern tip of the Philippines; Mindanao's turn had come.

To help protect his left flank as he moved northward, MacArthur had decided on an intermediate operation in the Moluccas, the islands lying between the Vogelkop Peninsula and Mindanao. On one of the islands, Halmahera, the Japanese Second Area Army was believed to have 30,000 troops. Morotai, the adjacent island, was estimated to have an enemy garrison of only about 1,000. MacArthur decided on Morotai; the invaders, designated the Tradewind Task Force, were to number some 61,000 men. Only about a third were combat troops; the rest were to build airfields or function as service personnel. The invasion was set for September 15. On September 12, MacArthur boarded the cruiser *Nashville* at Hollandia, bound northward to join the naval support force.

In the meantime, distant events were about to alter the entire future course of the Philippines campaign. On the 9th and the 10th of September, carrier planes from Admiral Halsey's Third Fleet attacked Mindanao, as prearranged. On the 12th, they attacked the central Philippines, including Leyte. On the 13th, Halsey reported to Nimitz, at Pearl Harbor, that the central Philippines were "wide open." He urged that the Mindanao invasion be canceled and that Leyte be invaded instead.

Nimitz passed the word on to the Joint Chiefs of Staff, then attending a conference in Quebec with Roosevelt, Churchill and the British military chiefs. General Marshall dashed off a message to MacArthur, asking his view of the proposed change. But the message went to Hollandia; the *Nashville*, with MacArthur aboard, was traveling under radio silence. From Hollandia, Lieut. General Richard K. Sutherland, MacArthur's chief of staff, replied in MacArthur's name, approving the proposal for a direct assault on Leyte.

On the 15th of September, the Tradewind Task Force landed unopposed on Morotai. Two hours later MacArthur came ashore to inspect the operation. Standing on the beach, he gazed out to the northwest, in the general direction of the Philippines. As one of his accompanying aides described the moment, it was "almost as though he could already see through the mist the rugged lines of Bataan and Corregidor." Then MacArthur spoke. "They are waiting for me there," he said. "It has been a long time."

THE NAVY'S FLOATING BASES

Mission accomplished, an F6F Hellcat fighter jerks to a standstill on the deck of the U.S. carrier Yorktown as sailors dash to detach steel arrester cables.

AN AWESOME WALLOP FROM SPEEDY CARRIERS

Vice Admiral Marc A. Mitscher, tactical wizard of Fast Carrier Task Force 58, follows the action from his flagship during a 1944 strike on Saipan.

On June 10, 1943, the U.S.S. *Essex,* first of a new, powerful class of aircraft carriers, steamed out of Pearl Harbor and plowed her way across the ocean to join the United States Pacific Fleet. The 27,000-ton flattop carried a load of planes and a formidable array of antiaircraft guns, including a dozen 5-inchers.

In the ensuing months, as America began to flex its industrial muscles, more such carriers were built. They became the core of a swift armada of battleships, cruisers and destroyers, all capable of doing better than 30 knots. Brought to the peak of effectiveness under the guiding genius of Vice Admiral Marc A. Mitscher, the fast-carrier task groups made available to U.S. military planners the most mobile and devastating naval striking forces that had ever been assembled. The carriers—usually two *Essex*-class carriers and two light carriers per task group—rode near the center with as many as 300 planes on board. Forming a defensive perimeter around them were heavy vessels such as battleships and cruisers, encircled in turn by up to 30 destroyers. So pulverizing were these groups in action that in one three-day strike on the Palau Islands in 1944 the planes from 11 carriers destroyed 150 aircraft and sent 100,000 tons of shipping to the bottom of the ocean—at a loss of only 25 planes.

The key to the fast-carrier operation was a highly efficient method of resupply that American planners had worked out to keep a task force at sea for as long as 70 days. At regular intervals "sea trains," composed of oilers and cargo ships, sailed from Pearl Harbor and other bases to refuel the carriers. When the oilers caught up with them they would rig oil hoses between the two ships and refueling would begin *(right).* Then, when their tanks were nearly drained, the supply ships would transfer what oil was left to another waiting oiler and hurry back to base for a new load. Each carrier group was refueled approximately every four days. The refueling operation provided a special dividend for the men in the carrier force: the oilers also brought mail and the latest movies.

Coupled by cables and oil hoses, the U.S.S. Lexington (right) and a Navy oiler churn through the water together at 10 knots during a refueling operation.

While ordnance men arm bombs on the hangar deck, where 40 planes with folded wings could be stored, off-duty crewmen (background) watch a movie.

FRANTIC ACTIVITY BEFORE A STRIKE

Life on board the fast carriers followed a regular routine that erupted into frenzied activity when the planes were launched on strike day.

Besides normal ship's duties, the "Big Day," as it was called, involved a staggering variety of special jobs. Some men wrestled bombs into bomb racks; others checked and loaded the planes' machine guns. Still others gassed up the planes and spotted them for takeoff. Radio engineers made final adjustments on the radios. Even the cooks stepped up the pace and prepared a special feast. The "big chow" consisted of thick steaks, fried eggs and potatoes, butter-dipped toast and, of course, black coffee.

Hangarmen roll a fighter onto an elevator that will lift it to the flight deck.

Prior to taking off for the strike, Navy pilots, sitting in a ready room below the flight deck, receive a last-minute briefing from air-intelligence officers

DRAMATIC DEPARTURES, AGONIZING ARRIVALS

When launch time approached, the action shifted to the carrier's flight deck, where the planes stood carefully parked in order of takeoff: big torpedo bombers at the stern; the dive bombers and level-flight bombers next; and the fighters farthest forward, ready to move out first.

At takeoff, the flight deck came alive. Plane directors motioned aircraft into position, and the flight-deck officer, with his black-and-white checkered flag, signaled them to go. Takeoff was a challenge: the deck was less than 400 feet long, a tenth of the runway length normally used on land.

Once the first deckload of planes was in the air, the flight-deck crews geared up immediately for the next strike—spotting more planes, topping off gas tanks, fusing bombs and checking machine guns. Coordination was essential. For landings as well as takeoffs, each crew wore a different colored shirt that quickly identified what it did: blue for plane handlers, red for ordnance men and fire fighters, green for the men who handled the arresting gear. Even those sailors who slid blocks under the wheels of the planes, the chockmen, had a special color—purple.

As soon as all of the planes had been launched, the crewmen began preparing the flight deck to receive returning aircraft. The flight-deck crew rigged a collapsible steel-net barrier across the deck in order to keep landing aircraft from crashing into any planes parked on it. Then the carrier steamed along a prearranged course so the returning aircraft could find her.

Ordnance crews (top) ready aircraft guns. Below, flight-suited pilots file confidently to their planes.

Preparing for takeoff, plane directors "spot," or park, Dauntless dive bombers, which would later taxi forward into a starting line as planes ahead were launched.

With a TBF Avenger revved up and ready to go, a plane director on the Lexington gives the okay to take off during a strike on Saipan. Apart from torpedoes, the Avengers often carried bombs; when possible, Navy pilots hit enemy airfields at dusk, knowing overnight repair would be difficult.

Launched by a catapult, a Dauntless dive bomber soars off the deck of one of Mitscher's carriers. Constantly developing new combat techniques, Mitscher withheld hitting Japanese fuel dumps until the last strike of the day, because the smoke raised by the bombs obscured other targets.

Dauntless dive bombers roar over Navy landing craft during the invasion of Saipan. On raids, the rear gunner would hold off enemy fighters, while the pilot took aim on the target

About to come under attack by planes of the U.S. Navy in November of 1943, Japanese warships maneuver frantically out of the harbor at Rabaul to head for open seas

HITTING THE ENEMY WHERE IT HURT

The planes that streaked off the decks of the fast carriers pounded Japanese forces from the Gilbert Islands to the Philippine Sea. They struck airfields and anchorages, attacked ships and flew close air support for assault landings. In one span of six weeks, carrier-based pilots flew more than 5,400 sorties, dropping no less than 2,000 tons of bombs.

In addition to massive doses of firepower, these strikes featured both speed and surprise. During one action, Mitscher put more than 200 planes in the air within 10 minutes. On another occasion, the first night-bombing attack on enemy shipping in the Navy's history, his torpedo bombers roared into the harbor at Truk and scored 13 direct hits. But the attack on Truk was expensive. The aircraft carrier *Intrepid* was hit by a torpedo and put out of action for six months. Mitscher's Task Force 58 lost 26 planes. Of 46 airmen shot down, only half were rescued. Others limped back to their carriers and crash-landed on the decks

A wounded gunner is lifted gently from his plane by carrier crewmen.

Rushing to assist the pilot from his cockpit, a Navy officer clambers up the side of a Hellcat enveloped in flames after its crash-landing on the U.S.S. Enterprise

6

In the middle of June 1944, the sun rose shortly before 6 a.m. in the Philippine Sea, burning off the night clouds and for a moment gilding the topsides of warships of the U.S. Fifth Fleet. It was the most powerful armada the world had ever known. From the towering superstructure of the new aircraft carrier *Lexington,* the flagship of the fleet's striking arm, Task Force 58, the visibility soon was 12 miles in all directions. High above, the wing tips of patrolling aircraft feathered a cloudless sky with twin contrails of white vapor. The 98,618 sailors and aviators of the fast-carrier task force welcomed the felicitous weather, which would make it easier to spot and shoot down any Japanese carrier planes. No one knew exactly where the enemy fleet was, but the men expected a fight soon. And indeed they would get one. Before the end of this operation, the aircraft of two mighty naval forces would battle it out with results that would determine the course of the war in the Pacific.

In addition to its Task Force 58—a vanguard of seven battleships, 21 cruisers, scores of destroyers and 15 fast carriers bearing 891 combat planes—the Fifth Fleet boasted no fewer than 535 vessels. Packed into troop transports were 127,571 fighting men: the 2nd, 3rd and 4th Marine divisions, the 1st Provisional Marine Brigade, the Army's 27th Division and reinforcing units.

The Marines and infantrymen had a clear-cut mission: they were to seize the Mariana islands of Saipan, Tinian and Guam, the next logical steppingstones in Admiral Nimitz' westward drive through the central Pacific. The Marianas, lying some 1,500 miles east of Manila Bay and only 1,300 miles southeast of Tokyo, were key strongholds in the Japanese defensive chain. By taking them, the Americans would cut the enemy's supply line, which stretched from Japan to its Pacific bastions in the south, and further isolate Truk, the Japanese stronghold in the Carolines, 600 miles southeast of Guam. Moreover, possession of the airfields in the Marianas would allow the Americans to employ the new B-29 bomber against Japan.

Guam was the primary objective of the Americans. In addition to its excellent airfields, the island could claim the best deepwater harbor in the Marianas. For more than 40 years Guam had been a United States possession. Then, two days after Pearl Harbor, Japanese invaders had overwhelmed the small Marine garrison stationed there and

BLOOD, SAND AND CORAL

seized the island. Recapturing Guam would have a symbolic effect in addition to the strategic one: it would be the first American-held territory to be recovered from the Japanese, and its occupation would boost the morale of American soldiers and civilians alike.

First Admiral Nimitz decided to strike at Saipan; the invasion of Guam would come three days later. Saipan was 100 miles closer to Japan and therefore more practicable as a base for bombing the homeland. The capture of Saipan, Nimitz also reasoned, would cut off Japanese air support to Guam and make the invasion there less costly.

Saipan was a well-developed tropical island, some 14 miles long and five miles wide, with towns, sugar plantations, terraced hillsides and a large Japanese civilian population. Volcanic in origin, it was dominated at its center by a 1,554-foot peak called Mount Tapotchau, the apex of the island's spiny mountain backbone. To the north and to the east, a series of high plateaus and rolling hills ended abruptly in pinched, steep coastal flats or sheer cliffs that dropped hundreds of feet to the sea; but to the south and to the west the land melted into a long coastal plain that was fringed with beaches.

The island's garrison had received few reinforcements since spring. Imperial General Headquarters had not expected an attack on the Marianas so soon; American air raids farther south on the Palau Islands, in the western Carolines, had deluded Japanese planners into thinking that the Americans would strike there first. Moreover, American submarines had played havoc with Japanese transports bound for Saipan with troops and supplies. On the eve of the invasion, Lieut. General Yoshitsugu Saito, the island's Army commander, had only 25,469 soldiers on hand. Vice Admiral Chuichi Nagumo, who had commanded the Japanese carrier strike forces in the Pearl Harbor attack and then had fallen into disfavor after his carriers were demolished at the Battle of Midway, had 6,100 naval troops at his disposal.

The U.S. plan of attack called for the 2nd and 4th Marine divisions to assault the beaches on the southwest coast of Saipan on June 15. Both divisions would push inland until they were well established on high ground. The 2nd Division, on the north flank, would then surge upward and capture Mount Tapotchau. Meanwhile, the 4th Division would head eastward across the island, cutting the Japanese off and capturing Aslito Airfield.

The invasion got off to a bad start. The gunnery officers on the new battleships had not been trained in shore-bombardment techniques and wasted much of their fire; the more experienced officers on the older battleships were given only one day to shell Saipan, and the island was too big, the targets too numerous and too widely dispersed, for them to knock out every gun position. As a result, Japanese mortars and artillery disabled amtracs as they swept shoreward. Adding to the Marines' problems, an unanticipated current deposited many men of the 2nd Division on the wrong beaches, where they milled about for hours. By nightfall, 553 of the 2nd Division were dead or missing and 1,022 were wounded.

Still, 20,000 Marines had made it ashore on the first day and they were well enough established to throw back two suicidal counterattacks that General Saito hurled at them under the cover of darkness. The 6th Marine Regiment of the 2nd Division counted 700 Japanese bodies in front of its lines at dawn.

In spite of his losses, General Saito had reason to feel reasonably optimistic. As the fighting raged, the Japanese First Mobile Fleet was steaming toward the Marianas under the command of Vice Admiral Jisaburo Ozawa. As soon as it had become evident to the Japanese that an attack on the Marianas was imminent, Ozawa had been sent northeast from his base on the island of Tawitawi off the coast of Borneo to wage what the Japanese admirals had been waiting for—"the decisive battle." Joining Ozawa was a contingent of warships—including the powerful new dreadnoughts Yamato and Musashi—that had been preparing to head for the island of Biak off New Guinea to relieve the garrison under attack there by MacArthur.

Thus, Ozawa now had at his disposal practically every remaining vessel in the Japanese Navy—nine carriers with 430 combat planes aboard, five battleships, 13 cruisers and 28 destroyers.

However formidable his force, the odds were still stacked against Ozawa. He possessed fewer planes than the Americans, and most of his veteran pilots had died in the Solomon Islands battles. The majority of his fliers had only two to six months' training and few had seen combat. Ozawa had an

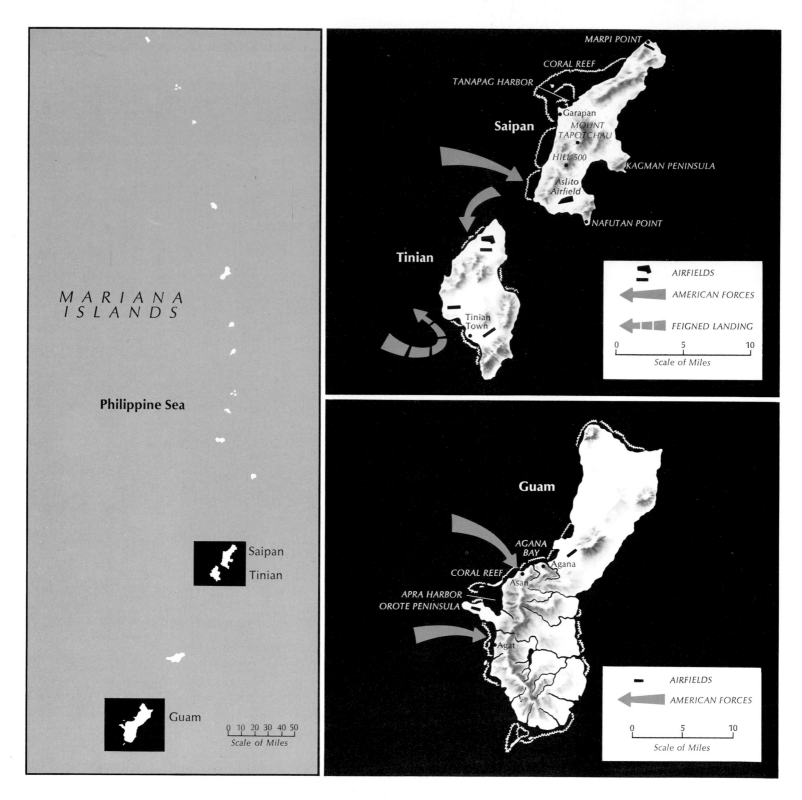

In the summer of 1944, American forces invaded Saipan, Tinian and Guam (above) in the Mariana Islands. The assault on the southwestern beaches of Saipan (upper right) was made by one Marine division attacking toward Mount Tapotchau and another forging straight ahead to capture Aslito Airfield. Then, on line with an Army division, the Marines staged an island-wide sweep northward, taking the town of Garapan and the seaplane base at Tanapag Harbor, and finally compressing the Japanese into the upper tip of the island. Next, in the assault on Tinian, some Marine landing boats made a feint toward the beaches at Tinian Town, while others landed on the tiny beaches at the northwest section of the island and the Marines moved southward from there. In the meantime, two separate forces landed on Guam (lower right) simultaneously, one cutting off the neck of Orote Peninsula and trapping the Japanese there, the other capturing the navy yard at Apra Harbor and the principal town of Agana.

even greater handicap that he did not know about. In their four days of preinvasion air strikes, beginning June 11, U.S. planes had destroyed most of the Japanese aircraft that would have supported Ozawa's operation from the fields of Saipan, Guam and Tinian.

The approach of the Japanese warships became known to Admiral Spruance, commanding the U.S. Fifth Fleet, on the night of June 15-16, when two of his submarines spotted the vessels in Philippine waters. Spruance, who had been preparing for the invasion of Guam on the 18th of June, quickly changed plans. He directed the transports to finish unloading men and supplies on Saipan by the 17th and then to run eastward to safety. Admiral Mitscher's fast-carrier fleet, Task Force 58, was sent into the waters 180 miles west of Tinian to await the Japanese.

Search planes from the Japanese First Mobile Fleet spotted Mitscher's task force on June 18 and at 8:30 the next morning, Ozawa launched his first raid: 45 bomb-carrying Zeros and eight torpedo bombers, covered by 16 Zero fighters. An hour and a half later, the American screening force sailing out ahead of Mitscher picked up the Japanese planes on radar when they were still 150 miles away. At that moment some of Mitscher's Hellcat fighters were over Guam, dogfighting with Japanese land-based planes. Over their radios the Hellcat pilots heard the old circus rallying cry "Hey, Rube!" They sped back to the fleet.

Task Force 58 turned to the wind and prepared to launch. Bombers roared off the flight decks and headed toward Guam to destroy airfields on the island so Ozawa's carrier planes could not land there for refueling. And Mitscher's 15 carriers started fast-moving, rotating schedules of takeoffs and landings that would keep a maximum number of fighters aloft throughout the day. At 10:36 a.m., 11 Hellcats, in the air early as part of the regular combat air patrol, gave the first "Tallyho," and dived toward the enemy.

What followed was a daylong romp for the American pilots, an air battle that has been known ever since as "The Great Marianas Turkey Shoot." Forty-two planes of the 69 in Ozawa's first raid were shot down. A few attackers fought their way through to the protecting battleships—the South Dakota was hit and 27 men killed—but none of the Japanese planes reached the fast carriers. Ozawa's second wave

followed: 128 planes, including 53 dive bombers and 27 torpedo bombers. There was another scramble of Hellcats, another series of wild melees high in the air and 70 more Japanese planes were down in the water, leaving a trail of oil slicks and burning debris 12 miles long. Six Japanese dive bombers and a handful of torpedo planes got through to the carriers, slightly damaging the Bunker Hill and killing three men. Twice more the Japanese launched their planes; twice more they ran into furious attacks from the Americans, the final one over Guam.

All told, Ozawa's carriers had put 373 planes into the air; only 130 had returned. About 50 Guam-based planes were shot down as well. In one day Japan's naval air arm had lost about three fourths of its planes—close to 300 in all. U.S. air losses amounted to 30 planes. American submarines, meanwhile, were dogging the Japanese fleet—with almost equally devastating results. They scored torpedo hits on two carriers, both of which sank later in the day. One of the flattops was the Taiho, Admiral Ozawa's flagship and the newest carrier in the dwindling Japanese fleet. As the Taiho settled in the water, a lifeboat ferried the admiral and his staff to another vessel.

Ozawa assumed that his missing planes had merely flown on to Guam to land and refuel and would return to the fleet in glory. He thus remained in the area, ready to resume the attack when his flight groups had reassembled. It was a costly mistake. Mitscher, with Spruance's approval, now went in pursuit of the crippled Japanese fleet. When it was spotted late in the afternoon of the second day, June 20, Mitscher launched 77 dive bombers, 54 torpedo bombers and 85 fighters against it, although he knew that he was running the risk of his pilots' not getting back to their carriers until well after dark. They reached the Japanese at twilight, and the Hellcats quickly disposed of the feeble fighter screen that Ozawa was able to muster. Then the American bombers bored in. Twenty minutes later the carrier Hiyo was sinking, other ships were seriously damaged —and 65 more Japanese planes had been shot down or damaged beyond repair. Finally recognizing defeat, Ozawa headed his battered fleet toward Japan. His gamble having paid off, Mitscher turned on all the lights on his ships to act as beacons for his fliers. (Fortunately for the Americans, there were no Japanese submarines lurking about.)

The twilight attack had cost the Americans 20 planes, but the cost was to escalate wildly just when the victorious pilots appeared to have returned safely from the battle. As the planes approached the brightly lighted carriers, they began running out of fuel. "Many planes—too many—announced that their gas was gone and they were going into the water," one returning pilot later wrote. "Seen from above, it was a weird kaleidoscope of fast moving lights forming intricate trails in the darkness, punctuated now and then by tracers shooting through the night as someone landed with his gun switches on, and again by suddenly brilliant exhaust flames or someone's turtleback light getting lower and lower until finally blacked out by the waves closing over it. A Mardi Gras setting fantastically out of place here, midway between the Marianas and the Philippines." Eighty of the 216 U.S. planes either fell into the sea when they ran out of fuel or crashed on carrier decks.

In all, the two-day battle cost the Americans 130 planes and 76 airmen. But for the Japanese those two days had been far more devastating. Of the 430 carrier planes Ozawa had started with, only 35 were still able to fly. Three of his carriers had plunged to the bottom of the Pacific, and other ships had been damaged severely. The Battle of the Philippine Sea broke the back of Japan's naval air force, and never again would its carriers do battle on a major scale.

Finally, Ozawa's defeat meant that there was no longer any hope of rescue for the Japanese on Saipan, although they did not know it at the time.

After eight days of fighting, the defenders had yielded most of the lower half of the island. To take the rest Marine Lieut. General Holland Smith, in overall command of the assault forces, ordered a massive island-wide thrust along the slopes and ridges of Saipan's mountain backbone. The 2nd Marine Division, on the left, would attack up the cruel slopes of Mount Tapotchau. On the right, the 4th Marine Division would move out northward, then curve to the east to capture the three-mile-long Kagman Peninsula. The attack in the center of the three-division front was assigned by General Smith to two regiments of the Army's 27th Division, which had landed on June 16.

On the morning of June 23 the Marines got off sharply and made good progress. But the center of the line sagged. The Army attack began late, sputtered and then stopped altogether. On the left and right, the advancing Marines were dangerously exposed by the failure of the 27th Division to keep up. There was nothing for them to do but halt, dig in and wait for the Army.

At this point, Howlin' Mad Smith was outraged. The next morning, he zipped off a curt dispatch to the 27th Division commander, Major General Ralph Smith, saying that he was "highly displeased" with the performance of the soldiers.

It was not the first time that the Marine Smith had found fault with the Army. On Makin, Howlin' Mad had become infuriated with the slow advance of the 27th Division, and Ralph Smith had borne the brunt of his short temper.

On Saipan as on Makin, the dispute stemmed from a basic difference in Army and Marine tactics. The Marines believed in moving swiftly, despite heavy casualties, to obtain their objectives. The soldiers were accustomed to cautious advances that kept casualties low.

When the 27th Division advance stalled again on Saipan on the afternoon of June 24, Holland Smith went aboard the cruiser *Indianapolis* to urge the dismissal of the Army general. "Ralph Smith has shown that he lacks aggressive spirit," he told his superior, Admiral Spruance, "and his division is slowing our advance. He should be relieved." Spruance agreed, and Ralph Smith was sent to Hawaii and later reassigned to the European theater.

Under fresh leadership the Army troops gradually got into step with the Marines, and by July 6 the American sweep northward had overrun the town of Garapan and the important seaplane base at Tanapag Harbor. From the heights of Mount Tapotchau, the attackers could now look down on the Japanese hopelessly compressed into the top third of the island. On that day, General Saito finally realized that all was lost. The weary old warrior, his beard long and matted, his clothing filthy, sat down in his cave headquarters and ate a farewell meal of canned crabmeat and *sake*. He walked to a flat rock, cleaned it off and sat down. With his samurai sword he sliced into his belly, and then his adjutant shot him in the back of the head. On another part of the island Admiral Nagumo, the commander of naval troops on Saipan, foregoing ritual, simply killed himself with a pistol.

Before killing himself, General Saito had issued a last message to his troops: "I advance to seek out the enemy.

Follow me!" The next morning, evidently determined to do just that, between 2,000 and 3,000 Japanese staged the most devastating banzai attack of the War. Fueled with *sake*, they rushed screaming into the 27th Division lines along the beaches at Tanapag Harbor and rolled like a wave over the frontline troops. Some Japanese had guns, but many carried no more than a couple of grenades, a long stick tipped with a bayonet or just a club. Still, they came in such numbers that the 1st and 2nd battalions of the 105th Infantry Regiment were quickly overwhelmed, cut off and carved into desperate pockets. The 1st Battalion commander, Lieut. Colonel William O'Brien, was killed while firing a heavy machine gun from a jeep. Sergeant Thomas Baker of the same unit was wounded, and when his buddies withdrew he asked to be propped against a tree and left there with his loaded pistol. The next morning he was found dead with eight lifeless Japanese around him.

One American soldier who faced the onslaught recalled later: "It reminded me of one of those old cattle stampedes in the movies. The camera is in a hole in the ground and you see the herd coming and then they leap up and over you and are gone. Only the Japs just kept coming and coming. I didn't think they'd ever stop." In some places the Japanese soldiers were forced to climb over piles of their own dead to get at the American soldiers and Marines. American machine gunners had to move their weapons to keep shooting, because the mounds of corpses blocked their view. But still the Japanese came on, swarming over Marine artillery positions in the rear even while 105mm howitzers fired into them at point-blank range. Among the attackers were men who until that morning had been hospital patients—soldiers in bandages and on crutches, some barely able to walk. Not until the wave reached a rear-area command post did its momentum cease. There it was finally halted by a pickup platoon of cooks, typists and staff officers. Two days later, when the mop-up was finished, 4,311 Japanese bodies were counted on the beaches at Tanapag.

Saipan was declared secure on July 9, but the final horror came after the fighting was over. At the northern tip of the island lay Marpi Point, a plateau some 833 feet above a shore of jagged coral rocks, and there hundreds of Japanese civilians joined the few remaining troops in an orgy of self-destruction. Despite loudspeaker assurances that the victors would treat captives well, parents threw their children off the cliffs and jumped after them. Whole families waded and swam out to sea to drown themselves. One group of 100 Japanese bowed to Marines watching from a cliff. Then they stripped, bathed, donned fresh clothing and spread a Japanese flag on a rock. One man distributed hand grenades, and one by one they pulled the pins and held the grenades against their bellies.

Some took their lives alone and quietly. War correspondent Sherrod witnessed the suicide of a youngster: "On the edge of the slippery, tide-washed rocks a Japanese boy of perhaps 15, attired in knee-length black trousers, walked back and forth. He would pause in meditation, then he would walk on, swinging his arms. He sat on the edge of the rocks, then he got up. He sat down again, waiting.

"When a high wave washed the rock, the boy let it sweep him into the sea. At first he lay face down, inert on the surface of the water. Then his arms flailed frantically, as if an instinct stronger than his willpower bade him live. Then he was quiet. He was dead."

At a cost of 16,525 Americans killed or wounded and some 29,000 Japanese dead, the Americans finally were in possession of an island within air striking distance of Japan. When the news of Saipan's fall reached Tokyo, the Navy adviser to Emperor Hirohito summed up everyone's anguish. "Hell is on us," he said. On July 18, Prime Minister Hideki Tojo, the one man most responsible for his country's entry into the War, proclaimed "an unprecedentedly great national crisis" and resigned, along with his entire cabinet. The newly appointed government, under Prime Minister Kuniaki Koiso, began to ponder what before had been officially unthinkable—whether to continue the War.

Saipan provided the Americans with the staging area, and artillery support, for the attack on Tinian, a slightly smaller and much less rugged island just three and a half miles to the south. As seen from the air, Tinian, with its network of sugar-cane fields, resembled a swatch of patchwork quilt. The same flat, gentle terrain that allowed extensive cultivation on the island also provided excellent sites for airfields; the Japanese had already constructed three and were working on a fourth—rich prizes the Americans eyed eagerly.

But Tinian's high, rocky coastline offered few possibilities for landing an invasion force. Seemingly the only beaches suitable for a landing were those at Tinian Town in the southwest corner, and the island commander naturally had concentrated his defenses there. If they elected to hit those beaches, the Americans could expect heavy casualties. Instead, they chose a most unlikely site—two tiny gaps of sand between cliffs of jagged coral on the northwest corner of the island. As Navy frogmen and Marines from Saipan had discovered, these minuscule beaches had been left virtually undefended; obviously the Japanese considered a landing on such a narrow front to be inconceivable.

The Americans would have to depend on surprise; if the Japanese realized what they were up to, they could easily plug the two gaps and destroy the landing force. Thus the attack on Tinian hinged on a massive ruse.

On July 24, after a thunderous preinvasion bombardment, a large invasion fleet appeared off Tinian Town. In clear view of the Japanese, landing boats started toward shore. When the boats pulled back a few hours later the Japanese thought that their shore batteries had repulsed an attack. But meanwhile, following artillery bombardment from Sai-

pan and napalm attacks from Saipan-based P-47s, two regiments of the 4th Marine Division had landed on the tiny beaches between the cliffs at the northwest tip of the island. By nightfall, delayed only briefly by the resistance of small Japanese units, 15,000 Marines were ashore. The trick had worked. The phony landing at Tinian Town had held the attention of the Japanese for hours; the hail of fire from warships and the big guns on Saipan had disrupted their communications and kept them pinned down. By the time they saw through the deception and rushed north to meet the invaders, the Americans had established a formidable defense perimeter a mile inland, and were able to repulse the counterattack the Japanese launched that night. In the next few days, tanks and infantry of the 4th and 2nd Marine divisions plunged southward against feeble resistance through the open, almost parklike countryside of Tinian, and the island fell within a week.

While Tinian was being taken with relative ease, a bloody battle was in progress on Guam 100 miles to the south. The largest of the Marianas, Guam is a rugged, 30-mile-long

chunk of limestone riddled with ridges and ravines and cloaked with dense, nearly impenetrable jungle verdure broken only by occasional rice paddies and patches of smooth tableland.

Everything on Guam of military value lay in a short stretch of coastline on the western shore: the principal town of Agana; Apra Harbor, an excellent anchorage with a navy yard; and Orote Peninsula, a heavily fortified rocky promontory on which the main airfield was situated. It was decided that two separate U.S. forces five miles apart were to attack simultaneously on July 21. The 3rd Marine Division would land on beaches north of the harbor and seize the navy yard. One regiment of the Army's newly arrived 77th Division and the 1st Provisional Marine Brigade would strike below the harbor and proceed to choke off Orote Peninsula at its narrow neck, trapping the Japanese there.

But when the Americans landed, they found Guam's terrain every bit as hostile as the Japanese. Even though the Americans had occupied Guam for 43 years, the available topographical maps were amazingly inaccurate, and the assault forces had only sketchy information about the obstacles they faced. Just beyond the beaches, the ground rose sharply into a corrugation of high ridges and cliffs from which Japanese artillerymen, with a bird's-eye view of the beaches, poured a rain of fire on the Marines. In the first few days of the battle, the American advance was agonizingly slow, marked by heavy casualties.

But late on July 25, the fifth day, Marines of the 1st Provisional Brigade captured the main coastal road that cuts across the neck of Orote Peninsula, thus sealing off the defenders of the spit of land. Realizing that his escape route had been blocked, the garrison commander on Orote called for a breakout. On the following night the desperate Japanese troops assembled noisily in a mangrove swamp just a stone's throw from the Marine lines. The preparations for the assault included, apparently, the consumption of a great deal of alcohol.

The Marines in the front lines were so close to the Japanese that they could hear shrieking, laughter and the breaking of empty bottles. So loud was the drunken din in the swamp that Marine artillerymen were able to use the noise to compute the range of targets at the edge of the swamp. "It sounded," someone later remarked, "like New Year's Eve in the zoo."

Shortly after midnight, the desperate revelry reached a crescendo, and the drunken Japanese rolled out of the swamp across open ground toward the Marine lines, the officers waving flags and swords, the enlisted men brandishing not only conventional weapons, but pitchforks, empty bottles and even baseball bats. At the sharp order of a Marine officer, a devastating artillery barrage descended on the charging Japanese. One American lieutenant later described what he saw: "Arms and legs flew like snowflakes. Japs ran amuck. They screamed in terror until they died." The survivors of this pinpoint bombardment turned tail and fled back into the swamp, where they were wiped out by readjusted artillery fire.

On the same night, five miles to the north, the 3rd Marine

U.S. Marines on Saipan examine the wreckage of a Japanese sugar refinery blasted by bombs and naval gunfire. Sugar was one of the leading products of Saipan, the most heavily settled and industrialized island in the Marianas.

Marine Lieut. General Holland "Howlin' Mad" Smith (holding helmet), commander of the V Amphibious Corps, discusses Saipan tactics with Admiral Raymond Spruance (far right), head of the Fifth Fleet, and Major General Thomas Watson, chief of the 2nd Marine Division.

Division was nearly thrown into the sea. In that sector a cooler Japanese head prevailed. Lieut. General Takeshi Takashina, the island commander, had realized that the wild suicide rushes that characterized last-ditch Japanese resistance in earlier Pacific battles were self-defeating. From his command post in the hills north of the harbor, he had carefully observed the Marine advance through huge telescopes. He sent out reconnaissance teams to probe for weak spots and he meticulously collected the men and equipment he would need for a coordinated counterattack.

During the night of July 25, Takashina's troops slipped through a gap his patrols had discovered between two regiments of the 3rd Division. They bypassed an entire American battalion and at dawn came tumbling out of the ridges to the beach near the division's headquarters. Truck drivers, Seabees and headquarters troops banded together to slow the Japanese onslaught. At daylight, the tip of this attack was finally blunted near the division's hospital, where the walking wounded had turned out with whatever weapons came to hand, and those who could not walk fired from their cots. By then, the Japanese drive, despite Takashina's careful planning, had become disorganized. For a while, the beachhead was engulfed with swirling small-unit actions. But many of the Japanese elements had lost contact with each other; some were without leaders, their officers having been killed. When the attack was over, 3,500 Japanese lay dead, and the beachhead was still in American hands.

The fight for Guam dragged on for two weeks. Even after the island was declared secure, small numbers of Japanese held out in the hills, guerrilla-style, for months—in some cases, for years.

With the Marianas won and the great Japanese naval base at Truk now cut off from support, the American strategists turned their attention to the last remaining obstacles in the westward drive. The Palau Islands in the western Carolines, 1,000 miles west of Truk and only 500 miles east of Mindanao, lay on the flank of any advance on the Philippines. Should they be invaded? In a high-level Navy conference on the question, the leading dissenter was Admiral Halsey. Arguing that the conquest of the Palaus would prove too costly, and fearing a repeat of Tarawa, he proposed bypassing the Palaus and striking directly at the Philippines. Nim-

itz, on the other hand, felt that the islands were too great a threat to ignore—and Nimitz was Halsey's superior.

Accordingly, plans were laid; the 1st Marine Division was to storm ashore on Peleliu Island, site of the largest air base in the Palaus, on September 15. Major General William Rupertus, the division commander, felt optimistic about the invasion. Addressing his officers after a landing rehearsal at Guadalcanal, Rupertus said: "We're going to have some casualties, but let me assure you this is going to be a short one, a quickie. Rough but fast. We'll be through in three days. It might take only two." But *Stalemate II,* as the operation was known, bore an all-too-prophetic name. The struggle for Peleliu would drag on for weeks, to rank with Tarawa as one of the bloodiest battles of the Pacific war.

Halsey's original contention that the Palaus could be bypassed was reinforced by a discovery that the Americans made just a few days before the scheduled landings. Softening up Japanese air bases in the Philippines in support of the Palaus operation, Halsey's pilots encountered only feeble opposition. Japanese air power in the western Pacific had all but collapsed, and suddenly the path seemed clear for a strike at the heart of the Philippines. This electrifying news spurred Halsey into action. Two days before D-day at Peleliu, he recommended that all impending operations in the western Pacific—including the Palaus and Mindanao in the southern Philippines—be canceled in favor of an immediate invasion of the central Philippine island of Leyte. Nimitz agreed, with one exception. He was unwilling to call off the attack on the Palaus. The invasion of Peleliu went ahead.

Almost all of the Palau Islands lie inside a coral reef. Many of them, volcanic in origin, rise several hundred feet above sea level and are covered with thick vegetation. Peleliu, within the southern tip of the enclosing reef, is shaped roughly like a lobster's claw. At its hinge, a wide flat area in the south, lay the airfield; the two pincers stretched east and northeast, toward the other islands of the group. Rising just north of the airfield and running along the entire northern pincer was Umurbrogol Mountain, a steep, bushy series of ridges riddled with caves.

To the Japanese, the Palaus were of major importance. All through the early part of the War, Japanese troops, vessels and planes bound for the Dutch East Indies and western

TRAGIC SPECTACLE AT THE EDGE OF THE SEA

A Japanese family paces the volcanic rocks of Marpi Point as other Japanese on a cliff above beg them not to make a suicidal leap into the sea.

Before they can resolve their inner conflict, the parents are hit by a Japanese sniper hidden in a nearby cave. Both were swept into the ocean.

Now orphaned, the horrified children flee from the scene of the tragedy. Later, several Japanese women led them from the rocks to safety.

As the U.S. ended its Saipan campaign, thousands of Japanese civilians chose suicide over capture, which was considered a fate worse than death. Some tossed grenades at each other, blowing up even their own children. More drowned themselves; many stoically joined hands, walked into the water and slipped under the waves.

One family, whose heart-rending drama was recorded by LIFE photographers Peter Stackpole and Eugene Smith, stood at the water's edge for 45 minutes trying to make up their minds. Then a Japanese sniper made the live-or-die decision for them.

New Guinea had staged through the well-developed naval and air bases in the group. Japan's administrative headquarters for all of the islands it controlled under the League of Nations mandate was located in the Palaus, and after Truk was neutralized by air attacks and the capture of the Marianas, the Combined Fleet moved its headquarters there for a brief period. In April, the crack 14th Division arrived from China. Its commander, Lieut. General Sadae Inoue, set to work building fortifications against a possible attack by Nimitz.

Inoue was aided by a topographical feature of Peleliu: its caves. Before the War the Japanese had mined the island for phosphates, and now they used mining techniques to enlarge the coral caverns that honeycombed Peleliu's ridgeline and to dig vast new ones—more than 500 in all. One of the underground complexes was big enough to hold 1,000 men; others were equipped with steel doors that slid open to allow artillery pieces to fire and then snapped shut again. Each cave was well stocked with food and ammunition.

Furthermore, the 6,500 Japanese combat troops on the island had been instructed in the new tactical doctrine employed by General Takashina on Saipan: there were to be no more hopeless suicide attacks at the beaches, no more wasteful expenditures of men and matériel in attempts to annihilate the enemy at the waterline. A powerful effort would still be made to knock out the American beachhead before it was consolidated, but if that failed Inoue had ordered his troops to withdraw to carefully prepared defense lines from which mortars and artillery could fire on previously registered targets. Troops who were overrun were to remain hidden, instead of killing themselves in their bunkers, so that at an appropriate moment they might attack the Americans from the rear. Inoue drilled his officers in seven separate counterattack plans, each to be set in motion by a distinctive flare or flag.

Merely dying for the Emperor while giving up the island of Peleliu would not help their cause, Inoue admonished his men. "Victory," he declared, "depends on our thorough application of recent battle lessons, especially those of Saipan. The Americans rely solely upon material power. If we repay them with material power it will shock them beyond imagination."

Ironically, Inoue himself missed the invasion. When it came, he was on another island overseeing the defenses for the entire Palau group. His subordinates on Peleliu, however, carried out his new defensive doctrine to the letter. It was a radical departure in Japanese military thinking, and the 1st Marine Division was to pay heavily for it.

Before the invasion got under way, bombers from MacArthur's bases in New Guinea and the neighboring islands pounded the Palaus in late August. They were succeeded by planes of fast carriers under Halsey's command. Then the battleships, cruisers and destroyers of the support force, under Rear Admiral Jesse B. Oldendorf, worked Peleliu over for three full days. After flattening what was left of the hangars, buildings and aboveground installations and rearranging the island's scenery, the naval gunners were ordered to let up, and Oldendorf announced that he had run out of targets. The fact is that the Japanese network of underground fortifications had barely been touched.

At least one veteran Marine commander did not share Oldendorf's confidence. As Colonel Lewis B. "Chesty" Puller was getting ready to go over the side of a transport to join his men on D-day, the skipper of the ship hailed him cheerfully.

"Coming back for supper?" he called out. "Everything's done over there. You'll walk in."

"If you think it's that easy," Puller growled, "why don't you come on the beach at five o'clock, have supper with me, and pick up a few souvenirs?"

The Marines struck from the west at the base of Peleliu's lobster claw, on a mile-long beach alongside the airfield. As they crossed the reef, three regimental combat teams abreast, they saw Umurbrogol end on, at their left, and it looked deceptively small and innocent. In some of the first-wave amtracs, Marines were singing. On the extreme left flank, the words of "Give My Regards to Broadway" could be heard coming from Company K of Puller's 1st Marine Regiment as the men rode shoreward.

When the final prelanding barrage moved inland and to the flanks of the Marines, the Japanese came out of their holes. From scores of undamaged mortars, artillery pieces and machine guns, the defenders of Peleliu dropped a curtain of lead and flying steel upon the reef. An amtrac was hit, and then others came under fire in quick succession. To the right, at the southern end of the beach, obstacles and mines forced the 7th Marine Regiment's amtracs and accompanying tanks into single file, making them easy targets. Many Marines had to wade ashore. On the left the 1st Marine Regiment found itself under fire from Japanese on a little rocky point of land jutting out from the beach. Only in the center, at the airfield itself, did the 5th Marine Regiment land almost intact.

On the heavy cruiser *Portland,* a gunnery officer watched through binoculars as a heavy steel door opened in the side of a ridge. A gun came out, fired at the beach and disappeared back inside the cave as the door swung shut. The officer directed five separate salvos against the hidden emplacement with the *Portland*'s 8-inch shells. Between salvos, the Japanese weapon emerged unscathed from its cave and pelted the Marine beachhead. The gunnery officer gave up finally in disgust. "You can put all the steel in Pittsburgh onto that thing," he said, "and still not get it."

Meanwhile, offshore, the burning amtracs and wading men created a scene reminiscent of the Tarawa landing. But there was a crucial difference: here there was no sea wall 20 feet from the water's edge. Moreover, Colonel Kunio Nakagawa, the Peleliu commander, had heeded General Inoue's orders and pulled the greater part of his infantry off the beach for a counterattack. Most of the Marines were thus able to dash inland as soon as they reached shore. Within hours, elements of the 5th Marines had struck completely across the southern edge of the airfield, and by late afternoon the 7th Marines had advanced, on a curve, toward the southern tip of the island. But the enemy fire on the reef had forced some of these units to land on beaches other than those intended; then they had become confused in the dense scrub jungle south of the airfield. Everywhere, the Marines were far behind the ambitious schedule that General Rupertus had set for them.

On the northern end of the beachhead, Colonel Puller's 1st Marines were in serious trouble. Almost all of his radios had been sunk when his command group amtracs were hit on the reef, making it impossible to call for help. A dangerous gap had opened in the lines of Puller's Company K, which had drawn the crucial job of anchoring the extreme northern flank of the division beachhead. Had Colonel Nakagawa spotted the gap, the Japanese could have surged right through it and rolled over the jumble of supplies and wounded and arriving men on the congested beach.

The gap developed because of a natural obstacle that had not shown up on any of the Marines' maps or intelligence reports. It was a steep, jagged coral ridge 30 feet high, 100 yards inland, studded with Japanese gun positions. Crossing the beach and rushing inland through bursting mortar fire, Company K's 2nd Platoon tumbled into a Japanese antitank trench in front of this ridge and stayed pinned down for hours, taking heavy casualties and losing contact with the rest of the company. North of the ridge, Company K's 3rd Platoon hit the beach and wheeled left to attack a rocky point of land jutting 25 yards into the sea from the northern end of the beachhead; in doing so they moved away from the Marines trapped in the trench—thereby widening the gap. But they had no choice. Their first mission was to silence the guns on the rocky point, which were creating havoc by raking the entire beachhead. It turned out to be K's last mission as well.

"The Point was a rocky mass of sharp pinnacles, deep crevasses, tremendous boulders," wrote the company commander, Captain George P. Hunt, afterward. "Pillboxes, reinforced with steel and concrete, had been dug or blasted in the base of the perpendicular drop to the beach. Others, with coral and concrete piled six feet on top, were constructed above, and spider holes were blasted around them for protecting infantry. It surpassed by far anything we had conceived of when we studied the aerial photographs." None of these defenses had even been damaged by the naval bombardment.

The Japanese guns on the point quickly cut the 3rd Platoon to pieces; by the time the unit had covered the 50 yards only a handful of men were fit to fight.

The 1st Platoon, Hunt's reserve, was ordered to follow up the 3rd in the assault on the point. Then Hunt left his shell-hole command post on the beach and headed for the point himself.

"The human wreckage I saw," he recalled later, "was a grim and tragic sight. Wounded and dying littered the edge of the coconut grove from where we had landed to the point. As I ran up the beach I saw them lying nearly shoulder to shoulder. I saw a ghastly mixture of bandages, bloody and mutilated skin; men gritting their teeth, resigned to their wounds; men groaning and writhing in their agonies; men outstretched or twisted or grotesquely transfixed in the attitudes of death; men with their entrails exposed or whole chunks of body ripped out of them. There was Graham, snuffed out a hero, lying with four dead Japs around him; and Windsor, flat on his face, with his head riddled by bullets and his arms pointed toward a pillbox where five Japs slumped over a machine gun."

The carnage marked the path of the 3rd Platoon, which had lost more than half of its men but had wiped out the Japanese covering the point from the beach. On the point itself five concrete pillboxes and a network of trenches were taking a heavy toll as Lieutenant William Willis and his

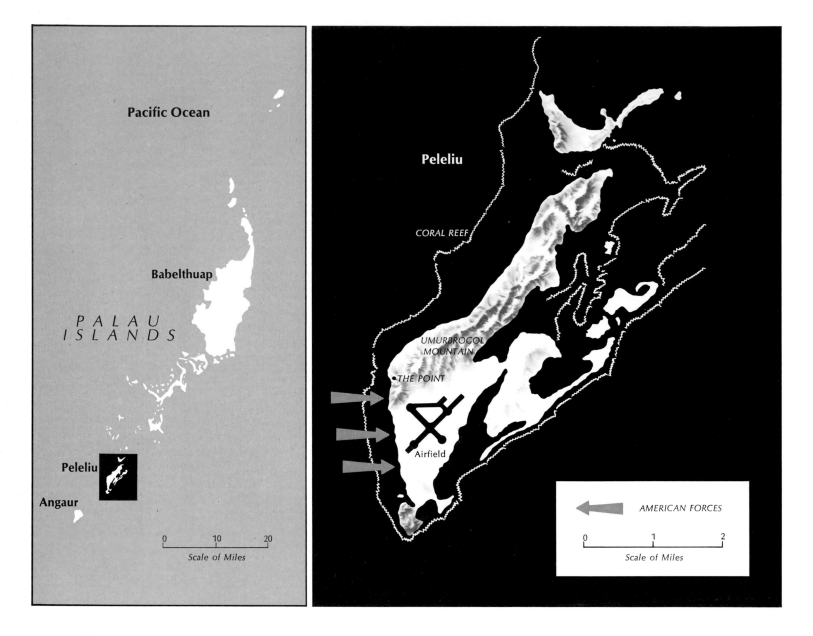

On September 15, 1944, the 1st Marine Division invaded Peleliu in the Palaus (above). Attacking with three regiments abreast (above right), the division immediately ran into trouble on the northern beachhead, where one company expended itself capturing a feature known simply as "the point," and other units of the 1st Marine Regiment were stopped cold by Japanese dug into the southern ridges of Umurbrogol Mountain. From the southern beachhead, the 7th Marine Regiment struggled southward to clean out resistance in the lower tip of the island. In the center, the 5th Marine Regiment thrust across the island and mopped up the eastern peninsulas and islets; next it doubled back and sliced along the western coastal flat to wipe out opposition in the northern tip. Then the regiment reversed direction again to attack Umurbrogol from the north while the 1st and 7th Marine regiments and the Army's 321st Infantry Regiment pushed against the mountain redoubt from the south.

1st Platoon, along with the survivors of the 3rd, stormed the craggy bluff on Hunt's orders. Each pillbox had to be knocked out individually, and the only way to do it was to crawl up close and throw in a grenade.

Hunt arrived to find the point taken, but Company K's ordeal was far from over. Less than two hours had passed since the landing, yet only 30 men remained alive and unwounded out of the 1st and 3rd platoons. This small remnant was completely isolated. Between the point and the helpless 2nd Platoon stuck in the antitank trench—from which Hunt had heard nothing—lay the gap, several hundred yards of craggy jungle into which the Japanese moved unseen and at will. Several times during the day Colonel Puller tried to shift reserve companies into the gap to tie in with Hunt—but at each attempt well-emplaced Japanese machine guns mowed down men moving along the antitank trench.

Gathering together two reserve companies and all the regimental-headquarters troops that could be spared, Puller established a secondary defense line south of the point. That did nothing for Hunt, but it offered some hope that a Japanese counterattack through the gap could be stopped.

Fortunately for the Americans, Colonel Nakagawa had not foreseen this opportunity. His carefully made counterattack plans called for action elsewhere, and late in the afternoon he set one of them in motion. At approximately five o'clock several hundred Japanese infantrymen emerged from the devastated hangar area north of the airfield and began to advance in a skirmish line toward the Marine positions. This was no screaming banzai charge of bunched-up men providing easy targets. Coolly, the veteran 14th Division troops kept well dispersed, and they sprinted from one chunk of concealing debris to another as they crossed the open ground of the airfield.

Scarcely had the Marines fired their first salvo of mortars when a new peril arose. As a corporal in Puller's 2nd Battalion described it: "From behind a bombed down hangar I saw a cloud of dust with the ugly snout of a Nippon tank at the head of it, then came another, then another from behind a bunker, another from here and one from there. Sure enough they are coming. Jap tanks pouring out of their hiding places, dodging and swirling crazily about. All of us

open fire with machine guns, automatic rifles, small arms, bazookas, or whatever we have. The Japs don't give up, they keep coming and coming fast, very close now."

Spitting fire from machine guns and 37mm cannon, the light tanks—at least 13 of them—whizzed through the advancing Japanese infantry and charged diagonally across the airfield at top speed. Puller's 2nd Battalion took them under flanking fire and two crashed. From the southern end of the field, four of the Marines' Sherman tanks, much heavier and more powerful than the Japanese vehicles, trundled onto the airfield and, with their 75mm guns blazing, charged into the midst of the enemy armored force. Then eight more Shermans joined the fray, and a Navy dive bomber swooped low and dropped a bomb on the Japanese.

The massed firepower was too much for the light Japanese tanks. Their armor was so thin that they were vulnerable to almost every Marine weapon. Nevertheless several of the tanks reached the Marine lines. The 2nd Battalion corporal recalled: "A tank rushed for the machine gun on my right. 'Stoney' stands up in the foxhole and lets go a burst of automatic fire. The tank was not ten feet away when it burst into flame, leaving a trailing fire as it still rolled forward. The lower half of a twisted and burnt Jap body fell not a pace from me. The Marine machine gunners jumped to safety just in time as the tank came crushing over their nest, smashing the weapon to bits. The tank gave a final lunge as it blew up about ten yards behind our lines." One of the Marines rushed up with his flamethrower, but a final spurt of bullets came from the burning tank and caught him in the chest.

Within minutes, Colonel Nakagawa's climactic effort had failed. Nearly all his tanks were destroyed and none of the infantrymen reached the Marines.

At dusk, an amtrac brought supplies to Captain Hunt's isolated men at the point and took away their wounded. Around midnight the Japanese launched a heavy mortar barrage and the Marines fired back blindly with their few machine guns. Their radio batteries had died and they had to endure hours of nerve-racking silence, punctuated by scuffling sounds in front of their lines, sniping and an occasional cry for corpsmen.

At first light the next morning, the Japanese opened up with another grenade and mortar barrage. Without a radio

Hunt could not call in mortar or artillery fire, and his men were falling one by one.

The attack mounted in fury until only about 20 Marines were left; then one of Hunt's men knocked out a Japanese mortar with a rifle grenade and the attack faltered. Suddenly the Marines were standing on the rocks firing at the backs of running Japanese. Supplies and reinforcements began to arrive—troops, mortars, an artillery-observation team, radios and a telephone line. In the afternoon the gap was finally closed.

Hunt counted his men and found that of the 235 in his company who had landed 48 hours earlier, only 78 had not been killed or wounded. Hunt's Company K was relieved and sent into reserve, but for the rest of the division the battle for Peleliu had hardly begun. The airfield, the most important objective, had been taken on the second day, but it could not yet be used because Japanese artillerymen on Umurbrogol's heights could blast anything that moved on it.

After his tank attack failed and his units in the south were cut off, Colonel Nakagawa withdrew all of his troops into the caves and pillboxes of his Umurbrogol bastion, there to hold out as long as he could. In the meantime, the 5th Marines, in spite of heavy losses, had managed to traverse the island by way of the exposed airfield and had begun to secure the beaches and sliver-like peninsulas on the eastern side of Peleliu. The 7th Marines were still slogging southward, pressing the Japanese into promontories that jutted out from the lower tip of the island. Thus it fell to Colonel Puller's 1st Marines, who had already suffered the heaviest casualties in the division, to make the first push against Umurbrogol.

During the preliminary naval gunfire, much of the vegetation on the peak had been blasted away. To the 1st Marines who reached Umurbrogol on September 17, the denuded ridges presented a nightmare scene. "Along its center, the rocky spine was heaved up in a contorted mass of decayed coral, strewn with rubble, crags, ridges and gulches thrown together in a confusing maze," runs the 1st Marine Division's official history. "There were no roads, scarcely any trails. The pock-marked surface offered no secure footing even in the few level places. It was impossible to dig in: the best the men could do was pile a little coral or wood debris around their positions. The jagged rock slashed their shoes and clothes, and tore their bodies every time they hit the deck for safety. Casualties were higher for the simple reason it was impossible to get under the ground away from the Japanese mortar barrages. Each blast hurled chunks of coral in all directions, multiplying many times the fragmentation effect of every shell."

Few of the many ridges and hills were more than 200 feet high, but on each of them, and in the steep ravines between them, were dozens of caves and pillboxes sheltering riflemen, machine gunners, mortars, rockets and field guns. When the Marines approached in the blistering heat, the Japanese would run a gun out of a cave, fire it and then pull it back in before the Marines could spot it.

On the 17th, Puller's 2nd Battalion managed to claw its way up the first of these ridges—only to find that the crest was a perfect target for Japanese gunners on the ridge a couple of hundred yards beyond. Later that day, Puller's 1st Battalion, aided by naval gunfire and tanks and bazookas, had to knock out 35 caves just to start up the forward slope of another ridge; in doing so, the battalion lost so many men that reserves and headquarters troops were hurriedly thrown into the line to hold the gains that night. The next morning, after just one day of fighting on the ridge, the battalion had to be taken out of the line briefly to reorganize and catch its breath.

Evidence of 35 caves on one slope alone and the fact that the 1st Marine Regiment had lost nearly half of its strength in the short space of three days of fighting should have tempered the optimism of the division's officers. But they continued to dispose their forces for a fast sweep up Peleliu's northern peninsula. They did not know, of course, about General Inoue's new tactics or the extent of Colonel Nakagawa's defenses.

The truth emerged on the 18th. A fierce Japanese counterattack forced Puller's 2nd Battalion partially off the ridge it had won the day before. Company B, which had been pulled from the line with the rest of the 1st Battalion only hours before, was ordered back into the fray in an attempt to outflank the Japanese pressing down on the 2nd Battalion. The company took one hill and then was thrown back before a formidable complex of jagged ridges. From then

Rockets blazing away, an LCI (Landing Craft, Infantry) launches an
attack on Peleliu. Immediately before the 1st Marine Division's landing,
18 of these gunboats blanketed the beaches with fire. Four others,
armed with mortars, pounded potential trouble spots beyond the beaches.

on Umurbrogol came to be known in the Marine Corps as Bloody Nose Ridge.

By the sixth day, September 20, the 1st Marine Regiment was finished as a fighting outfit on Peleliu. In its 1st Battalion only 74 men were left out of three companies, and every platoon leader had been hit. The regiment had sustained more than 1,700 casualties. As one of its exhausted men put it: "We aren't a regiment. We're the survivors of a regiment."

As a contingent of the 1st Marines boarded a hospital transport a week later, a close-shaven, starched Navy officer asked the men if they had any souvenirs to trade. One gaunt and battle-weary Marine stood silent for a moment and then reached down and patted his own rear. "I brought my ass outta there, swabbie," he said. "That's my souvenir of Peleliu."

On September 20, the entire 7th Regiment—elements of which had been fed into the weakening lines on Umurbrogol since the third day of fighting—was thrown against the impregnable ridges on the island. It made no more headway than the 1st. Clearly the Marines on Umurbrogol needed help.

At that point the Army lent a hand. The 81st Division had just completed a relatively easy campaign on Angaur Island, 10 miles to the south. One of its units, the 321st Regimental Combat Team was available. On September 23, the 321st relieved Puller's remnants.

On September 25, the 5th Marines marched through the Army's newly established lines on the western flank of Umurbrogol and, bypassing the treacherous ridges, struck northward through the narrow coastal flat to the upper tip of the island. Led by tanks and amtrac-mounted flamethrowers, and calling in naval gunfire with precision, the regiment captured the entire northern section of Peleliu with relative ease and with comparatively few casualties in just five days. Then it doubled back to attack Umurbrogol's tenacious defenses from the north. Little by little, the 321st combat team and the 5th and 7th Marine

regiments tightened a noose around Nakagawa's redoubt.

For every inch of tortured coral they bought, the Americans paid dearly.

On October 4 the Japanese allowed the 48 men of Company L, 7th Marines, to scale one 100-foot-high ridge unmolested. When all of the Marines were on the exposed crest, the hidden enemy opened up from three sides with mortars, antitank guns and withering small-arms fire. Three men were killed instantly; the platoon leader, Second Lieutenant James E. Dunn, was one of the first to fall. "Bullets tore him from his grip on the cliffside where he was trying to withdraw his men to safer positions," combat correspondent Jeremiah O'Leary recorded, "and he fell to his death on the ravine floor many feet below."

At the base of the peak, Company K tried desperately to cover the isolated platoon of Company L, but it could only guess at some of the Japanese gun positions.

"The wounded crawled behind rocks or just lay motionless, bullets hitting them again and again," O'Leary wrote. "Others cried pitifully for help and begged their comrades not to leave them there." Medical corpsmen on the crest of the ridge worked feverishly to drag the wounded out of the storm of fire. One stood up and shouted: "Take it easy! Bandage each other. Get a few out at a time." Then he, too, was killed.

Throwing away their weapons, the frantic Marines clawed their way back down the cliff. Some were hit and fell off the peak; others slipped in their haste and tumbled down, ripping their flesh on the jagged coral. The horrified commander of Company L, Captain James V. Shanley, watched them falling. "For God's sake," he screamed to Company K, "smoke up that hill!"

Under the cover of billowing phosphorus from smoke grenades, some of the men let themselves drop, taking their chances on the fall. The wounded on the ledge urged their buddies to jump. "You've done all you can for us," one shouted. "Get outta here." Realizing that the wounded would never survive if they were left behind, several Marines rolled their injured buddies off the ledge. One man, his foot caught in a vine, hung head down and helpless until another Marine kicked him loose.

On the ravine floor, two wounded Marines tried to help each other across an exposed draw to the safety of a tank Captain Shanley had called in. Arm in arm, they hobbled slowly across the draw, but they were too weak to make it. They fell together, and the Japanese opened fire on them. It was more than Shanley could take. Fighting off a lieutenant who tried to hold him back, he sprinted into the draw, picked up one of the men, carried him through Japanese fire and laid him gently in the lee of the tank. As he raced to get the other man, a mortar shell exploded behind him and he crumpled to the ground, fatally wounded. Seeing Shanley fall, his executive officer, a second lieutenant, rushed to his aid. He was hit by an antitank shell, and fell dead beside the captain.

Some of the men high on the ledge tried to climb down. A few descended without getting hit and made it across the ravine to the tank. Two quickly volunteered to return with stretchers to the base of the cliff to carry out the wounded. Both were killed. The debacle at Ridge 120 lasted about three hours and 15 minutes. When it was over, only 11 of the original 48 Marines had survived.

In the words of the 1st Division report, the combat had now become "a battle of attrition—a slow slugging yard by yard struggle to blast the enemy from his last remaining stronghold in the high ground." Long-range flamethrowers mounted on tanks charred hundreds of caves and pillboxes, but many tanks poking into the ravines were knocked out of action before they could fire. Hills were captured and lost and captured again. Cave mouths were sealed with explosives—but the Japanese often escaped through tunnels. Once the ridges overlooking the airfield were cleared of Japanese, Marines Corsair fighter planes could fly close support missions for the troops—but their bombs and bullets had little effect on the Japanese underground. At one point a Marine battalion commander established a command post directly above a Japanese cave. From beneath his feet the aroma of cooking drifted upward. Provoked, he ordered his men to lower a TNT charge on a rope to the cave mouth. The charge exploded and collapsed the shelter.

By the end of October more Army troops replaced the 5th and 7th Marines, both of which had lost about half their strength. But of Colonel Nakagawa's force of 6,500 only 700 remained. The 81st Infantry Division, whose 323rd Regiment had earlier captured Ulithi, an atoll to the north in the Caroline chain, took over the Peleliu operation.

Major General Paul J. Mueller, the 81st's commander, resolved to proceed slowly and methodically, without risking a man unnecessarily. Every advance was preceded by artillery, mortar and napalm attacks. Armored bulldozers cleared routes for tanks. Soldiers inched forward on their bellies, pushing sandbags ahead of them for protection. To get into one troublesome area, the Army's engineers laboriously rigged a fuel pipeline 300 yards long with a nozzle that enabled an operator to squirt flame on a Japanese position like water from a hose. Finally, after more than a month of this grinding action, soldiers of the 323rd Infantry Regiment attacked a Japanese-held ridge from three sides and cleaned it out. Three days earlier, in his underground command post, Colonel Nakagawa had burned his regimental colors and shot himself. It was all over.

The battle for Peleliu claimed the lives of 1,252 Marines and 277 soldiers; another 5,274 Marines and 1,008 soldiers were wounded in the fighting. Ten thousand Japanese soldiers and civilians perished. So well protected had been the Japanese by their caves and tunnels that it took an average of 1,589 rounds of heavy and light ammunition to kill each of Nakagawa's men.

"It seemed to us," one Marine officer said later, "that somebody forgot to give the order to call off Peleliu. That's one place nobody wants to remember." And the battle went largely unnoticed back in the States. While Marines and soldiers were still locked in a tragic struggle with the enemy, another event in the Pacific had drawn the world's attention. MacArthur, with attendant fanfare, had returned to the Philippines.

THE AGONY OF PELELIU

"Then I ran slanting up the beach for cover," Wrote Tom Lea, the artist who painted this invasion scene.
"I fell flat on my face just as I heard the whishhh of a mortar I knew was too close. On the
upper edge of the beach, it smashed down four men from our boat. One figure seemed to fly to pieces.
With terrible clarity I saw the head and one leg sail into the air."

AN ARTIST PAINTS WAR'S HORROR

When the U.S. 1st Marine Division landed on Peleliu Island in September 1944, among the assault troops in the first waves was a noncombatant named Tom Lea, an artist and writer for LIFE. Lea was a veteran correspondent. By this stage of the War, he had chronicled life aboard a destroyer in the North Atlantic and on an aircraft carrier in the South Pacific. He had hopped around the globe—England, North Africa, Italy, India and China—painting pictures of Allied pilots and their planes. But mostly his travels had taken him, as he later put it, "on the backroads of war, where there was not much firing in anger." He had seen no ground combat, and nothing in his experience could prepare him for the grisly drama about to unfold on those six square miles of coral in the western end of the central Pacific.

Almost from the moment he stepped ashore on Peleliu, Lea was confronted by death. "I saw a wounded man near me," he wrote. "His face was half bloody pulp and the mangled shreds of what was left of an arm hung down like a stick, as he bent over in his stumbling shock-crazy walk. The half of his face that was still human had the most terrifying look of abject patience I have ever seen. He fell behind me, in a red puddle on the white sand."

Under fire himself, Lea found it impossible to use the pencils and sketch pads in his knapsack. "My work there consisted of trying to keep from getting killed and trying to memorize what I saw and felt." Lea survived a Japanese mortar barrage on the beach, dodged sniper fire in the jungle and, crouched in a foxhole, waited out a Japanese banzai charge in the darkness. He experienced, as he later wrote, "the sheer joy of being alive."

On the evening of his second day on Peleliu he returned to a ship offshore and feverishly put down, in words and sketches, the scenes that were seared into his consciousness. Later, at home in Texas, from his rough pencil sketches he painted the scenes that appear on these pages. Accompanied by excerpts from his own narrative, the paintings bring starkly to life the horror and pathos that characterized combat in the terrible island fighting of the Pacific.

During a lull in the fighting on Peleliu Island in 1944, Tom Lea, a LIFE artist, takes a breather with some of his Marine buddies beside a shell crater.

"As we passed sick bay, it was crowded with wounded, and somehow hushed in the evening light.
I noticed a tattered marine standing quietly by a corpsman, staring stiffly at nothing. His mind had crumbled
in battle, his jaw hung, and his eyes were like two black empty holes in his head. Down by
the beach again, we walked silently as we passed the long line of dead marines under the tarpaulins."

"I do not know what time it was when the counterattack came. I heard, in pauses between bursts of fire, the high-pitched, screaming yells of the Japs as they charged, somewhere out ahead. The firing would grow to crescendo, drowning out the yells, then the sound would fall dying like the recession of a wave. Looking up, I saw the earth, the splintered trees, the men on their bellies all edged against the sky by the light of the star shells like moonlight from a moon dying of jaundice."

"We found the battalion commander. By him sat his radioman, trying to make contact with company commands. There was an infinitely tired and plaintive patience in the radioman's voice as he called code names, repeating time and time again, 'This is Sad Sack calling Charlie Blue. This is Sad Sack calling Charlie Blue.'"

"The padre stood by with two canteens and a Bible, helping. He was deeply and visibly moved by the patient suffering and death. He looked very lonely, very close to God, as he bent over the shattered men so far from home. Corpsmen put a poncho, a shirt, a rag, anything handy, over the grey faces of the dead and carried them to a line on the beach to await the digging of graves."

"We saw a Jap running along an inner ring of the reef, from the stony eastern point of the peninsula below us. Our patrol cut down on him and shot very badly, for he did not fall until he had run 100 yards along the coral. Another Jap popped out running—and the marines had sharpened their sights. The Jap ran less than 20 steps when a volley cut him in two and his disjointed body splattered into the surf."

"There were dead Japs on the ground where they had been hit. We walked carefully up the side of this trail littered with Jap pushcarts, smashed ammunition boxes, rusty wire, old clothes and tattered gear. Booby traps kept us from handling any of it. Looking up at the head of the trail I could see the big Jap blockhouse that commanded the height. The thing was now a great, jagged lump of concrete, smoking."

KEEP 'EM FLYING
Emergency Strip Repair
36TH CONST. BATT.

THE "CAN DO" SEABEES

A crew of hardy Seabees of the U.S. Navy's 36th Construction Battalion takes a brief breather from the day's job of repairing an airstrip on Bougainville.

THE U.S. NAVY'S MASTER BUILDERS

The island-hopping war the Allies fought in the South Pacific depended in large measure on a rough-and-ready breed of engineers who proudly called themselves "the goddamnedest, toughest road gang in history." Members of the U.S. Navy's Construction Battalions, and known as Seabees from the initials, these versatile performers could magically transform the thickest jungle or most barren atoll into a full-blown air and naval base, build roads and railroads, and clear underwater obstacles.

The speed and ingenuity of the Seabees became legendary throughout the Pacific. Recruited from the ranks of American workers—many from the construction industry—the 260,000 Seabees were for the most part already masters at their trades when they signed up. They were outfitted in an incongruous mix of combat gear from all the services—Seabees liked to call themselves "Confused Bastards"—and received little formal military training. But they operated so near the front lines that they often joined in the fighting.

The Seabees lived by a simple code: "Can do!" No job was too big or too difficult for them to accomplish. They converted the muddy mangrove swamps of Merauke, Dutch New Guinea, into a finished airstrip in eight days. On Tinian in the Marianas, they moved more than 11 million cubic yards of mud, rock and coral to build the world's biggest bomber base—six strips, each a mile and a half long. Seabees constructed fuel tanks, barracks and hospitals; they pushed through highways and railways—on Guam carving out and surfacing 100 miles of road in 90 days. They worked so hard and with so little regard for creature comforts that one of their officers said they "smelled like goats, lived like dogs and worked like horses." But so essential were they to Allied operations that U.S. Secretary of the Navy James Forrestal said in 1945: "The Seabees have carried the war in the Pacific on their backs."

The Seabees' insignia (above) was a bee blazing away with a Tommy gun while carrying wrench and hammer. Their principal weapon was the bulldozer, one of which—photographed below minus its blade—was known as "Old Faithful," and saw so much action throughout the Pacific that the Seabees hoped eventually to parade it down the streets of Tokyo (which was misspelled "Tokyio" on the side of the bulldozer).

A burly, bare-chested Seabee depresses the handle of a detonator to blast coral into bits. The coral was used to surface an airstrip on Eniwetok in 1944.

Supervising an unloading operation, a *Seabee stevedore watches a truck swing through the air while another Seabee steadies the rear at a New Guinea port.*

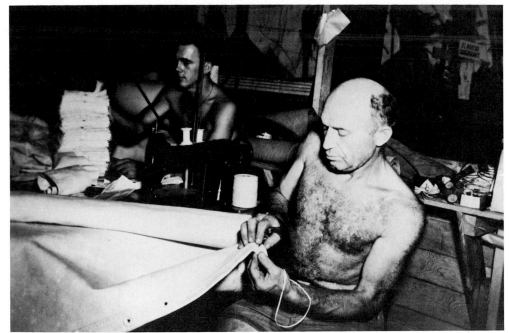

Mending a tarpaulin, a Seabee applies sewing skill he acquired as a civilian garment manufacturer.

SPECIALISTS IN EVERYTHING UNDER THE SUN

"They can build tank traps with sticks of macaroni, repair a lady's wrist watch with a Stilson wrench, or pitch hay with a one-prong fork," wrote an Arkansas newspaperman of the Seabees during the War.

The Seabees demonstrated their ingenuity in innumerable—and often zany—ways; no task was too small. Seabee craftsmen actually did double as watchmakers, replacing broken watch crystals with plexiglass from downed planes. In a pinch they could also perform as shoemakers, cutting rubber soles for boots from tires. Seabee dentists repaired broken dental plates by applying a mixture of ground rubber and cement, then leaving the plates in a carpenter's vise overnight. A Seabee machinist even made two stars out of U.S. quarters to serve as insignia for an Army general.

Masters of the fine art referred to in the Navy as "pack-ratting"—saving cast-off equipment to use again—the Seabees cut power-shovel teeth from scrap metal, improvised truck mufflers from worn-out bazookas, and turned steel pontoons into ovens for their galleys. They fired 75mm armor-piercing shells from Sherman tanks to blast dynamite holes 10 feet deep in quarry walls, and they used their helmets as shovels to fill runway bomb craters.

As their reputation for working magic with limited materials grew, Ernest J. King, the tough-minded Chief of Naval Operations, paid them the ultimate compliment: "Your ingenuity and fortitude have become a legend in the Naval Service."

November 29, 1943: *Airstrip site is dense jungle before Seabees start work.*

December 8: *Stumps are uprooted after*

December 13: *The airstrip is covered end to end with Marston mat.*

December 18: *Crushed coral is spread on*

FROM JUNGLE TO AIRFIELD IN THREE WEEKS

The Seabees had a reputation not only for the speed with which they could build almost anything, but for working unfazed by the fighting going on around them. On Bougainville, as part of the crucial Allied campaign against Rabaul, New Britain, the Seabees landed with the Marines and started surveying the dense jungle for a bomber strip even before the Japanese had been driven from the area. They dodged bullets, and worked around bomb-disposal crews, who were unearthing time bombs, to proceed with their task.

First the ground was cleared of the nearly impenetrable growth of tropical trees and vines. Trees had to be cut down and the stumps blasted out. Once the rises had been flattened and the bogs filled, a "Marston mat"—interlocking strips of honeycombed steel 10 feet long and 16 inches wide—was laid over the raw earth. Then finely crushed coral was plowed on top of the matting and soaked with salt water to form a cement-hard surface.

Working day and night, the Seabees had the 8,000-foot strip ready for use three weeks from the time they broke ground.

the jungle has been bulldozed.

December 11: *Seabees work through the night grading the airfield.*

the mat and then regraded.

December 19: *Satisfied Seabees watch the first plane leave the field.*

Sawing lumber, a Seabee on Guadalcanal uses his foot and a cant hook to position one of the logs.

Laying a pipeline, Seabees install a floating fuel link that will be used by oil tankers off Tinian.

Burying a power line, Seabees use a trenching machine to carve a pathway for a cable at Eniwetok.

MAKING DO WITH LITTLE—OR NOTHING

On the islands where the Seabees landed, construction supplies were often limited to those at hand, including captured Japanese equipment. They set up their own sawmills to produce lumber, and their own metalworking shops to manufacture parts for machines, housing and docks. And they made abundant use of island coral to pave roads and surface airstrips.

The Seabees were challenged at every turn. To fuel ships riding at anchor beyond impassable reefs, they strung huge pipelines. To protect electric lines from bombings, they buried them. On Guadalcanal they built an ice-making facility out of Japanese parts and christened it the "Tojo Ice Factory." In operation, it provided more than 560,000 pounds of ice for hospitals and soft drinks.

The Seabees put in 10-hour days with no respite from their labors. Airfield construction crews cat-napped in shallow trenches beside the strips they were building. One Seabee who worked in the Palaus recalled: "The crabs and ants kept me awake most of the night—until about 3 a.m., when the guns and mortars were just incessant; then *they* kept me awake." But the adaptable Seabees took their backbreaking work in stride and bragged about how tough they were. "I wasn't born," one of them said; "I was quarried!"

Testing a new railroad, *Seabees go for a trial run on a mile-and-a-quarter-long narrow-gauge line they built in three days to haul supplies on Guadalcanal.*

Assembling a fuel tank, *Seabees on Tinian bolt together sheet-metal sections for the foundation. The huge tanks stored aviation gasoline for B-29 bombers.*

Building a mess hall, *shirtless men lay a concrete floor before erecting a prefabricated structure. Construction crews competed to set new speed records.*

A MAGIC BOX FOR CAUSEWAYS AND DOCKS

To carry out one of their most difficult jobs, the docking and unloading of ships in the shallow, reef-girdled waters of the South Pacific islands, Seabees employed a multipurpose steel pontoon. A prefabricated boxlike structure five feet wide, five feet tall and seven feet long, the Seabee pontoon weighed about a ton, floated in a foot and a half of water, and could support up to 20 tons without sinking. The pontoons could be strung together to form causeways and bridges. When equipped with huge outboard or inboard motors, they became barges for towing ships and ferrying cargo. They could be converted for use as storage tanks and even ovens.

The Seabees also fashioned floating dry docks of the pontoons for PT-boat repairs, and they joined together great numbers of the steel boxes to form docking berths *(left)* for oceangoing vessels. The Seabees' exploits even endeared them to the Marines, traditionally sparing of their praise. The Commandant of the Corps, Lieut. General Thomas Holcomb, said that the Marines had seen the Navy's construction men "performing miracles"; other Marines expressed it differently *(below)* but with no less feeling.

Joined pontoons *form a floating dock large enough to accommodate a pair of ships at the harbor of Banika in the Russell Islands. The Seabees' job did not end at the edge of the docks that they put together: Seabee stevedores were responsible for the loading and unloading of ships.*

Marine Raiders *on Bougainville offer a tribute to the Seabees. The Seabees themselves liked to boast that the Marines would find Seabee-built streets not only in Tokyo but also in Heaven (where, according to the celebrated Marine hymn, they would eventually stand guard).*

ACKNOWLEDGMENTS

The index for *Island Fighting* was prepared by Mel Ingber. The editors also wish to thank Master Sergeant Thomas Ashley, Photo Archives Chief, Marine Corps History and Museum Division, Washington Navy Yard, Washington, D.C.; Australian War Memorial, Melbourne, Australia; Dana Bell, U.S. Air Force Still Photo Depository, 1361st Audio-Visual Squadron, Arlington, Virginia; Carole Boutté, Senior Researcher, U.S. Army Audio-Visual Activity, The Pentagon, Arlington, Virginia; Walter Cate, U.S. Air Force Still Photo Depository, 1361st Audio-Visual Squadron, Arlington, Virginia; James N. Cedrone, Audio-Visual Archivist, John F. Kennedy Library, Waltham, Massachusetts; George W. Craig, Supervisory Archives Technician, Photographic Archives, Marine Corps History and Museum Division, Washington Navy Yard, Washington, D.C.; V. M. Destefano, Chief of Reference Library, U.S. Army Audio-Visual Activity, The Pentagon, Arlington, Virginia; Marylou Gjernes, Curator, Center of Military History, Department of the Army, Alexandria, Virginia; Charles R. Haberlein Jr., Photographic Section, Curator Branch, Naval History Division, Department of the Navy, Washington Navy Yard, Washington, D.C.; Norman Hatch, Chief, Audio-Visual Division, Office of Public Affairs, Department of Defense, The Pentagon, Washington, D.C.; Agnes F. Hoover, Photographic Section, Curator Branch, Naval History Division, Department of the Navy, Washington Navy Yard, Washington, D.C.; Tom Lea, El Paso, Texas; William H. Leary, National Archives and Records Service, Audio-Visual Division, Washington, D.C.; Walter Lord, New York, New York; J. M. Mackenzie, Historian, Royal Australian Navy, Melbourne, Australia; Marion McNaughton, Still Art Curator, Center of Military History, Department of the Army, Alexandria, Virginia; Ray Mann, Historian, Ships History Branch, Naval History Division, Department of the Navy, Washington Navy Yard, Washington, D.C.; Colonel Misao Matsumoto, Military Attaché, Embassy of Japan, Washington, D.C.; Marguret Price, Australian War Memorial, Melbourne, Australia; Beverly Schurr, Librarian, Embassy of Australia, Washington, D.C.; Henry Shaw, Chief Historian, Marine Corps History and Museum Division, Washington Navy Yard, Washington, D.C.; George Silk, Westport, Connecticut; Brigadier General Edwin Simmons, Director, Marine Corps History and Museum Division, Washington Navy Yard, Washington, D.C.; Julie Streets, Archivist, Naval Facilities Engineering Command, Historical Information Office, U.S. Naval Construction Battalion Center, Port Hueneme, California; Regina Strothers, Film Library Assistant, Photographic Archives, Marine Corps History and Museum Division, Washington Navy Yard, Washington, D.C.; Lieut. Colonel Russell Tiffany, Executive Officer, Marine Corps History and Museum Division, Washington Navy Yard, Washington, D.C.; Jim Trimble, National Archives, Washington, D.C.; Marie Yates, U.S. Army Audio-Visual Activity, The Pentagon, Arlington, Virginia.

BIBLIOGRAPHY

Adams, Henry H., *Years of Expectation, Guadalcanal to Normandy.* David McKay Company, Inc., 1973.

Barbey, Daniel E., *MacArthur's Amphibious Navy, Seventh Amphibious Force Operations 1943-1945.* United States Naval Institute, 1969.

Birdsall, Steve, *Flying Buccaneers, The Illustrated Story of Kenney's Fifth Air Force.* Doubleday & Company, Inc., 1977.

Brown, David, *Carrier Operations in World War II,* Vol. II: The Pacific Navies. Ian Allan Ltd., 1974.

Buggy, Hugh, *Pacific Victory.* Australian Ministry for Information. No Date.

Butterfield, Roger, *Al Schmid Marine.* Farrar & Rinehart, Incorporated, 1944.

Cant, Gilbert:
  America's Navy in World War II. Farrar & Rinehart, Incorporated, 1944.
  The Great Pacific Victory, From the Solomons to Tokyo. The John Day Company, 1946.

Castillo, Edmund L., *The Seabees of World War II.* Random House, 1963.

Cave, Hugh B., *We Build, We Fight: The Story of the Seabees.* Harper & Brothers, Publishers, 1944.

Craven, Wesley Frank, and James Lea Cate, eds., *The Army Air Forces in World War II,* Vol. IV: *The Pacific: Guadalcanal to Saipan.* The University of Chicago Press, 1944.

Dexter, David, *Australia in the War of 1939-1945, The New Guinea Offensives.* Australian War Memorial, 1961.

Donovan, Robert J., *PT 109.* McGraw-Hill, 1961.

Eichelberger, Robert L., *Our Jungle Road to Tokyo.* The Viking Press, 1950.

Feldt, Eric A., *The Coastwatchers.* Oxford University Press, 1946.

Gallant, T. Grady, *On Valor's Side.* Doubleday & Company, Inc., 1963.

Griffith, Samuel B., II, *The Battle for Guadalcanal.* Ballantine Books, 1963.

Halsey, William F., and J. Bryan III, *Admiral Halsey's Story.* McGraw-Hill Book Company, Inc., 1947.

Heinl, Robert Debs, Jr., *Soldiers of the Sea.* United States Naval Institute, 1962.

Hess, William N., *Pacific Sweep, The 5th and 13th Fighter Commands in World War II.* Doubleday & Company, Inc., 1974.

The History of the U.S. Marine Corps Operations in World War II. Historical Division Headquarters, U.S. Marine Corps:
  Garand, George W., and Truman R. Strobridge, *Western Pacific Operations,* 1971.
  Hoffman, Carl W., *The Seizure of Tinian,* 1951.
  Hough, Frank O., *The Assault on Peleliu,* 1950.
  Hough, Frank O., and John A. Crown, *The Campaign on New Britain,* 1952.
  Hough, Frank O., Verle E. Ludwig and Henry I. Shaw Jr., *Pearl Harbor to Guadalcanal,* 1958.
  Rentz, John N., *Bougainville and the Northern Solomons,* 1948.
  Rentz, John N., *Marines in the Central Solomons,* 1952.
  Shaw, Henry I., Jr., and Douglas T. Kane, *Isolation of Rabaul,* 1963.
  Shaw, Henry I., Jr., Bernard C. Nalty and Edwin T. Turnbladh, *Central Pacific Drive,* 1966.

Hough, Frank O., *The Island War.* J. B. Lippincott Company, 1947.

Howlett, Robert, *Battleground South Pacific.* Charles E. Tuttle Co. No Date.

Huie, William Bradford, *Can Do! The Story of the Seabees.* E. P. Dutton & Co., 1944.

Hunt, George P., *Coral Comes High.* Harper & Brothers, 1946.

Isely, Jeter A., and Philip A. Crowl, *The U.S. Marines and Amphibious War.* Princeton University Press, 1951.

Ito, Masanori, with Roger Pineau, *The End of the Imperial Japanese Navy.* W. W. Norton & Company, Inc., 1956.

James, D. Clayton, *The Years of MacArthur,* Vol. II: *1941-1945.* Houghton Mifflin Company, 1975.

Johnston, Richard W., *Follow Me!* Random House, 1948.

Jungle Warfare. The Australian Military Forces, Australian War Memorial, 1944.

Kenney, George C.:
  General Kenney Reports, A Personal History of the Pacific War. Duell, Sloan and Pearce, 1949.
  The Saga of Pappy Gunn. Duell, Sloan and Pearce, 1959.

King, Ernest J., *U.S. Navy at War 1941-1945.* Official Reports to the Secretary of the Navy, United States Navy Department, 1946.

Krueger, Walter, *From Down Under to Nippon.* Combat Forces Press, 1953.

Leckie, Robert, *Strong Men Armed.* Random House, 1962.

Lockwood, Charles A., and Hans Christian Adamson, *Battles of the Philippine Sea.* Thomas Y. Crowell Company, 1967.

Lodge, O. R., *The Recapture of Guam.* Historical Division Headquarters, U.S. Marine Corps, 1954.

Long, Gavin, *Australia in the War of 1939-1945, The Final Campaigns.* Australian War Memorial, 1963.

Lord, Walter, *Lonely Vigil, Coastwatchers of the Solomons.* Viking, 1977.

MacArthur, Douglas, *Reminiscences.* McGraw-Hill Book Company, 1964.

McCarthy, Dudley, *Australia in the War of 1939-45,* Vol. V: *South-West Pacific Area First Year, Kokoda to Wau.* Halstead Press, 1959.

Macintyre, Donald, *Aircraft Carrier: The Majestic Weapon.* Ballantine Books, Inc., 1968.

McMillan, George, *The Old Breed.* Infantry Journal Press, 1949.

Masashi, Ito, *The Emperor's Last Soldiers.* Coward-McCann, Inc., 1967.

Mayo, Lida, *Bloody Buna.* Doubleday & Company, Inc., 1974.

Morison, Samuel Eliot:
  History of United States Naval Operations in World War II. Little, Brown and Company.
  Volume V, *The Struggle for Guadalcanal,* 1964.
  Volume VI, *Breaking the Bismarcks Barrier, 22 July 1942—1 May 1944,* 1975.
  Volume VII, *Aleutians, Gilberts and Marshalls,* 1975.
  Volume VIII, *New Guinea and the Marianas,* 1959.
  Volume XII, *Leyte,* 1970.

Newcomb, Richard F., *Savo.* Holt, Rinehart and Winston, 1961.

Okumiya, Masatake, Jiro Horikoshi and Martin Oaidin, *Zero!* E. P. Dutton & Co., Inc., 1956.

Papuan Campaign, The Buna-Sanananda Operation. Military Intelligence Division, War Department, 1944.

Paull, Raymond, *Retreat from Kokoda.* Heineman, 1958.

Pogue, Forrest C., *George C. Marshall: Organizer of Victory.* The Viking Press, 1973.

Potter, E. B., *Nimitz.* Naval Institute Press, 1976.

Potter, E. B., and Chester W. Nimitz, eds., *The Great Sea War.* Bramhall House, 1960.

Pratt, Fletcher, *The Marines' War.* William Sloane Associates, Inc., 1948.

Reigelman, Harold, *Caves of Biak.* The Dial Press, 1955.

Reports of General MacArthur: Volume I: *The Campaigns of MacArthur in the Pacific,* 1966.
  Volume II: *Japanese Operations in the Southwest Pacific Area,* 1966.

Reynolds, Clark J., *Fast Carriers: The Forging of an Air Navy.* McGraw-Hill Book Company, 1968.

Robinson, Pat, *The Fight for New Guinea.* Random House, 1943.

Sherrod, Robert:
  History of Marine Corps Aviation in World War II. Combat Forces Press, 1952.
  On to Westward. Duell, Sloan and Pearce, 1945.
  Tarawa, The Story of a Battle. The Admiral Nimitz Foundation, 1973.

Smith, Holland M., and Percy Finch, *Coral and Brass.* Charles Scribner's Sons, 1949.

Smith, S. E., ed., *The United States Marine Corps in World War II,* Vol. I. Ace Books, 1973.

Stafford, Edward P., *The Big E.* Random House, 1962.

Stamps, T. Dodson, and Vincent J. Esposito, eds., *A Military History of World*

War II, Vol. II. United States Military Academy, 1953.

Steichen, Edward, *The Blue Ghost*. Harcourt, Brace and Company, 1947.

Sunderman, James F., ed., *World War II in the Air: The Pacific*. Franklin Watts, Inc., 1962.

Taylor, Theodore, *The Magnificent Mitscher*. W. W. Norton & Company, Inc., 1954.

Toland, John, *The Rising Sun*. Random House, 1970.

Tregaskis, Richard, *Guadalcanal Diary*. Random House, 1943.

The United States Army in World War II, The War in the Pacific. Office of the Chief of Military History, Department of the Army:

   Crowl, Philip A., *Campaign in the Marianas*, 1960.

   Crowl, Philip A., and Edmund G. Love, *Seizure of the Gilberts and Marshalls*, 1955.

Miller, John, Jr., *Cartwheel: The Reduction of Rabaul*, 1959.

Miller, John, Jr., *Guadalcanal: The First Offensive*, 1949.

Milner, Samuel, *Victory in Papua*, 1957.

Morton, Louis, *Strategy and Command: The First Two Years*, 1962.

Smith, Robert Ross, *The Approach to the Philippines*, 1953.

Vader, John, *New Guinea: The Tide is Stemmed*. Ballantine Books, Inc., 1971.

Vandegrift, A. A., and R. B. Asprey, *Once a Marine*. W. W. Norton & Company, Inc., 1964.

Wigmore, Lionel, *Australia in the War of 1939-1945: The Japanese Thrust*. Australian War Memorial, 1957.

Willoughby, Charles A., and John Chamberlain, *MacArthur 1941-1951*. McGraw-Hill Book Company, Inc., 1954.

Zimmerman, John L., *The Guadalcanal Campaign*. Lancaster Publications, 1949.

PICTURE CREDITS

Credits from left to right are separated by semicolons, from top to bottom by dashes.

INDEX